What Your Colleagues Are Saying . . .

Teaching reading is the responsibility of all teachers, but how? This is the book that highlights the critical skills regardless of age or curricula. It emphasizes the active view of reading, the critical nature of reading for purpose, starts from what the reader brings to the text, and acknowledges that reading tasks and purposes can be unique to content areas. Packed with great ideas, grounded in research, and written for the teacher who wants to increase their impact on their students to share the passion for learning.

John Hattie, Melbourne Laureate Professor Emeritus

Teaching reading and learning to read are enormously complex tasks. It certainly involves phonics, but so much more. Jennifer Serravallo does a masterful job of unpacking what is involved in becoming a proficient reader. Equally important, she provides remarkably clear and readable examples, with supporting detail, of how to teach those many essential competencies involved in reading instruction. It's one thing to talk about what needs to be done to create readers; it's quite another to actually show how it's done in the classroom. Clearly Jennifer Serravallo is a master of both! If you're interested in putting the science of reading into action, this book is for you.

Timothy Rasinski, Ph.D., Professor Emeritus, Literacy Education

We know that teaching reading is rocket science but aren't always sure how to fly the ship. This is the instruction manual. It's the guide you need to right the ship and ensure that students learn to read at high levels. You'll find practical ideas and examples that help you maneuver the complex world of literacy learning with ease.

Douglas Fisher, Professor, San Diego State University

This book is packed with tools, tables, tips, and practical lesson structures that support predictability and teacher decision-making. With student engagement front and center, Jen shows us that we don't have to choose between structured and responsive teaching. Kids need both!

Kari Yates, Author, Leadership and Literacy Consultant

Once in a generation a teacher's teacher comes along and makes plain what adults can do to ensure children thrive. Jen is that teacher, and this book is required reading for all of us who believe every child can develop powerful literacies, and want a role to play in that development.

Rachael Gabriel, Professor of Literacy Education,
Neag School of Education, University of Connecticut

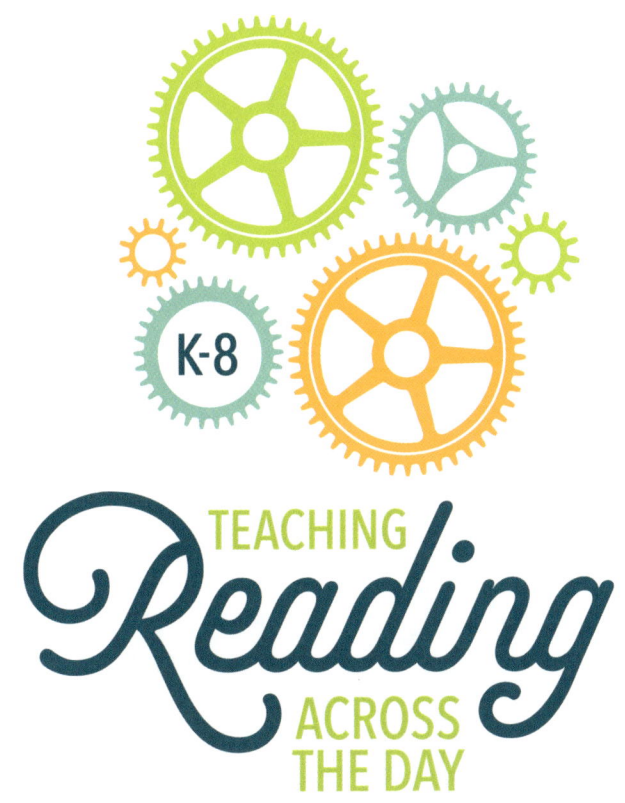

TEACHING
Reading
ACROSS
THE DAY

K-8

JENNIFER SERRAVALLO

K-8

TEACHING
Reading
ACROSS
THE DAY

Methods and Structures for Engaging,
Explicit Instruction

CORWIN Literacy

FOR INFORMATION:

Corwin

A SAGE Company

2455 Teller Road

Thousand Oaks, California 91320

(800) 233-9936

www.corwin.com

SAGE Publications Ltd.

1 Oliver's Yard

55 City Road

London EC1Y 1SP

United Kingdom

SAGE Publications India Pvt. Ltd.

Unit No 323–333, Third Floor, F-Block

International Trade Tower Nehru Place

New Delhi 110 019

India

SAGE Publications Asia-Pacific Pte. Ltd.

18 Cross Street #10-10/11/12

China Square Central

Singapore 048423

Vice President and
  Editorial Director: Monica Eckman

Director and Publisher: Lisa Luedeke

Editor: Katie Wood Ray

Associate Content Development Editor: Sarah Ross

Product Associate: Zachary Vann

Production Editor: Laura Barrett

Copy Editor: Erin Livingston

Typesetter: C&M Digitals (P) Ltd.

Proofreader: Theresa Kay

Interior Designer: Gail Buschman

Cover Designer: Rose Storey

Marketing Manager: Megan Naidl

Marketer: Rebecca Eaton

Video and Photography: Nick Christoff

Printed in the United States of America

Library of Congress Control Number: 2024936087

ISBN: 978-1-0719-2460-0

This book is printed on acid-free paper.

24 25 26 27 28 10 9 8 7 6 5 4 3 2 1

Contents

Acknowledgments   xiii

About the Author   xv

Introduction   1

PART 1: FOUNDATIONS   17

1 Teaching Reading Across the Day   19

Reader Models   20

Texts, Tasks, and Sociocultural Context   25

    Texts   25

    Tasks   27

    Sociocultural Context   28

Teach Strategies and Build Knowledge—Together   30

2 Engaging, Explicit Instruction   33

What Research Says About Engaging, Explicit Instruction 33

Lesson Structures for Explicit Teaching   38

Making Decisions Within Lesson Structures   42

    Focused Practice Versus Orchestration 42

    Planning and Responsiveness   43

    Methods for Scaffolding   45

Choosing What to Teach: Standards, Curriculum, and Student Needs 50

    Using Lesson Structures to Adapt a Program or Curriculum 50

    Using Lesson Structures to Support Individual Needs 51

Grouping Students for Instruction   54

    Whole-Class Lessons   54

    Small-Group Lessons   54

    Individual Lessons   55

Selecting Texts for Instruction and Practice   56

PART 2:
LESSON STRUCTURES 59

3 Read-Aloud Lessons 61

Picture It: A Third Grade Read Aloud in Science 61

An Overview 65

What Research Says About Read-Aloud Lessons 66

Knowledge and Vocabulary Building Within Read-Aloud Lessons 68

Planning 69

    Texts 69

    Think Aloud 70

    Student Engagement 72

Structure and Timing 75

Responsive Teaching 76

Lesson in Action: Small-Group Read-Aloud Lesson, Fourth Grade, Social Studies 78

Lesson in Action: Whole-Class Read-Aloud Lesson, First Grade, English Language Arts 80

Lesson in Action: Whole-Class Read-Aloud Lesson, Fifth Grade, Science 82

Spin It: Video Aloud 84

Take It to Your Classroom 85

4 Phonics and Spelling Lessons 87

Picture It: Introducing /sh/ to a Group of First Graders 87

An Overview 93

What Research Says About Phonics and Spelling Lessons 95

Knowledge and Vocabulary Building Within Phonics and Spelling Lessons 96

Planning 97

    Formative Assessment and Progress Monitoring 97

    Tools and Materials 104

    Student Engagement 107

    Activities and Games 109

    High-Frequency Words 114

Structure and Timing 116

Responsive Teaching 118

Lesson in Action: Small-Group Phonics and Spelling Lesson, First Grade, /o/ 120

Lesson in Action: Whole-Class Phonics and Spelling Lesson, Second Grade, VCe Review 122

Take It to Your Classroom 124

5 Vocabulary Lessons 127

Picture It: Second Graders Expand Their Vocabulary With a Morphology Lesson 127

An Overview 131

What Research Says About Vocabulary Knowledge and Instruction 132

Planning 134

    Choosing Focus Words 134

    Explaining 137

    Applying: Deep Processing 138

    Extending 140

Structure and Timing 144

Responsive Teaching 145

Lesson in Action: Whole-Class Vocabulary Lesson, Fifth Grade, Science 146

Lesson in Action: Small-Group Vocabulary Lesson, Second Grade, Social Studies 148

Take It to Your Classroom 150

6 Focus Lessons 153

Picture It: A Small Group of Fourth Graders Learns a Strategy to Support Their Reading Engagement 153

An Overview 157

What Research Says About Focus Lessons 158

Knowledge and Vocabulary Building Within Focus Lessons 160

Planning 161

    Articulating a Strategy 161

    Texts for Demonstration 162

    Texts for Student Engagement 162

    Visual Anchors 163

Structure and Timing 164

Responsive Teaching 166

Lesson in Action: Individual Focus Lesson (Conference), Sixth Grade, Social Studies 168

Lesson in Action: Whole-Class Focus Lesson (Mini-lesson), Fourth Grade, Science 170

Lesson in Action: Small-Group Focus Lesson (Strategy Lesson), First Grade, English Language Arts 172

Spin It: Student-Led Focus Lessons 174

Take It to Your Classroom 176

7 Shared-Reading Lessons 179

Picture It: Second Graders Practice Fluency and Comprehension With Poetry 179

An Overview 182

What Research Says About Shared-Reading Lessons 183

    Comparing Shared Reading, Close Reading, and Read Aloud 184

Knowledge and Vocabulary Building Within Shared-Reading Lessons 185

Planning 186

    Texts 188

    Skills and Strategies 189

Structure and Timing 191

Responsive Teaching 192

Lesson in Action: Small-Group Shared-Reading Lesson, First Grade, English Language Arts 194

Lesson in Action: Whole-Class Shared-Reading Lesson, Second Grade, Social Studies 196

Spin It: Fluency-Oriented Reading Instruction (FORI) Lessons 198

Take It to Your Classroom 199

8 Close-Reading Lessons 201

Picture It: Seventh Graders Study a Multimodal History Text 201

An Overview 205

Knowledge and Vocabulary Building Within Close-Reading Lessons 207

What Research Says About Close Reading 208

Planning 210

    Texts 210

    Deciding What to Teach: Content 211

    Deciding What to Teach: Strategies 213

    Deciding How You Will Read 214

Structure and Timing 216

Responsive Teaching 217

Lesson in Action: Small-Group Close-Reading Lesson, Sixth Grade, English Language Arts 218

Lesson in Action: Whole-Class Close-Reading Lesson, Fifth Grade, Science 220

Spin It: Expand the Definition of Text 222

Take It to Your Classroom 223

9   Guided Inquiry Lessons   225

Picture It: Fifth Graders Reflect and
Set Goals   225

An Overview: Guided Inquiry Lessons   229

What Research Says About Guided Inquiry   231

Knowledge and Vocabulary Building
Within Guided Inquiry Lessons   232

Planning   233

     Conversation Fishbowl   233

     Craft Study   233

     Goal Setting   235

Structure and Timing   238

Responsive Teaching   239

Lesson in Action: Individual Goal
Setting Guided Inquiry Lesson, Second
Grade, English Language Arts   240

Lesson in Action: Whole-Class
Conversation Fishbowl Guided Inquiry
Lesson, Fourth Grade, English
Language Arts   242

Lesson in Action: Small-Group Craft
Study Guided Inquiry Lesson, Sixth
Grade, English Language Arts   244

Spin It: Expand the Definition of Text   246

Take It to Your Classroom   247

10   Reader's Theater Lessons   249

Picture It: Third Graders Practice
Reading a Script About Ancient Egypt   249

An Overview: Reader's Theater Lessons   252

What Research Says About
Reader's Theater   254

Knowledge and Vocabulary Building
Within Reader's Theater Lessons   255

Planning   256

     Groups   256

     Texts   256

     Weekly Schedule   259

Structure and Timing   260

Responsive Teaching   261

Lesson in Action: Small-Group
Reader's Theater Lesson, First Grade,
English Language Arts   262

Lesson in Action: Small-Group
Reader's Theater Lesson, Fourth Grade,
English Language Arts   264

Take It to Your Classroom   266

11 Conversation Lessons

11 Conversation Lessons   269

Picture It: Fifth Graders Take Part in a Book Club   269

An Overview: Conversation Lessons   272

What Research Says About Teaching Conversation Skills   273

Knowledge and Vocabulary Building Within Conversation Lessons   274

Planning   275

     Texts   275

     Grouping   276

     Skills and Strategies   278

Structure and Timing   280

Responsive Teaching   281

Lesson in Action: Whole-Class Conversation Lesson, Sixth Grade, English Language Arts   282

Lesson in Action: Partnership Conversation Lesson, Second Grade, English Language Arts   284

Lesson in Action: Small-Group Book Club Conversation Lesson, Fifth Grade, Science   286

Take It to Your Classroom   288

Appendix: Lesson Planning Templates   289

References   301

Index   321

Visit the companion website at
https://companion.corwin.com/courses/2024_TRAD
for access to video and downloadable resources.

Note From the Publisher: The author has provided content throughout the book that is available to you through QR (quick response) codes. To read a QR code, you must have a smartphone or tablet with a camera. We recommend that you download a QR code reader app that is made specifically for your phone or tablet brand.

Acknowledgments

I am so excited to be publishing my first book with Corwin Literacy and am especially grateful to everyone there, especially Lisa Luedeke, Elena Nikitina, Monica Eckman, and Mike Soules, for welcoming me and supporting me. Lisa, I am very grateful that you've trusted me throughout this process, and I deeply appreciate all of your guidance, responsiveness, and care.

Thanks to Rebecca Eaton for your thoughtful strategy and tireless work to spread the word about the book; to Gail Buschman, thank you for the engaging, colorful, navigable interior and for your collaboration and flexibility; to Rose Storey for the perfect cover; to Erin Livingston for all of your attention to detail—it is a clearer book because of your careful work; to Laura Barrett for the many ways you supported me and this work throughout the production process and for tolerating all of my newbie questions! I've learned so much from you; and to Sarah Ross and Zack Vann for all of your critical behind-the-scenes work with various tasks.

Katie Ray, I never want to write a book without you by my side! I love that you hold me to the highest standards, challenge me in ways that help my writing be better, and offer helpful critiques from big-picture ideas to noodling at the word level until everything is just right. I so appreciate you.

To my research assistants, Elaine Les and Yasmine Perry, thank you for the time and the care you gave to helping me identify the best studies, evaluate them, and use them to inform this manuscript throughout the process. (And thank you to Dr. Jennifer Urban for the introduction!)

This book comes to life because of the photographs, videos, and teaching vignettes from the classrooms I've been fortunate to spend time in. Thank you to school and district leaders and teachers in NBTS for welcoming me into your schools to teach lessons while cameras were rolling. I know I've said this a million times, but your classrooms are such special places and I love working with your students. Thank you especially to Jeannine Lanphear, Nicole LaTorre, Melissa Kopko, Nancy Porcelli, Christina Debari, Brianna Ryan, Katelyn Kohut, Kimberly Mory, Alexis Defilippo, Yasmeen Cocab,

Anthony Bruno, Janton Shorter, Katelyn Dwyer, Jess Norbut, Mercy Chang, Ann Kingsley, Laurie Stewart, Vicki Caputo, Brianna Bisconti, Lauren Runge, and Carly Cummings. And the biggest thanks of all to the incredible kindergarten, first-, second-, third-, fourth-, fifth-, and sixth-grade students of John Adams and Linwood! I can't wait for a world of teachers to learn from your brilliance in the Lesson in Action videos.

Deep gratitude to Nick Christoff for capturing the teaching and learning on video and in photos. The book would not be what it is without either and it was an absolute joy working with you throughout the process. You took such care with every single detail as if the book were your own. Thank you. Thanks also to Thomas and Lasso, Inc. for assisting with capturing the footage.

Thank you to my colleagues and members of my consulting team whom I lean on to be sounding boards, thought partners, and critical friends, especially those of you who pitched in with student work examples or read early versions of chapters and offered feedback: Emily Strang Campbell, Katherine Cetrulo, Gina Dignon, Angela Forero, Macie Kerbs, Clarisa Leal, Elisha Li, Lea Leibowitz, Jerry Maraia, Rosie Maurantonio, Lainie Powell, Cristy Rauseo, Leah Steiner, and Molly Feeney Wood.

Thanks to Mark Weakland for reviewing the phonics and spelling chapter.

Thank you—above all and always—to my family.

About the Author

© Fumie

Jennifer Serravallo is a *New York Times* bestselling author, award-winning educator, literacy consultant, frequent invited speaker at state and national conferences, and former member of the *Parents Magazine* editorial board. In 2023, she launched her podcast, *To the Classroom: Conversations With Researchers and Educators*. Jen is best known for creating books and resources rooted in research that help make responsive, strategic, differentiated literacy instruction possible for all educators.

Her latest books are *Teaching Reading Across the Day: Methods and Structures for Engaging, Explicit Instruction* (2024), *The Reading Strategies Book 2.0* (2023), *Teaching Writing in Small Groups* (2021), *A Teacher's Guide to Reading Conferences* (2019), and *Understanding Texts and Readers* (2018). Her books and resources are used around the world; *The Writing Strategies Book* (2017) and *The Reading Strategies Book* (2015, 1st edition) have been translated into French, Chinese, and Spanish.

Her comprehension assessment and teaching resources, *Complete Comprehension: Fiction* (2019) and *Complete Comprehension: Nonfiction* (2019), help teachers make sense of comprehension, especially in whole-chapter books and book-length nonfiction texts.

Jen holds a BA from Vassar College and an MA from Teachers College Columbia University, where she has also taught graduate and undergraduate classes.

Follow Jen on X (@jserravallo) and Instagram (@jenniferserravallo), learn more from her website/blog: www.jenniferserravallo.com, and join the Reading and Writing Strategies Facebook Community.

Introduction

We read all day long: We read fiction and feel lost in a book. We read emails filled with instructions we need to follow or that require a thoughtful response. We read the latest coverage of a tragic war halfway around the world and consider each journalist's perspective. We read to prepare dinner from a recipe, administer a child's medication correctly, and stay in touch with text message after text message on our phones. Reading is a critical life skill for us all, not merely something we do in school during an English language arts (ELA) block. Reading well opens possibilities. Struggling to read limits them—across our day and throughout our lifetimes.

Because reading is so critically important, the job of teaching students how to read well belongs to all of us. Reading well across disciplines and within varied contexts will help students to be versatile, flexible, deep readers who can better learn from their reading, transfer skills across subjects, and use strategies to meet the unique demands of reading in each content area. The depth and breadth of skills and knowledge that students will need to be proficient is not something they will only develop in the ELA block while reading literature; they need opportunities and support with thoughtful instruction in reading all day long. They also need teachers across their day (and across disciplines) who understand readers and reading and who can make instructional choices supporting not only students' knowledge development but also their reading skill development.

With all of the varied goals, skills, strategies, knowledge, and vocabulary that students need to learn (no matter the text or subject), as teachers, we need predictable, efficient, trusted structures for explicit and engaging teaching—structures that draw on the research and also make room for the *art* of teaching or what Paige et al. (2021) define as the "teacher's decision making that involves selection, differentiation, and delivery of engaging and efficacious reading instruction" (pp. 1–2). Structures that can be used no matter your curriculum or subject area. Structures we come to know so well that they streamline our planning and help students focus their attention on *what* we're teaching, not *how* we're teaching it, which helps to manage the cognitive load and aid learning.

⚙ What You'll Find in Parts I and II

Part I includes two chapters that explore foundations for this book. Chapter 1 builds the case for teaching reading across the whole day. Using the Active View of Reading model (Duke & Cartwright, 2021), you'll explore various aspects of reading you'll help your students develop and then consider the role that texts, tasks, and sociocultural context play in the act of reading. Chapter 2 takes a close look at explicit instruction as I unpack key recommendations from the last several decades of research, introduce you to the nine lesson types you'll read about in Part II, and offer a crash course in key decisions you'll make, no matter what lesson type you choose. I also share advice for when to teach lessons to the whole class and when to focus instruction with smaller groups. This chapter concludes with a general discussion of text selection for instruction and independent practice.

After exploring these foundations, each of the nine chapters in **Part II** focuses on one type of lesson. The order of the chapters is not significant, and in fact, you could read them in any order you choose. Once you understand the purposes of each type of lesson, you'll choose the ones that will best serve your students and the content you need to teach, likely using a blend of them across each school day. In each chapter, we'll explore how to identify a lesson focus and plan for an engaging explicit lesson, including considerations for text selection; how to monitor progress within a lesson to know if students are meeting your goals; how to ensure your lessons are supporting students with reading skills and strategies while also helping them build knowledge and grow their vocabularies; how to pace the lesson for maximum engagement; and how to plan for responsive teaching, including anticipating possible misunderstandings and how to offer feedback to guide students as they learn.

Note that throughout every chapter, I've tried to show *and* tell, providing both explanation and examples across a wide range of grade levels, subject areas, and different group sizes. So, while a lesson example (either a teaching vignette or video) might be with, say, a small group of first graders in a science classroom, if you focus on the teaching moves and the lesson structure, you will see they apply to any grade level, subject area, or grouping—even if you're an eighth-grade teacher teaching an ELA lesson to a whole class.

In each chapter in Part II, you'll find a repeated structure with familiar sections.

Picture It

Each chapter starts with a teaching vignette and the lesson plan behind it. The callouts in this section note the hallmarks of each lesson type and key takeaways to make the teaching effective, efficient, and engaging.

An Overview

In this section, you'll find an explanation of the lesson type, along with research highlighting its essential elements and why and how this kind of teaching has a positive impact on students.

What Research Says

Each chapter is filled with research. In this section, you'll find a short summary of key findings that are aligned to, and that provide support for, the lesson type that is the focus of the chapter.

Knowledge and Vocabulary Building

In every lesson, you won't only be planning for your students' reading skill development—you'll also consider the goals you have for knowledge and vocabulary building. In this section, you'll find advice, ideas, considerations, and research to inform this aspect of your planning and instruction.

Planning

Next, you'll read about how to prepare, whether you're planning a lesson from scratch or adapting a lesson from a core program or existing curriculum. You can reference that lesson's planning template in the appendix or online as you learn about text considerations for both your demonstrations and student practice as well as other tips unique to each lesson type.

Structure and Timing

This section includes a quick guide to timing for each part of the lesson as well as tips for making it as impactful as possible.

Responsive Teaching

Here, you'll find key things to look for to help you anticipate how students might respond to the various parts of the lesson and sample prompts, redirections, questions, and responses to keep students moving toward your lesson objective.

Lesson in Action

With the online video that accompanies each chapter, you can watch me teach at least two complete lessons. For each lesson, you'll find annotations on a lesson plan that highlight my planning decisions, things I noticed when I watched the video, responsive decisions I made on the spot that deviated from the plans, ideas for what I'd do differently if I had a do-over, thoughts about what I'd teach next based on how students responded, and more. I hope these offer you not *perfect* examples but rather realistic examples of how to plan and deliver lessons, bringing the structures you'll read about to life while also responding to the students in front of you.

Spin It

In a few of the chapters, you'll read about ways to innovate with the lesson structure—for example, by changing up the text types or by offering students a chance to lead the lesson.

Take it to Your Classroom

These sections offer key takeaways and things to think about from the chapter as you bring what you've read to life with your students.

From start to finish, this book highlights research in the teaching of reading. I believe teaching should be informed by empirical research to ensure that we are developing all facets of reading, making appropriate text decisions, and making choices based on what will have the best chance of working for the most students. While writing this book, I read hundreds of studies and synthesized and translated the key findings into practical ideas you can use in your classroom. That said, I also think there are limitations to what research can tell us, and we need to be mindful of where the science leaves off and the art of teaching needs to pick up. The moment-to-moment decisions we make as teachers during lessons and the interactions we have with students during a lesson can have the biggest impact on their learning and growth. So, we need to respect the science and the promising findings published in research journals while also trusting the collective knowledge that comes from our practice and experiences with children in classrooms every day.

Students in our classrooms are unique with diverse backgrounds, strengths, and needs, and we must create lessons (or tailor lessons from an existing program or curriculum) with individual students in mind. Throughout the book, you'll find advice for planning *before* you teach a lesson, such as the amount of scaffolding you'll use to introduce the lesson, what activities and tasks you'll plan for students to do, or how you'll pace the lesson. But, as I say throughout the book, you should also expect to be surprised by what happens *during* the lesson and be prepared to respond in the moment with prompts, feedback, or new examples to make the lesson objectives even clearer for students.

We need to respect the science and the promising findings published in research journals while also trusting the collective knowledge that comes from our practice and experiences with children in classrooms every day.

⚙ What You'll Find in the Online Resources

The videos available in the online resources are a critical component of this book. When you pause to watch the examples of teaching included with each chapter, you can envision the principles, elements, pacing, structure, and moves of each lesson type. You'll see a variety of grade levels and content areas represented, which should help you to notice what stays the same, regardless of the content or age of the students.

The lessons were filmed in five classrooms across two days in two New Jersey schools, one that serves students in Grades K–4 and the other with students in Grades 5–6. As a guest in these classrooms, I visited each briefly the week prior to filming, and I planned my lessons based on information I learned about the children from my visit and their teachers. I also aligned all the lessons to the content area, ELA, and phonics curricula and scope and sequences of each class. I used a few of the lesson texts provided by the curriculum, but the majority of texts I chose to align with the current topics and skills students were studying.

Table 0.1 provides an overview of the video lessons you'll find online, though you'll want to watch the video examples when you are prompted to do so at the end of Chapters 3–11. Notice the variety of whole-class and small-group lessons, the range of grade levels, and that lessons were filmed during English language arts, science, and social studies classes.

Table 0.1   An Overview of Lesson Videos Available Online

Chapter	Video Number and Title
Read-Aloud Lessons	**3.1** Small-Group Read-Aloud Lesson, Fourth Grade, Social Studies **3.2** Whole-Class Read-Aloud Lesson, First Grade, English Language Arts **3.3** Whole-Class Read-Aloud Lesson, Fifth Grade, Science
Phonics and Spelling Lessons	**4.1** Small-Group Phonics and Spelling Lesson, First Grade, /ŏ/ **4.2** Whole-Class Phonics and Spelling Lesson, Second Grade, VCe Review
Vocabulary Lessons	**5.1** Whole-Class Vocabulary Lesson, Fifth Grade, Science **5.2** Small-Group Vocabulary Lesson, Second Grade, Social Studies
Focus Lessons	**6.1** Individual Focus Lesson (Conference), Sixth Grade, Social Studies **6.2** Whole-Class Focus Lesson (Mini-lesson), Fourth Grade, Science **6.3** Small-Group Focus Lesson (Strategy Lesson), First Grade, English Language Arts
Shared-Reading Lessons	**7.1** Small-Group Shared-Reading Lesson, First Grade, English Language Arts **7.2** Whole-Class Shared-Reading Lesson, Second Grade, Social Studies
Close-Reading Lessons	**8.1** Small-Group Close-Reading Lesson, Sixth Grade, English Language Arts **8.2** Whole-Class Close-Reading Lesson, Fifth Grade, Science
Guided Inquiry Lessons	**9.1** Individual Goal Setting Guided Inquiry Lesson, Second Grade, English Language Arts **9.2** Whole-Class Conversation Fishbowl Guided Inquiry Lesson, Fourth Grade, English Language Arts **9.3** Small-Group Craft Study Guided Inquiry Lesson, Sixth Grade, English Language Arts
Reader's Theater Lessons	**10.1** Small-Group Reader's Theater Lesson, First Grade, English Language Arts **10.2** Small-Group Reader's Theater Lesson, Fourth Grade, English Language Arts
Conversation Lessons	**11.1** Whole-Class Conversation Lesson, Sixth Grade, English Language Arts **11.2** Partnership Conversation Lesson, Second Grade, English Language Arts **11.3** Small-Group Book Club Conversation Lesson, Fifth Grade, Science

Lesson Plans and Templates

You'll find complete lesson plans to accompany both the Picture It teaching vignettes that begin each chapter, and each of the Lesson in Action video lesson examples in Table 0.1. These complete plans, as well as the templates I used to plan each lesson type are available in the book's appendix (for photocopying) and online in grayscale (in writeable PDFs to type into or for easy printing if you prefer to plan by hand; see Figure 0.1).

Figure 0.1   Sample Planning Templates

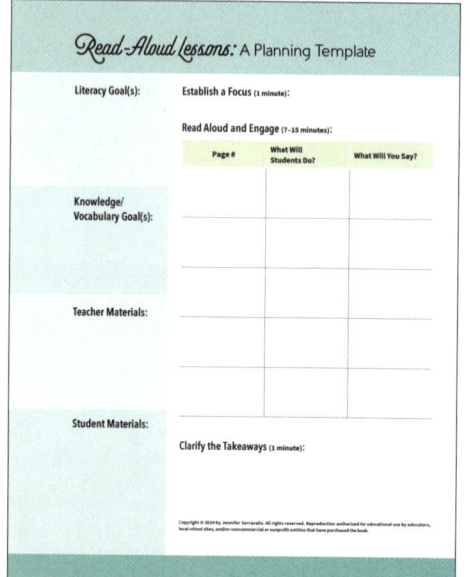
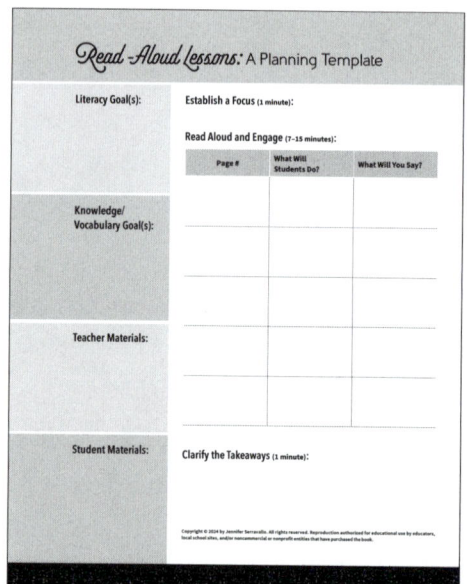
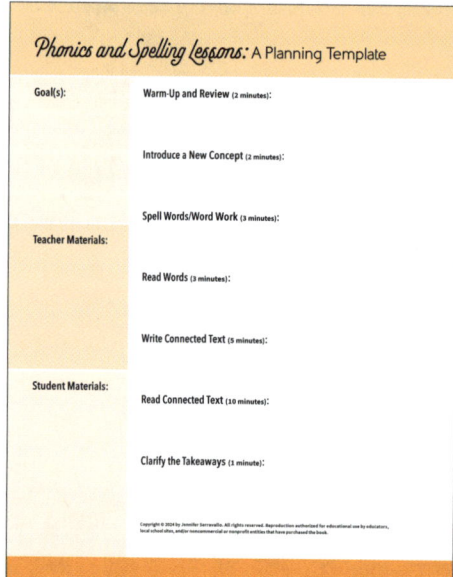
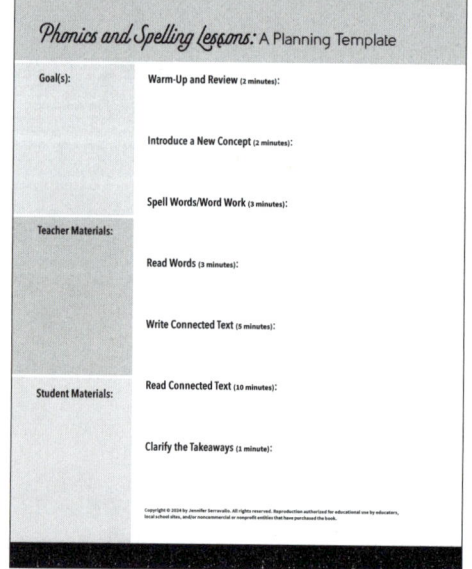

✳ Using *Teaching Reading Across the Day* as Professional Learning and/or as a Supplemental Resource

The advice, lesson types, and ideas throughout the book stand on decades of research on effective teaching and can be helpful in a wide range of classrooms and for teachers at every point in their career—from first-year teachers to experienced educators looking to fine tune; from classrooms using new core reading programs to those creating their own curriculum from scratch; from teachers of kindergarten through eighth grade; from ELA teachers to teachers of content studies such as science or history (see Table 0.2).

Table 0.2

If . . .	How This Book Can Help . . .
You recently adopted a new core reading program.	Even with a scripted program, you'll make choices—you'll modify a long lesson to fit within your time constraints, swap out a text for another that's more relevant or engaging, tailor your responses during lessons to the students in front of you, and more. Often, you'll keep the text and task the program suggests but need to use a different lesson structure with more or less scaffolding. In this book, you'll find practical, use-tomorrow advice and many other modifications necessary to adapt any program.
You embrace (or have been asked to embrace) the science of reading and want clarity around what it looks like in practice.	Much of the science of reading research tells us what happens in the brain of a reader and what areas of reading instruction to focus on. I've read the research—there are over 300 citations throughout this book—and have used that, together with countless hours of teaching in classrooms around the country and working with hundreds of educators over decades, to suggest methods, structures, and practices that honor both the science of reading and the art of teaching reading.
You're a content area teacher (i.e., science, social studies) and you assign reading, read aloud to students, or include texts in your lessons in another way.	Though a primary purpose for assigning reading in the content areas may be to help students learn content, most students will benefit from explicit instruction about how to read discipline-specific texts and will need guided practice to do so. The teaching methods and practices in the nine lesson structures in this book are designed to help students develop the skills to both read and engage meaningfully with texts *and* to learn content from the texts.
You work in a district where you create your own curriculum maps and lesson plans from scratch.	If you're designing lessons from the ground up, you'll need streamlined templates to help you plan efficiently and advice for how to maximize effectiveness. After reading this book, you'll know nine lesson structures and an assortment of methods to use within each that you can use to teach reading about any topic in any subject, text, or grade level.

(Continued)

Table 0.2 (Continued)

If . . .	How This Book Can Help . . .
You are looking for ways to boost student engagement during lessons.	The most effective lessons are ones in which students are highly active and engaged—some research suggests that the most effective teachers elicit three to five opportunities for simple responses (quick choral responses, gestures such as a thumbs up, or holding up a response cards) and at least one opportunity for a complex response (turn and talk, writing a response on a whiteboard, or partner reading) *per minute* of each lesson. This book is filled with suggestions and concrete examples of how to engage students in lessons and then respond with feedback and prompts to keep them active.
You want practical, tangible examples—written lesson plans and videos—of what effective research-based reading instruction looks like.	Many books about research-based instruction tell about it, but few show it with concrete examples. This book contains more than 30 sample lesson plans in K–8 ELA, science, and social studies classrooms, along with video of me teaching about two dozen lessons to show what the plans look like in action. The videos were filmed across two days, all in one take, with very minimal editing. Watching them, I thought of things I would have done differently, and I have ideas for follow-up (included as commentary alongside the plans). My goal was to show not perfect lessons but rather the reality of what it means to be informed by all the best research and have the most well-intentioned plans but then need to modify and make on-the-spot decisions when teaching.
You want practical ideas for how to bring more intentional knowledge building and vocabulary development into each lesson.	Research has consistently found that knowledge and vocabulary are critical to comprehension. All of the lesson structures in this book, and all of the written and video lesson examples, show how to balance explicit teaching of strategies with intentional knowledge and vocabulary building. In addition, an entire chapter is devoted to explicit teaching of vocabulary.
You have students reading below grade level, but you know they need experience with grade-level texts.	All students need experience with grade-level texts every day. Depending on the level of text each student can read independently and their background knowledge of the topic they are reading about, they may need more or less scaffolding with that text. Several of the lesson structures in this book offer the support your students need to engage with a text that is more complex than what they can read independently.
Your students need support with foundational skills, including phonics and fluency.	Whether you teach Grades K–2 (where all or most of your class will need support with these skills) or Grades 3–8 (where only certain students might need support), the lesson structures in this book can help. Lesson structures for phonics and spelling, reader's theater, shared reading, or focus lessons that can be centered around word reading or fluency strategies will keep your teaching streamlined and student engagement high.
You are in a preservice program learning to be a teacher or are new to the teaching profession.	The advice throughout the book is based on decades of research with hundreds of links to peer-reviewed studies and is presented clearly and with helpful scaffolds (i.e., lesson templates, video examples) to make it accessible. The lesson structures make planning more streamlined and focused and teaching more intentional, and the guidance for responsiveness and offering feedback supports the on-your-toes decision-making that is critical to effective instruction.

⚙ Using *Teaching Reading Across the Day* With Other Books I've Authored

The information in this book adds to and complements my previous work on reading instruction but can also be a helpful resource for anyone unfamiliar with my past work (see some connections to my most recent publications in Table 0.3). Note that *Conferring With Readers* (2007), *Teaching Reading in Small Groups* (2010), *The Literacy Teacher's Playbook: 3–5* (2012), *The Literacy Teacher's Playbook: K–2* (2013), *The Reading Strategies Book* (2015), and *Connecting With Students Online* (2021) are all out of print at my request. While these books contain some information that is still relevant and helpful, there is at least some information in each book that is outdated or does not represent my latest thinking. The titles in the following table are aligned to current research. If you have *Teaching Reading in Small Groups*, for example, you should retire it and transition to *Teaching Reading Across the Day* for more updated, comprehensive, and research-aligned advice about how to plan and lead small-group (and whole-class!) lessons.

Table 0.3

If You Have/Have Read/Have Used	How *Teaching Reading Across the Day (TRAD)* May Help
The Reading Strategies Book 2.0 (*RSB2.0*, 2023)	*TRAD* will help you bring the research-based strategies from *RSB2.0* to life in your classroom. *TRAD* offers dozens of videos to see the incorporation of strategies in a variety of lesson structures for a range of ages and will help you see how strategies are one part of a well-crafted lesson that should also include intentional knowledge and vocabulary building. You can use the charts, strategies, and prompts from *RSB2.0* to simplify and streamline planning using the templates and advice from *TRAD*. *RSB2.0*'s skill progressions can help you monitor progress during all the lessons described in *TRAD*. Between these two books, there are over 1,000 citations to peer-reviewed research; they make a perfect text set to help with both *what* to teach and *how* to teach it in any classroom.
A Teacher's Guide to Reading Conferences (*TGRC*, 2019)	In *TRAD*, I cover lesson structures for whole-class and small-group teaching (with occasional mention of one-on-one instruction). In *TGRC*, I offer advice for mostly one-on-one conferences, though I explore small-group strategy lessons (also known as *focus lessons* in *TRAD*) and book clubs (also known as *conversation lessons* in *TRAD*). Both *TGRC* and *TRAD* offer video examples of a variety of types of lessons.
Understanding Texts and Readers (*UT&R*, 2018)	In *UT&R*, I focus on quantitative and qualitative leveling and expectations for reader response aligned to text complexity for second- to sixth-grade text levels. It also includes skill progressions aligned to comprehension goals. The content in *UT&R* could inform text selection and help you monitor progress in comprehension as you plan lessons as described in *TRAD*.
Complete Comprehension: Fiction (*CC: F*, 2019) and *Complete Comprehension: Nonfiction* (*CC: NF*, 2019)	*CC: F* and *CC: NF* are assessment, evaluation, and teaching kits focused on increasingly complex whole works of fiction and nonfiction. In the Teach portion of each resource, there are video examples of some (but not all) of the same lesson types found in *TRAD* (close reading, read aloud, focus lessons, etc.). However, the primary focus of *CC: F* and *CC: NF* is not on the lesson structures, so *TRAD* could help you teach more explicitly, efficiently, and with increased engagement based on the information you glean from *CC: F* and *CC: NF*.
The Writing Strategies Book (2017) and *Teaching Writing in Small Groups* (*TWiSG*, 2021)	These two books, one about writing strategies (*what to teach*) and one about writing instructional methods (*how to teach*), could work well to round out a classroom that uses the lesson structures in *TRAD*. In truth, many of the structures I explore in *TWiSG* can be used as whole-class lesson structures, just as many of the structures in *TRAD* work well in either a whole-class or small-group format.
No other books by Jennifer Serravallo	*TRAD* can be your introduction to my approach to engaging, efficient, explicit instruction in literacy! Like all of my work, *TRAD* is designed to offer practical advice and clear examples no matter the grade level you teach, your subject area, or your approach to literacy instruction.

The advice, lesson types, and ideas throughout the book stand on decades of research on effective teaching and can be helpful in a wide range of classrooms and for teachers at every point in their career.

PART 1

Foundations

Teaching Reading Across the Day

There's an old adage that students learn to read until third grade, and after that, they read to learn. But in truth, we never stop learning to read and, ideally, we learn from our reading from the very start. Because of this, students need reading instruction at every grade level and across the day: We should bring instruction about *how to read* and opportunities to do so into our content areas, and we should bring opportunities to build knowledge and vocabulary into our literacy block (Bryant et al., 2001; Greenleaf et al., 2011; Hwang et al., 2022; Hwang, Cabell et al., 2023; Hwang, McMaster et al., 2023; McKenna & Robinson, 1990; Swanson et al., 2014; Vaughn et al., 2013).

Successful reading requires a complex, interconnected set of word reading skills, executive functioning skills, and the use of comprehension skills and strategies together with deep and varied knowledge—from knowledge about words (i.e., phonics, morphology, vocabulary) to knowledge related to culture and content to knowledge about genre, topic, language, verbal reasoning, and theory of mind (Cervetti & Hiebert, 2015; Cervetti & Wright, 2020; Graesser et al., 1994; Kintsch, 1986; Moll et al., 1992). Reading happens with a text, for purpose(s), and always within context(s). To develop this depth and breadth of skills and knowledge, experience the varied purposes and contexts for reading, and develop facility with reading any kind of text, all teachers should be reading teachers and students should be reading across the day.

⚙ Reader Models

For decades, researchers have created models to synthesize and organize research findings. You may be familiar with the Simple View of Reading (Gough & Tumner, 1986), which posits that reading comprehension is the product of word recognition and language comprehension; Scarborough's Rope (Scarborough, 2001), which unpacks word recognition and language comprehension strands included in the Simple View's broader categories; the Componential Model of Reading (Joshi & Aaron, 2000), which includes cognitive, psychological, and ecological factors related to reading; the Construction-Integration Model (Kintsch, 1988), which explains how readers create a mental model for comprehension; the Direct and Indirect Effects Model of Reading (DIER; Kim, 2020, 2023), which highlights hierarchical, dynamic, and interactive relationships among elements; and/or the Active View of Reading (Duke & Cartwright, 2021), which includes the contributions of executive functioning skills and bridging processes (overlapping areas between word recognition and language comprehension) to proficient reading (see Figure 1.1).

Figure 1.1   Duke and Cartwright's Active View of Reading (2021)

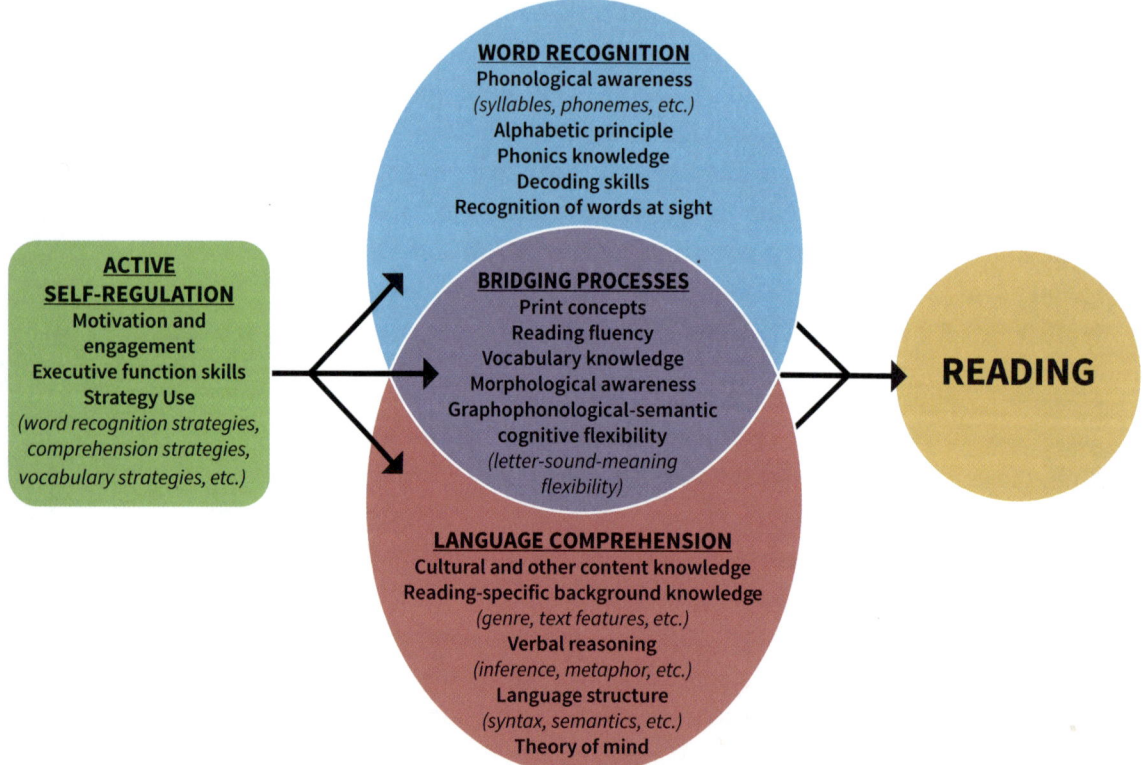

Source: Used with permission of John Wiley & Sons from, *The Science of Reading Progresses*, Duke, Nell K.; Cartwright, Kelly B., 56, 2021 permission conveyed through Copyright Clearance Center, Inc.

An understanding of any of these models can help us conceptualize research-based components that would be important to include in a comprehensive approach to literacy instruction within English language arts (ELA) and the content areas. These models can also help us choose reading resources and curricula, plan lesson content effectively, and guide our assessments as we attempt to pinpoint sources of reading difficulty.

Take a look at Table 1.1 on pages 21–24 to see a quick explanation and example of each of the components from the Active View of Reading model, a model that is both current and comprehensive. Notice how most of the components include both skills (which I'll define as *proficiencies*, something a reader is able to do) as well as knowledge (something a reader needs to know). Knowledge is a part of nearly everything—even the ability to use and apply strategies (a reader's goal-directed actions) requires a knowledge of those strategies. As you read through Table 1.1, consider the application of each of these components when reading literature or informational texts, when reading during an ELA class, or when reading during history, science, math, or any other content area.

Table 1.1 Explanations and Examples of the Components Detailed in the Active View of Reading

Component from the Active View of Reading	Quick Explanation	One Example
Active Self-Regulation		
Motivation and engagement	Approaching a text with a desire to read it, being interested in the topic, having a positive self-concept about reading, finding value in the reading Engagement may overlap with executive function skills	I am excited to read this book because I'm interested in the topic, and I have a plan to talk about it with my friends later.
Executive function (EF) skills	Includes skills such as cognitive flexibility, working memory, inhibitory control, attention, and planning	I can hold information in my mind from chapter to chapter, remembering important information. If I get distracted while reading, I can refocus my attention.
Strategy use	Taking an active approach to reading means using strategies as needed. *Strategies* are conscious actions or steps a reader can take to help with anything from reading words accurately to comprehension	I realize that I don't understand what I just read, so I'm going to back up, reread, and pause after each sentence to check my understanding before moving on.

(Continued)

Table 1.1 (Continued)

Component from the Active View of Reading	Quick Explanation	One Example
Word Recognition		
Phonological awareness	Attention to the sounds in spoken words; most helpful for reading is phonemic awareness	I know the word *lighter* has four phonemes, or sounds: /l/ /ī/ /t/ /ûr/ .
Alphabetic principle	An understanding that the sounds in spoken language can be represented by written letters	I know that I can spell /t/ with the letter t.
Phonics knowledge	Knowledge of sound-letter (phoneme–grapheme) correspondences In English, there are around 44 phonemes (sounds) but there are around 250 graphemes (letters or letter groups that correspond to a single sound)	I know how to spell *lighter* with seven letters, even though it has four phonemes.
Decoding skills	Being able to break words apart (segment) and blend sounds to correctly pronounce words using phonetic and/or morphological knowledge	If I don't know the word *lighter*, I can go through the word, pronouncing it part-by-part—/l/ /ī/ /t/ /ûr/ or light-er—then blend the sounds together to say lighter.
Recognition of words on sight	Eventually, all words should become *sight words*, words that a reader knows right away without having to decode them. Usually, a word becomes a sight word after a reader orthographically maps the word, connecting letters, sounds, and meaning	I slowed down to decode *lighter*, and the next time I see it, I'll know it right away and don't need to segment and blend. I can just read it.

Component from the Active View of Reading	Quick Explanation	One Example
Bridging Processes		
Print concepts	Understanding conventions of printed language, such as knowing how to hold a book with the spine on the left; knowing to read the text left-to-right, top-to-bottom; knowing what the punctuation marks on the page direct a reader to do, and so on	When I am reading a page with multiple lines of print, I start at the top left, read across the page, then go to the next line to continue my reading.
Reading fluency	Accurate and automatic word reading and reading with proper phrasing, pace, and prosody (expression, intonation, emphasis) informed by the meaning of the text	As I read this character's dialogue, I think about how he's feeling and use expression in my voice to match it. I read it smoothly and it sounds like someone talking.
Vocabulary knowledge	Understanding words in a text Readers need to be able to correctly pronounce the word and know its meaning, especially related to the context of the text in which they encounter it	I can pronounce the word *row* and I know it can mean to use oars to move a boat. But in this context, it describes an argument between two people.
Morphological awareness	Awareness of meaning-based units in words and using that knowledge to figure out what a word means and its likely pronunciation	I know that *spect* often means *observe*, *in-* means *into*, and *-ion* changes a verb to a noun, and this knowledge helps me to break the word *inspection* into parts to read it and to figure out its meaning.
Graphophonological–semantic cognitive flexibility	A reading-specific EF skill that involves the ability to manage and shift attention continuously between letter–sound information and meaning information associated with printed words	As I'm reading, I pay attention to what the words say and how to read them.

(Continued)

Table 1.1 (Continued)

Component from the Active View of Reading	Quick Explanation	One Example
Language Comprehension		
Cultural knowledge	What readers understand about people, social norms, practices, experiences, and more related to the culture(s) they interact with or are part of	This story is set in an urban middle school in present-day United States—similar to where I live and go to school—so I can bring what I know to help me visualize the story, but the character's cultural background (first-generation Chinese American) is different from mine, so I'll be learning about that culture from the text.
Content knowledge	Information readers bring to a text about a topic and concepts related to a topic, which they may have learned from a variety of experiences (lessons in school, books they've read, shows they've watched, experiences, and so on)	This textbook chapter is about planets in our solar system, so I'll use what I know from the Magic School Bus book I read about this topic and remember what I learned on my trip to the planetarium to help me understand this text.
Reading-specific background knowledge	Knowledge of a genre and its elements; for example, how texts of that genre are typically structured	This book is a mystery and I know there is always a detective who collects clues, gets tricked by a red herring somewhere along the way, and eventually figures out the mystery. I'll use what I know about that predictable structure to pay attention to the important details.
Verbal reasoning	Using reasoning to make inferences, including when readers encounter figurative language	I know that the phrase *hit the road* doesn't literally mean to hit the street with a stick, based on the context and how the phrase is used.
Language structure	Understanding the organization of information within a sentence and how the information connects with other information	In the sentence, "Katie was ready for her race—the hardest event she'd ever tried—because of her dedicated practice," I understand that the information offset in em-dashes is meant to offer extra background information, a parenthetical. I know that *her* and *she* refers to Katie, the subject of the sentence.
Theory of mind	Making inferences about a character's feelings, actions, motivations, and more People develop this in life, and readers apply it when reading texts	I can understand why the character locked her sister out of her room, even though she didn't say why, because in an earlier chapter, her sister took her favorite sweater without asking and got a stain on it.

Source: Adapted from Duke & Cartwright (2021).

⊛ Texts, Tasks, and Sociocultural Context

The Active View is a reader model because it details what the reader brings to the text, what's in the reader's mind, and what the reader does. But notice the authors are also very clear that reading is not *only* about the reader: They include an important note that "reading is also impacted by text, task, and sociocultural context" (Duke & Cartwright, 2021, p. S33). These additional factors are critical to consider when planning reading instruction.

Texts

Just as we evaluate what a reader brings to a text, we can and should evaluate what each text demands of the reader. You can evaluate the level of complexity to ensure you're choosing appropriate texts for your grade level, and you can also evaluate the information, concepts, and content in the text to make decisions about what to highlight in your lessons.

All students need experience every day with grade-level texts. But how do we know when a text is "grade level"? Unfortunately, it's not a simple thing to determine. Different leveling systems help us assign numeric and alphabetic levels to texts based on various criteria, with correlation charts that match level ranges to grade levels. While these leveling systems can "get you in the ballpark" (Hiebert, 2011, p. 2), none of them are completely scientific or as precise as we may assume.

Quantitative leveling is done by computers that count (*quant-*) aspects such as word length and numbers of syllables, word frequency and repetition, sentence length, text length, and overall cohesion (how much the words within the selection relate to each other). Though it may seem like we'd get a perfect result every time, consider this: *Horrible Harry and the Birthday Girl* (Kline, 2016), a text that a second grader might choose to read, has about the same Lexile level as *The Grapes of Wrath* (Steinbeck, 1939). The computer only sees the shorter sentences and simpler language of Steinbeck's work, not the complex themes and ideas in the text. Another example: the dystopian thriller *The Running Man* by Stephen King (1982) is the same Lexile level as *Trixie the Halloween Fairy* (Meadows, 2009) from the Rainbow Magic series—one is OK to hand to a first grader and the other would give most of them nightmares!

Qualitative leveling, on the other hand, evaluates (*qual-*) aspects of texts only humans can judge (though I wouldn't be surprised if an AI tool exists or is currently in development), such as levels of meaning or text purpose, text structure and organization, language conventionality and clarity, text content, themes and ideas, literary features, sentence complexity, and knowledge demands. While these text qualities are much more helpful for planning instruction—knowing the themes of a narrative are complex could help me choose strategies for helping a reader to understand them, knowing the sentence complexity is challenging could help me think of supports for sentence fluency, and so on—it's important to remember that even people with expertise in a given qualitative leveling system will, at times, arrive at a different level for the same text. They may, for example, weigh different elements more heavily than others or skew the level up or down based on their own background or bias about what makes for an age-appropriate theme.

So again, while not a perfect science, using one or more leveling systems can give you a general sense of grade-level appropriateness, but then you'll need to read any text you plan to use for instruction and consider its content in relation to what your students know and are able to do. For example, consider the following questions:

* How relevant is this text to my students' interests and identities?

* Does the information in the text align to what we're studying?

* What knowledge does the author assume the reader has (and do my students have it)?

* What challenges and complexities are in the text, and what strategies might my students need as they engage with it?

In addition to reader–text questions such as those in the list above, in Chapters 3–11, you'll find additional advice and considerations for text selection and use specific to each lesson structure.

Tasks

Any act of reading also includes a task (or a purpose): Why is the reader reading this and what will they do with the text or ideas from the text once they've read it? Based on a task or purpose, the way we read, the depth with which we read—even how we read—might be different. Consider, for example, how you read an email that you open when you're not sure if it's spam. Or how you're reading this book or any others that you are studying for helpful information for your teaching craft. Or how you read a cherished letter from a loved one.

In school, tasks can vary widely from asking readers to work on reading words accurately (as you will in phonics and spelling lessons), to asking them to summarize the key information from the text, to preparing for discussion groups about the text, to reading deeply to analyze and interpret

an author's craft, and more. When you teach, you almost always assign the task, but you also want to help nurture students to be self-directed, independent, and motivated readers who establish their own goals, purposes, and plans for their reading. You'll want them, for example, to decide to pick up a book because they want to get lost in the world of the story or to choose a text to learn new information about a topic they are passionate about.

Reading tasks and purposes might be unique to certain content areas, from ELA to math to science or history. When I read a math problem, my task is to understand what information is important to solving the problem and what is ancillary, to organize the information and come up with a sequenced plan for solving it, and then to reread to double check that I applied all the information from the problem in my solution. When I read a history textbook, I am thinking as a historian—linking events together, determining causes and effects, and remembering key historical figures and their roles in the events of history. And when I read a poem as inspiration to write my own poetry, I might study an author's use of figurative language and infer about their decision-making to inform my own decisions.

Sociocultural Context

Reading isn't something that only happens "inside the head" of the reader (Tierney & Pearson, 2021). Instead, outside factors mediate reading, contributing to and impacting the way a reader approaches a text and the meanings a reader derives from the text. The social context (who the reader is reading with or talking to about their reading) and cultural context (what cultural background and experience the reader brings to the reading and how aligned the text is to what the reader knows and considers interesting and important) shapes their reading experience, their purposes for reading, and how they read.

Social factors can influence children's experiences as readers in the classroom, including whether or not they have conversations with teachers and peers about specific texts, such as during literature circles or whole-class conversations. The general attitudes and culture around reading in the classroom can also influence readers. For example, are we, in this classroom, a community of readers who recommends books to each other, makes time to share texts together, and gets excited about new titles, or is reading something we do only from textbooks when assigned?

Factors outside of school can also impact readers' experiences—cultural norms and community perspectives about reading, how family and community members talk (or don't talk) with students about specific texts, what purposes they see for reading outside school, and more. For example, in certain cultures, oral storytelling plays an important role, and storytellers are valued and respected. A reader who comes from such a culture and has grown up hearing and enjoying stories told again and again might easily connect with narrative texts. We can also consider language practices that are common and/or valued within a community—such as translanguaging between English and Spanish in a multilingual household—and the extent to which the students' reading experiences align to that linguistic context (España & Herrera, 2020). As teachers, we need to develop what Ladson-Billings (1995) calls *cultural competence*, where we strive to know as much as possible about the cultures of the students we teach, "utilize students' culture as a vehicle for learning" (p. 161), and "work back and forth between the lives of students and the life of school" (Ladson-Billings, 2006, p. 36).

While most standards and standardized assessments don't consider sociocultural context, we must acknowledge that reading doesn't exist within the vacuum of the classroom, so neither should our reading instruction. When we learn about the social, cultural, and linguistic backgrounds and rich funds of knowledge that students bring to school and to their reading (Moll et al., 1992), provide opportunities for students to be social around their reading (Guthrie et al., 2012), and acknowledge that "literacy practices are purposeful and embedded in social goals and cultural practices" (Barton et al., 2000, p. 8), our reading instruction will be more meaningful and complete (Nieto, 2017; Souto-Manning, 2010; Souto-Manning & Martell, 2016).

⚙ Teach Strategies and Build Knowledge–Together

Instruction during ELA and across the day in various subjects and content areas needs to support students with the full complex range of skills and strategies they need to read successfully while also acknowledging their existing knowledge and building on it. Students will need experience reading a wide range of texts (different genres, text types, and levels of complexity) with varying levels of support from you, for assorted tasks and purposes, in differing social contexts.

The ultimate goal of reading is comprehension, and we know from research that readers need both knowledge and strategies to make meaning of texts. Knowledge alone is not enough; children need strategies both to *activate* their knowledge and to *integrate* and *mediate* knowledge (e.g., summarizing, inferring) while reading to form a coherent mental model of the text (Cervetti & Wright, 2020; Cromley & Azevedo, 2007; Kintsch, 1988). Strategies alone are not enough, either. Research has shown that when we ask students to try new strategies during reading instruction, doing so in texts where they have background knowledge (because the texts are connected to content area studies or because students already know about the topic) and/or where they are motivated and engaged will reduce cognitive load and support their facility with the new learning (Peng et al., 2023; Willingham, 2006). It's also important to remember that while there is a robust research base for strategies, as Robertson writes, "strategies are not the end goal of instruction. Rather, strategies are vital tools that enable readers to access textual information, accomplish learning goals, and acquire knowledge" (2021, p. 146).

Over time, you'll help your students build their knowledge of people, places, and things through your content studies and through the texts you carefully select for demonstration as well as with those you choose or offer for guided and independent practice. Importantly, students learn *from* their reading; in short, reading begets knowledge and knowledge sets you up to read with more comprehension and purpose (Bråten & Samuelstuen, 2004; Braunger & Lewis, 1997; Hwang et al., 2022), something Pearson calls the "virtuous cycle" (Serravallo, 2023a).

Engaging, Explicit Instruction

Explicit instruction means to teach with intention and clarity in a structured and systematic way. During lessons, students should be highly *engaged* and active. The teacher must be responsive to student needs, adjusting plans as necessary to help students move toward learning targets.

What Research Says About Engaging, Explicit Instruction

The idea of explicit instruction—and research to support it—has been around for decades; researchers and practitioners define and describe it in slightly different (though mostly complementary) ways. For example, Hollingsworth and Ybarra (2017) stipulate eight lesson design components, Rosenshine (1986, 2012) lists ten principles of effective instruction, and Archer and Hughes (2011) identify sixteen elements of explicit instruction, though there are notable overlaps among them all.

The recommendations for explicit instruction offered by Rosenshine (1971, 1986) and others (Kirschner et al., 2006; Paas & Sweller, 2012; Robertson,

2021) draw largely from cognitive science and research on "master teachers" (Amendum, Li, Hall et al., 2009; Rosenshine, 2012). The recommended elements can guide us to plan and deliver instruction that is clear and supportive and that reduces working memory load so new learning can be stored in long-term memory. Figure 2.1 lists essential elements of instruction that inform the lessons in this book (drawn from the research I've mentioned) with descriptions of what each one looks like in practice. You'll see evidence of these elements throughout the lesson vignettes you read and the lesson videos you watch in Chapters 3–11.

Research has shown that explicit instruction is valuable and important for many children and in many contexts, though incidental learning will also happen all the time. To take one example, children grow their vocabularies by more than 3,000 words each year, while a very small percentage of the new words they learn can be attributed to a teacher teaching them the words directly (Adams, 1990). Instead, they learn words from experiences, conversation, during content studies, in the context of their own self-selected reading, and more. Still, research suggests that using explicit instruction to teach *some* words and teaching about morphology to learn *about* words is beneficial, too (Crosson & McKeown, 2016; Goodwin & Ahn, 2013). While the lessons in this book will help you to teach a variety of content and skills explicitly, remember and expect that students will be learning outside of your lessons, too!

Lesson structures give you the flexibility to innovate, the space to respond to students in the moment, and the ability to improvise as needed.

Figure 2.1 Elements of Engaging, Explicit Instruction

While various researchers, practitioners, and theorists identify principles and elements of explicit instruction differently (Hollingsworth and Ybarra, 2017; Rosenshine, 2012; Archer and Hughes, 2011), the following nine undergird what you'll learn about engaging, explicit instruction in this book.

Connect existing knowledge to new knowledge.

Begin lessons by establishing a focus; during this time, orient students to the relevance of the lesson and remind them of what they've learned previously that connects to today's learning. Throughout the lesson, connect new information to what students already know to help them form conceptual networks. Honor students' backgrounds, perspectives, and responses throughout the lesson.

Use a gradual release of responsibility.

When presenting new information, provide clear models and explanations ("I do") and guide student practice with coaching, questioning, and feedback ("we do") before asking students to work independently on similar tasks ("you do"). These three can happen within one lesson and/or across lessons.

Break down concepts into clear steps or strategies.

Our working memory, where we process information, can only handle a bit at once, so present a small amount of new material at a time and break things down into concrete, actionable how-tos or strategies. Then, guide students step-by-step through strategies.

Offer clear demonstrations, models, explanations, and instructions.

Students benefit from seeing an example that meets the expectation (a model), from hearing why the model meets expectations (explanation), and/or from watching someone voice their process as they create that example (demonstration). When you assign tasks for guided or independent practice, the instructions should be clear and should match the demonstration.

Ensure active engagement during all parts of the lesson and regularly check for understanding.

Set students up to be actively involved throughout the lesson (reading chorally with you, responding verbally or with gestures, stopping and jotting, turning and talking, and so on). When students have many opportunities to respond to questions, practice, and reflect on their process, you can check for understanding and monitor progress. Checking for understanding does *not* mean simply asking, "Does everyone understand? Are there any questions?" but rather setting students up to demonstrate what they know and are able to do and assessing them on the spot.

Offer clear feedback in response to what students need.

Get feedback from students during active engagement by considering the following questions: What do they understand/misunderstand? What are they doing automatically? Where does their work fit within the skill progression guiding my evaluation and progress monitoring? What more do they need to demonstrate they've met the lesson goal(s)? Then respond, coaching and prompting them toward mastery and providing critical and complimentary feedback. Aim for a high success rate during guided practice *before* asking students to work independently so they don't make errors that become entrenched.

Provide scaffolds when tasks are difficult.

Provide supports that are absolutely necessary for students to access challenging or novel content and skills and then remove supports as soon as possible. Scaffolds may be verbal, such as thinking aloud and prompting, or you may offer physical scaffolds such as checklists, graphic organizers, or a model of the completed task. To plan for scaffolds, you'll need to anticipate student errors and make plans for addressing them.

Differentiate to meet students' needs.

Differentiate within any lesson by anticipating students' various needs and providing different access points, scaffolds, and feedback. You can also offer students additional practice (e.g., by pre-teaching or reteaching lessons for a small group) and/or lessons on content or strategies to fill in gaps or challenge students beyond whole-class lessons.

Support student collaboration and independent practice.

Students need ample opportunities to practice (both independently and with peers) what they learn during lessons. Practice leads to fluency and automaticity with new skills and information, moving learning from working memory to long-term memory. Monitor students' practice to ensure they are practicing correctly. Collaborative work also gives students opportunities to get feedback from peers and to explain their process aloud and has been shown to increase engagement.

⚙ Lesson Structures for Explicit Teaching

I'm a structure lover, and with so much ground to cover—from reading skills and strategies to vocabulary and content knowledge—and such limited time, I find that structures save the day. When you use a small repertoire of lesson structures with similar methods and moves, your teaching is more efficient and more likely to engage students as they actively work toward goals.

Predictable lesson structures aligned to clear purposes also save valuable planning time and focus your teaching—and students' attention—on content rather than procedures. Once students recognize the structure of a lesson and know your expectations and their role, you can get to the good stuff faster. This means lessening students' cognitive load: Working memory can be stressed when students wonder how the lesson is going to go or what they are supposed to do; familiar routines allow students to home in on the content you're teaching (Cervetti & Wright, 2020; Garnett, 2020; Kirkland & Saunders, 1991; Lovell, 2020; Sweller, 1988). Lesson structures give you the flexibility to innovate, the space to respond to students in the moment, and the ability to improvise as needed.

The lesson structures you'll find in this book are my go-tos for teaching reading across the whole day from English language arts (ELA) to content areas. Each lesson involves a mix of planning (where you'll consider your objectives and anticipate what your students will need) and responsiveness (where you'll pay attention to student's responses to your teaching and adjust accordingly). This responsiveness can sometimes feel like improvisation—not unlike theatrical improvisation, in fact. If you've ever been to an improv show, you were probably amazed at how the actors on the stage took suggestions from the audience and—with no rehearsal—created a narrative with the suggested content that not only made sense but was also funny! The truth is, behind the scenes, these actors are innovating within structures (also known as "improv games") that they've practiced many times. They are so comfortable with how these games go that they can take just about any new content, fold it in, and make it work.

Similarly, in this book you'll learn the high-leverage moves you can count on to deliver powerful lessons again and again. For example, once you know how to plan a read-aloud lesson and the teaching moves to deliver the lesson and engage and respond to students, you can follow the same predictable structures with any text. The structures stay the same; the content changes. And as with theatrical improv where the actors need to pay attention to the other actors to both act and react, when you're in the midst of teaching, a lot of your moves will depend on how your students react and respond to what you've planned. You'll be teaching content within a structure but then flexibly adapting, prompting, and offering feedback based on what students say and do during the lesson.

While all the lesson structures align to elements of engaging, explicit instruction you read about (see Figure 2.1), each has unique characteristics and purposes. Of these nine predictable lesson structures, some will help you target one focused strategy, reducing cognitive load and supporting mastery learning (Peng et al., 2023; Schnotz & Kürschner, 2007; Sweller, 1988). Others will help you show readers how to do the necessary work of orchestrating and integrating many strategies (Barron et al., 1998; Duke & Cartwright, 2021; Kim, 2020, 2023). Some structures offer readers a lot of support with new learning, while others provide ongoing guided practice—different amounts of scaffolding are important at different points of learning as you gradually release to independence (Pearson & Gallagher, 1983). Some are very teacher-directed and require more planning, while others lean heavily on responsiveness, requiring you to think on your feet and base your teaching on what you notice students need. You'll likely use all the structures at different times across the day and across units. In your planning, aim to choose different lesson structures while keeping in mind how what you choose matches your purpose. See Table 2.1 on pages 40-41 for an overview of the lesson structures you'll learn about in Chapters 3–11.

Table 2.1 Lesson Structures, Descriptions, and Purposes

Chapter Number	Lesson Type	What Is It?	Who Is It For? When and Why Would I Choose It?
3	Read-aloud lessons	When you read aloud a text (or excerpt), engage students in thinking about its meaning using questions and invitations to discuss and respond, and scaffold students' understanding by thinking aloud, including defining words as needed	Any time you read aloud to students, you can explicitly model strategies and engage students in the active processing of texts. Read-aloud lessons build comprehension, vocabulary, and knowledge, and they set students up for strong conversation
4	Phonics and spelling lessons	Lessons to help children develop phonemic awareness (the ability to isolate and blend sounds in words), decode words, and spell words	An essential, daily lesson type for beginning readers who are still developing word-reading skills. Use for readers in upper grades as needed
5	Vocabulary lessons	Lessons to help students learn meanings of specific words, meaning-based parts of words (i.e., morphology), and how word meanings connect to other word meanings (i.e., semantic connections)	Teach vocabulary lessons regularly, as all students are always growing their vocabularies; this is especially critical for multilingual learners
6	Focus lessons	Brief, targeted lessons to deliver explicit instruction about an individual strategy	A highly versatile lesson type to teach strategies aligned to any goal or skill in any grouping at any time of day
7	Shared-reading lessons	When you engage children in choral and echo reading of a text-on-display with all eyes on the same physical copy; you'll pause the reading to prompt, redirect, and question readers to support their engagement with the text and their skill development	Best suited for beginning readers, shared-reading lessons support accurate word reading, fluency, and comprehension

Chapter Number	Lesson Type	What Is It?	Who Is It For? When and Why Would I Choose It?
8	Close reading lessons	When you engage students in deep, careful, slow reading, pausing to prompt, redirect, and question readers to support their engagement with the text and their skill development	Close-reading lessons are for more experienced and advanced readers, helping them engage with complex texts and/or do deeper analysis and interpretation
9	Guided inquiry lessons	Lessons to support students to develop a "notice and name" habit of mind, discovering and drawing conclusions from texts, conversations, images, and/or their own work (to set goals) and more	Guided inquiry lessons put students squarely in the driver's seat of their learning, are highly engaging, and (for some children) better help the learning to stick (Farrell et al., 1999; Kuhlthau et al., 2015; Margunayasa et al., 2019)
10	Reader's theater lessons	Students read and reread scripts to prepare for a low-stakes performance while you provide strategies and feedback (including vocabulary support) to help them	These highly engaging lessons are helpful for students of all ages who are working to develop reading fluency
11	Conversation lessons	Students discuss texts in pairs, groups, or as a whole class while you provide support and feedback	Conversation lessons make sense (at all grade levels) any time students are discussing, whether in brief turn-and-talks with a partner, or in longer conversations in a group or with the whole class

⚙ Making Decisions Within Lesson Structures

Once you've decided on the kind of lesson you need to plan to match your purpose, then within each structure, you have choices about how many objectives students learn and practice (focus versus orchestration), how much you pre-plan and how much you respond in the moment (planning and responsiveness), and how much support you offer students before and while they are practicing (methods for scaffolding). Let's think about each of these choices next.

Focused Practice Versus Orchestration

Sometimes you'll want your instruction to be laser-focused on one new skill or strategy. For example, if your students are learning to summarize informational texts with a problem–solution text structure for the first time, you'll want them to practice with texts that have that organization. You might choose focused practice when the learning is new and you're trying to reduce cognitive load and support mastery with a new skill or strategy. Focus lessons (see Chapter 6) are designed for this kind of practice, and reader's theater lessons offer targeted practice with fluency (see Chapter 10). You could also choose to plan a read-aloud lesson, close-reading lesson, or shared-reading lesson to offer repeated practice with the new skill (see Chapters 3, 8, and 7, respectively).

But when proficient readers read, we don't do only one thing at a time— we don't only decode words with a long-*o* sound or only infer about a character. As the Active View of Reading framework (Figure 1.1) makes clear, we *orchestrate* many skills and strategies to read words fluently and comprehend text, and students also need lessons that teach them how to manage this orchestration as they read. In most cases, your read-aloud lessons, shared-reading lessons, and close-reading lessons will offer this kind of practice, while whole-class conversation lessons (Chapter 11) and many guided inquiry lessons (Chapter 9) will also fall into this category. In phonics and spelling lessons (Chapter 3), it's important students have opportunities to decode and spell words in isolation, but also apply those skills to writing and reading connected text.

Planning and Responsiveness

The more teacher-directed a lesson is, the more decisions you have to make before you teach the lesson. If it's a lesson where you're going to demonstrate and have students practice how to orchestrate multiple skills and strategies as they read, then you'll have even more planning decisions to make. How many of these decisions you need to write down and how much detail about each one you need to note depends on your experience and how much you feel you *need* to write in order to teach the lesson well. Over time, as the planning decisions for different lesson types become a habit of mind, you should find that you need to include fewer and fewer written details in your plans, though you will continue to think through each of these planning decisions every time you teach a lesson.

I've included resources to help you think about planning throughout the book. In every chapter, you'll find a Planning section where I detail some of the before-teaching decisions you'll make, such as planning which text(s) you'll use, what your think alouds may sound like, and the sorts of prompts and questions you might use to guide practice. In the Picture It section that

Figure 2.2 Conversation Skill Progression

Active listening, staying on topic, taking turns

↓

Preparing ideas that will lead to strong conversation, staying accountable to the topic under discussion, and elaborating on ideas

↓

Asking questions, inviting quieter speakers, and keeping the conversation going

↓

Taking risks, debating, and thinking flexibly when encountering new opinions, ideas, and/or information

opens each chapter, you'll see callouts that highlight some of the planning decisions the teachers made in these model lessons. In the Lesson in Action sections, you'll see my plan, watch a video of me teaching a lesson, and read my reflections after the lesson. In the online resources and in the appendix, you'll find blank planning templates specific to each lesson structure.

As important as planning is to the success of a lesson, there is only so much you can plan for. You'll predict what you think you need to say and do to meet the objectives of the lesson, but you can't anticipate everything. You'll need to watch your students' level of engagement and attention and decide in the moment to quicken the pace or cut out some of what you had planned to cover. You might ask a question and get very different responses than you expected, so you'll need to call students' attention back, rephrase, and adjust. You might realize that your demonstration didn't quite land the way you thought it would, and you'll need to offer another example or quick demonstration on the fly. You'll listen to students and give them feedback on how they are understanding the lesson and prompts to coach them along. This kind of responsiveness to the students in front of you during guided practice is, in many ways, the most exciting and critical part of each lesson!

Keeping skill progressions in mind (as in Figure 2.2, adapted from Serravallo, 2023b) can help you monitor progress during a lesson and make decisions about what feedback to offer students. For example, when listening to and observing students in conversation, you might realize they are taking turns but not yet building on ideas. You can point to the part of the progression that best describes what they are currently doing, then look ahead to see what you might offer them as a strategy and/or prompts—in this case, preparing and elaborating on ideas.

In every chapter, you'll find a section called Responsive Teaching (see Figure 2.3) with some advice and examples of the kinds of responsiveness you might need in each lesson type. I hope this supports you as you think about and, in some ways, *anticipate* the kinds of if/then scenarios common to each lesson. You'll also see callouts in the Picture It and Lesson in Action sections as I detail the ways the teachers and I had to be flexible, change our plans, or offer prompts and questions to respond to students while teaching.

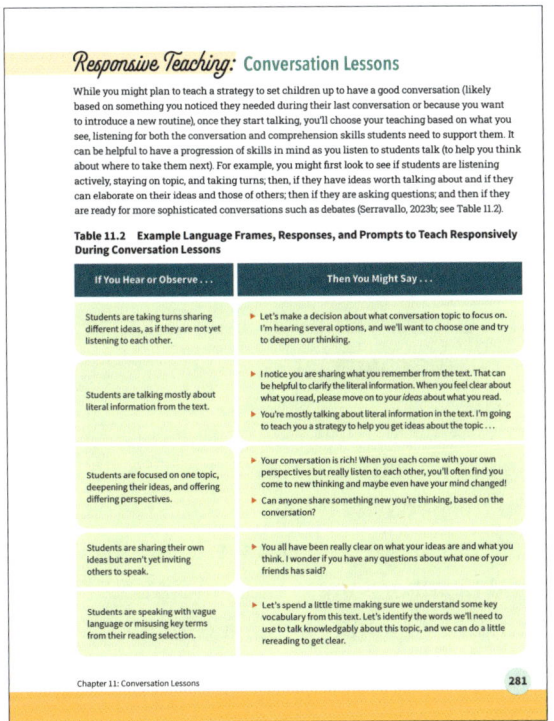

Figure 2.3   Responsive Teaching Example

Look for the Responsive Teaching page in each of the chapters in Part II for advice on what to look for and how you might respond during guided practice.

Methods for Scaffolding

Within each lesson structure, you can choose how much support you'll offer students. Sometimes it will make sense to offer a lot of teacher support up front in the lesson—for example, when the strategy or concept you're teaching is new or when you've learned that your students do better with more in-depth explanations and models for this type of content. At other times, your lesson will be planned more to support guided practice as you gradually release responsibility toward independence (Pearson & Gallagher, 1983).

In each of the lesson structures, you'll be teaching strategy(ies) skills, or concept(s), and you can choose from a range of methods that offer more or less up-front support before students begin practicing. Demonstration offers the most support, followed by shared practice and example and explanation, and then guided inquiry, which requires the most student independence. Regardless of which method(s) you use, to make the learning more transferable, always clearly state the steps of the strategy (or main idea of the concept) one last time before students begin practicing. Once you are guiding practice, you'll decide how much support to offer with prompts and feedback.

Demonstration

In a demonstration, you *show* and *tell*. You begin by telling students what you are going to show them and then explicitly state the steps you're going to demonstrate. It will sound something like this: "There are times when a character will act 'out of' character—where they'll surprise us or show a different side to themselves. In moments like this, we should pay attention because they help us understand the complexity of the character. We can reread that scene and think, 'How would I describe the character in this moment?' I'm going to read the next section to you, and I am going to think aloud as I use these steps to think about the character."

Next, you'll think aloud, modeling *each step* of what you want students to do (rather than, for example, reading a long chunk of text, explaining all the thinking you did, and pointing out at the end how it happened). This explicit step-by-step demonstration helps readers to see *how* you were able to create the model you did, not merely the end result or a great example. Another way to demonstrate is to offer a non-example by making a mistake or modeling confusion and then explaining to students how you can use the strategy to clarify your thinking or revise your lesson.

Shared Practice

In shared practice, you and your students practice together. For example, if you are teaching students how to take effective notes to use as a summary of an informational text, you might explain the strategy like this: "Think about your purpose. Why are you reading this text? What information are you hoping to learn? Then, read a short chunk and think, 'What of what I just read aligns to my purpose?' Next, jot a short summary of what you read that matches your purpose. Let's try this together." You would then read a section of the text chorally and ask students, "What aligns to our purpose? What should I write down?"

As students offer suggestions, you can choose to do all the scribing or you can share the pen (or keyboard) and let them help you. If they offer something that isn't a great example of what you're trying to model, help them revise their notes so that what you end up with is a good example for everyone.

Example and Explanation

With an example and explanation, you give your students a vision for what it looks like to have used a skill or strategy successfully or what understanding of a concept looks and sounds like. As a method, offering an example and explanation takes less time and offers a bit less support than a demonstration because you won't be doing the work in front of students, voicing over each step as you go. Instead, you'll present an already-completed example along with an explanation of how it exemplifies the lesson objective. For example, you might share a skill progression with a sample of completed student work that aligns to skill progression language. While you might summarize what the student did to create the example, students won't be watching you work through steps to create it in real time as they would in a demonstration.

Guided Inquiry

While guided inquiry can be its own lesson type (see Chapter 9), you might also use guided inquiry as a method in other types of lessons, such as a focus lesson. When using inquiry, you guide students to notice and name something that can serve as an example for the lesson you're teaching. For example, you might show students an excerpt of dialogue in a narrative and ask them to think about how the dialogue reveals character, or you might show them a sample of a reader's notes and ask them to notice ways the notes capture the main points of an article. Similarly, students can be guided to inquire about specific patterns in language; for example, looking at a long list of words to understand when to use -*tion* versus *sion* to spell /shun/ at the end of words.

Prompting and Feedback

Guided practice during lessons is critical, and as you read earlier, it's important that as students practice, you monitor and correct any misunderstandings so that their imperfect practice or misconceptions don't become stored in long-term memory. Also, let students know when they are on the *right* track so practices and knowledge become automatic. Keep in mind that effective feedback has the following characteristics:

* **Actionable and instructive.** Feedback should offer students a clear how-to next step toward a goal, either prompting them to try something or naming something they are doing that they should continue to do (Hattie, 2009; Sadler, 1989).

* **Brief.** The less you say, the more time and space students have to do the work. Say only as much as students need to be able to keep practicing, trying, and working through the task. That said, there are times when short prompts aren't enough and you'll need to offer another example, lead students through another round of shared practice, or be wordier with your prompts. When you do find yourself offering a great deal of support in one lesson, you'll probably want to repeat the lesson with decreasing support as a bridge to independence.

* **Specific and relevant.** Make sure the questions, prompts, and feedback you offer are aligned with the lesson goal(s) (Hammond, 2015; Schunk & Rice, 1991). You can offer success criteria in the form of a student- or teacher-authored example or skill progression descriptors to help keep your feedback focused (Hattie & Clarke, 2018).

* **Timely.** Whenever possible, prompt *in the moment* so students can be clear about what they did well or so they can course correct before practicing and reinforcing an error (Hammond, 2015; Hattie & Clarke, 2018).

* **Generalizable.** While feedback needs to be relevant and aligned to the lesson goal(s), try to word it so students can apply it across contexts and in other texts.

* **Encouraging.** It's important that you communicate your belief that students are capable (Bandura & Cervone, 1983), and deliver feedback in a low-stress, supportive environment where there is a strong relationship between teacher and student (Hammond, 2015; Howard et al., 2020) to positively impact a reader's "self-efficacy, [and] self-regulatory proficiencies" (Hattie, 2009, p. 275).

Whether you're teaching a whole class or small group, different individuals will likely need different levels of support at different times with different lessons or even at different moments within a lesson! You also might anticipate that students need one level of support and then, during the lesson, you find you need to amp your support up or tamp it down, based on your students' responses. Always remember that the goal is to ensure student mastery of concepts and move them toward more independent work.

In general, prompts that reiterate multiple steps of a strategy offer more support, as will a short demonstration or brief explanation. Prompts that are brief, open-ended, or provide students with positive feedback on what they are already doing will support them in being more independent with what they are learning in the lesson (see Table 2.2).

Table 2.2   Prompts With Varying Levels of Support

Strategy: Stop after every paragraph or short section. Think, "How can I say what I learned in my own words?" Jot a note in the margin. At the end of the article, read back over your margin notes and think, "So, what's this article mostly about?"

Examples of Prompts That Offer More Support

- Don't write the same thing the author wrote; think about it and try to say it in your own words.
- Look back across each of your jots. Now think about what they all have in common. What's the article mostly about?
- Let me give you another example of what I might jot in the margin.

Examples of Prompts That Offer Less Support (As Students Become More Independent)

- Stop there, jot a note.
- What's this article mostly about?
- State the main idea.
- Where will you stop to jot your ideas?
- Yes! I notice you're jotting ideas.

Source: Example strategy and prompts from *The Reading Strategies Book 2.0* (Serravallo, 2023b), based on research by Ellis and Graves (1990), Hagaman et al. (2010), Katims and Harris (1997), Lauterbach and Bender (1995), and Schumaker et al. (1984).

⚙ Choosing What to Teach: Standards, Curriculum, and Student Needs

The lesson structures in this book are flexible containers in which any reading content can go, whether that content comes from whole-class expectations (such as those for standards and curriculum) or is based on your assessments of small-group or individual needs.

Using Lesson Structures to Adapt a Program or Curriculum

You can use the structures in this book to plan your own lessons from scratch, of course, or you may adapt lessons from a published curriculum or other resources you currently use. After all, rarely can you use a lesson exactly as written because the people who created it don't know your students! To adapt a lesson, you might need to choose a text that's more relevant and responsive to your students, tweak the pacing to fit the time constraints of your schedule, or reduce or increase the number of lesson objectives to be more focused or offer additional opportunities for orchestration. At times, you may choose to use the general information and content from a lesson in your program but plug it into one of the lesson structures you'll read about in this book to streamline your teaching (because a different structure might yield more clarity or engagement for your students) or to modify the level of support you offer. For example,

* if you notice a text in the curriculum is too complex for students to tackle without support, you might choose a close-reading or shared-reading lesson to guide students through it;

* you might decide to slow down students' processing of a text and incorporate more discussion, so you plan a conversation lesson with the whole class or in smaller discussion groups after reading the text together;

* you might notice the lessons in the program are moving too quickly, so you plan to insert some lessons to reteach strategies aligned to the same objective following a focus lesson structure; or

* you might notice that the lessons are very content-heavy but don't offer students much in the way of transferable strategies to support their understanding and decide to add in a read-aloud lesson to model and guide practice with strategies, using a text from the curriculum.

Similarly, if you're working with standards-aligned curriculum you and your colleagues have developed (instead of an outside program), you probably have your lesson topics and student activities mapped out, but you can use the lesson structures in this book to help you plan how to deliver the content. Having a repertoire of familiar teaching structures allows you to adapt in myriad ways.

Using Lesson Structures to Support Individual Needs

Whether you're following a program or have created your own curriculum in-district, you will always need to respond to the students in front of you, adding in whole-class, small-group, and/or one-on-one lessons to teach key concepts, vocabulary, skills, and knowledge you know your students need. To determine those needs, you can conduct simple formative assessments or study the data from any standardized assessments you give and create a summary document to see your class at a glance (see two examples on pages 102–103).

Just as it's helpful to think about lessons as structures, I find that thinking about assessment in a structured way leads to more powerful planning and instruction. As I assess students' reading skills, I think about what they need in terms of goals—categories or types of reading work they could use support with during ELA and across the day in content areas. Table 2.3 on the next two pages shows a list of reading goals from *The Reading Strategies Book 2.0* (Serravallo, 2023b), correlated to components from the Active View of Reading (Duke & Cartwright, 2021) explored in Chapter 1, and some recommendations for assessments you might use to learn more about your readers in that area.

Assessing your readers, of course, doesn't only happen with capital-A assessments offered at a moment in time; assessment is ongoing. In every lesson, you'll study your students' responses to your teaching, evaluate what they understand and are able to do in light of your goals, respond in real time, and/or make or adjust plans for the next lesson(s).

Table 2.3   Reading Goals and Example Assessments

Reading Goals (Serravallo, 2023b)	Active View of Reading Components (Duke & Cartwright, 2021)	Assessment Examples
Emergent literacy and language development	Bridging process: print concepts Language comprehension	▶ Oral language assessment ▶ Use Sulzby's (1985, 1991) stages of emergent reading to evaluate a child's retelling of a story
Engagement and motivation	Active self-regulation	▶ Engagement inventory (Serravallo, 2023b) ▶ Interest survey (Serravallo, 2023b)
Reading with accuracy	Word recognition	▶ Letter/sound identification assessment (CORE Learning, 2018) ▶ CORE phonics screener (CORE Learning, 2018) ▶ Listen to a student read aloud and make notes about how they work to decode unfamiliar words ▶ Spelling inventory (Invernizzi et al., 2017) ▶ Word or sentence dictation
Fluency	Bridging process: fluency	▶ Oral Reading Fluency (ORF) assessment ▶ Listen to a student read aloud and analyze their work using the National Assessment of Educational Progress (NAEP) Fluency Scale or Rasinski's (2004) Multidimensional Fluency Scale
Comprehension in narrative: understanding plot and setting, character, and themes **Comprehension in expository: understanding main topics and ideas, key details, and text features**	Language comprehension	▶ Whole-book or short-text assessment, ask questions aligned to different goals (Serravallo, 2018) ▶ Ask questions during an assessment conference ▶ Ask students to write about their reading (summarize, annotate, jot ideas, and so on) and evaluate what they've written ▶ Listen to students discuss a text and evaluate the quality of their ideas and comments

Reading Goals (Serravallo, 2023b)	Active View of Reading Components (Duke & Cartwright, 2021)	Assessment Examples
Vocabulary and figurative language	Bridging process: vocabulary knowledge	▶ CORE vocabulary screener (CORE Learning, 2018) ▶ Ask students to explain the meaning of words from texts that offer contextual support for those meanings to notice the strategies they use when they come to unfamiliar words
Conversation	N/A	▶ Observe students during whole-class, small-group, and partner conversations
Writing about reading	N/A	▶ Annotations and notes ▶ Extended writing in a notebook, such as summaries or reading responses

⚙ Grouping Students for Instruction

You can use the lesson types in this book to teach your whole class and small groups and sometimes when you're working one-on-one with students. You'll likely teach in different groupings across the day, based on your purposes and your students' needs.

Whole-Class Lessons

Often, you'll choose whole-class instruction when what you're teaching aligns to your standards, is part of your whole-class curriculum, and/or is instruction that most students are likely to need.

Whole-class instruction can have many benefits. When you bring all your students together, they can interact, collaborate, and learn from one another, fostering a strong sense of community. Whole-class instruction also enables you to follow a systematic scope and sequence where skills and knowledge progressively build over time and your instruction is aligned to grade-level content and skills (Kuhn, 2020; Lawrence-Brown, 2004). And finally, since all of your students explore the same literary works, historical events, or scientific discoveries during whole-class lessons, the shared references and common knowledge can lead to deeper discussions and connections.

During whole-class lessons, you can and should still consider the range of needs and diverse backgrounds within your class and provide varying points of access, differentiated feedback, prompts, intentional knowledge or language supports, and/or options for demonstrating their learning, critical principles of Universal Design for Learning (Cast, n.d.; Rappolt-Schlichtmann, 2020).

Small-Group Lessons

In most classrooms, children have a diverse range of skills and goals, have different learning needs, and would benefit from different levels of repetition with concepts. Therefore, whole-class instruction alone won't meet everyone's needs and small-group instruction is essential.

Small groups are most effective when they respond to student needs and their composition is flexible and changes regularly (Walpole & McKenna, 2017).

When you group children by need, you can be more targeted with your instruction (Conradi Smith et al., 2022; Tilly, 2008; Vernon-Feagans et al., 2010), tailoring instruction to students' unique strengths and weaknesses (Kosanovich et al., 2007).

In small-group instruction, you can pre-teach or reteach concepts you will be teaching to the whole class, increasing instructional density, repetition, and guided practice for those who need it (Elbaum et al., 1999; Foorman & Torgesen, 2001). Small groups also offer opportunities to provide support or enrichment in areas outside of the scope of your whole-class instruction. Working with fewer children at once means your feedback can be more immediate, targeted, and frequent than in whole-class settings (Vernon-Feagans et al., 2010). This real-time interaction can enhance student engagement and motivation to participate (Amendum, Li, & Creamer, 2009), fostering a positive learning environment, which is important for all students but especially for those who may struggle (Foorman & Torgesen, 2001). Studies have found positive impacts of small-group instruction on students with executive functioning needs (Diamond & Lee, 2011; Meltzer & Krishnan, 2007), students reading below grade level and in need of Tier 2 or Tier 3 intervention (Burns & Gibbons, 2008; Hatcher et al., 2006), and beginning learners (Wasik, 2008), as well as students who are working on goals related to word-level reading and accuracy (Gersten et al., 2017; Neitzel et al., 2022; Wanzek et al., 2016), fluency (Begeny et al., 2018), and vocabulary and comprehension (Connor et al., 2014; Wanzek et al., 2017). In short, small-group instruction can benefit all students.

Individual Lessons

If you tutor students one-on-one or offer individualized intervention during the school day, many of these lesson structures will work just as well for one-on-one instruction as they do for larger groups. For classroom teachers, you will find that some of these lesson structures work well for individual conferring (i.e., focus lessons, using guided inquiry lessons to set goals, engaging in close reading with a short excerpt of text). However, other lesson types are too time intensive to use with only one student in the general education classroom setting (for example, a read-aloud or phonics and spelling lesson), and still others require that students work together in groups (i.e., conversation lessons, reader's theater lessons).

⚙️ Selecting Texts for Instruction and Practice

My general advice is that across the day—in ELA and during content studies—you'll want to use a variety of texts in terms of genre, complexity, length, text type, and topic. You'll also want to ensure your texts are inclusive, relevant, identity-affirming, and culturally responsive and sustaining, and support knowledge and vocabulary building. Sometimes you'll select the text; other times, the text will come from your curriculum or program; and still other times, children will choose what they read for practice. Sometimes you'll select a text that students won't be able to read well without your support, and other times, you'll choose a text they can read with accuracy and automaticity so they can practice their reading fluency and/or deepen their comprehension or analytical reading skills.

Your students will be reading texts in your ELA block, of course, but they should also be reading in their content area studies alongside inquiry-based projects, problem-based learning, historical reenactments, field trips, lab experiments, and so on. Research has shown that when hands-on experiences such as these are paired with reading, students' understanding of content, knowledge of vocabulary, and ability to write about what they've learned is substantially higher (for one example, see Goldschmidt & Jung, 2011).

During both ELA and content area studies, students need to read deeply to support knowledge building. Create content-rich, conceptually coherent text sets (see Figure 2.4) that allow children to explore similar vocabulary and topics connected to the same or related concepts (Cervetti & Hiebert, 2015; Duke et al., 2021; McKeown et al., 1992).

You'll also want to support broad reading, allowing students an opportunity to explore topics, authors, and genres that interest and engage them. Students who read widely and have knowledge of a broad range of topics fare better on measures of reading comprehension and subject area tests (Elleman & Oslund, 2019; Whitten et al., 2019). And don't discount narrative texts for knowledge building and strategy instruction! Narrative texts contribute to knowledge in important ways, helping students both to learn factual information—think about encountering a new time or place in historical fiction as the author provides rich descriptive detail—and to learn about people—important to the development of social understanding and skills related to theory of mind (Biber & Conrad, 2019; Heath et al., 2017).

Figure 2.4   An Example of One Teacher-Curated Multimodal, Multi-Genre, Conceptually Coherent Text Set

This teacher-curated text set includes a variety of informational, narrative, and poetic texts; a range of text complexity; and different formats, including books, articles, and videos. Together, they help readers explore various conceptual threads related to Native American activism centered on water protection, the dangers of oil pollution, and specific historical and current events related to these issues. Readers will encounter similar terminology, expand their understanding of the concepts, and interact with texts through a variety of modalities. Some of these texts may be best for lesson structures with greater teacher scaffolding, while in others, the teacher may plan to ask students to read with more independence and discuss in collaborative groups.

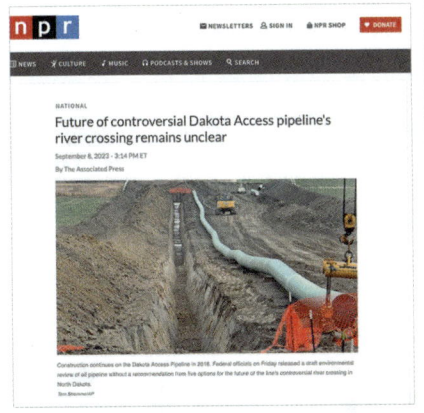

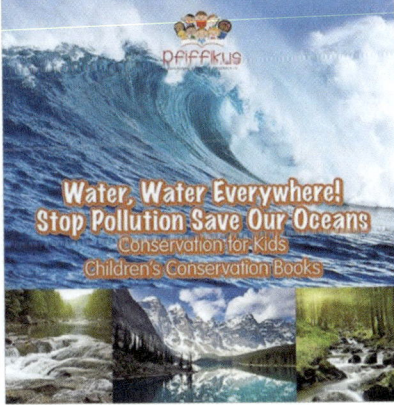

Lesson Structures

Read-Aloud Lessons

Picture It: A Third Grade Read Aloud in Science

Ms. Sayed gathers her class in the classroom meeting area; a copy of *Behold the Beautiful Dung Beetle* by Cheryl Bardoe, flagged with sticky notes, waits on her lap. "Third graders, we've been studying life cycles and ecosystems and how plants and animals live in interdependent ways. I found a book I think you're going to love that helps us focus all we've learned on a tiny creature that you might find fascinating or gross—or maybe *beautiful*, as this author does. I'll read to you so you can decide for yourself! Listen carefully and get ready to talk about your thinking with your partner."

When planning, Ms. Sayed noticed many opportunities in the book to model and engage children in using strategies to figure out new vocabulary words from context. After reading the first page, she smiles at the collective "Ewww!" from the children and then asks them to turn and talk about why the author uses the words *waste*, *dung*, *feces*, and *poop* within one sentence. She explains, "Sometimes an author will help us understand new words by using words they expect us to know that are synonyms for that new word right there in the same sentence." Two page turns later, she thinks aloud, "Hmm . . . *elytra* . . . that's a word we haven't seen before," and shares how she knows what the word must mean because the author uses the keyword *called* and em-dashes to alert us to the definition (protective top wings).

Because you can use any kind of books or texts in a read-aloud lesson, it's a great structure to use across the day to support readers in all content areas.

Read-aloud lessons show students how to orchestrate different skills and strategies as they read. Planning ahead and deciding what you will teach and how you will teach it is key to a successful lesson.

Make sure the text supports the strategies you want to teach, then be ready to state the strategies clearly and concisely as needed.

Read aloud is one of the best structures for modeling what readers notice and how they think.

In addition to its challenging vocabulary, the dung beetle book is rich with description and ties in perfectly with their life science curriculum's disciplinary core ideas, so Ms. Sayed also planned ahead to model strategies for making sense of the nonfiction content of the book. Two page turns later, she has students check their understanding by summarizing what they've learned so far with a turn and talk. First, she scaffolds their thinking: "Everyone, think for a moment about the different organisms we've read about so far in this book. List them across your fingers, whispering to yourself." Ms. Sayed pauses a moment and watches and listens as students think to themselves. Then she responds, "Yes, I heard *elephant, dung beetle, bacteria.* Third graders, can you please turn to your partner to explain the connections between these organisms? How and why are they important to each other?" As the students shift their bodies, sitting knee-to-knee with their partners, Ms. Sayed gets up to move around, listen in, and coach the readers as they talk. For some, this coaching is based on content: "Remember to talk about what we learned from the book and connect the information the author shared." For others, it's to support their conversational skills: "Daquan, can you say back the main point you heard Jasmine say and then add on to that with your own idea?"

After a few minutes, Ms. Sayed calls the children's attention back. "Even though this book doesn't have subheadings, the subtopic is going to shift in this next part. As I read, think, 'What is this new part mostly about?'" Ms. Sayed reads another handful of pages, modeling expressive reading, engagement, excitement, and awe at each new piece of information. Children respond with rapt attention and the occasional auditory outburst of "Woah" or "Ew!" or a slight giggle. Ms. Sayed then thinks aloud, "So let's stop here for a moment. I'm going to list a few things across my fingers that we just learned." She recounts some key facts she had read about rollers, tunnelers, and dwellers. "So now, let's do some thinking work with our partners to put that information together. If you were to come up with a heading announcing what this part is mostly about, what would you write?" The third graders then turn and share ideas, and Ms. Sayed again

Turn and talk is a predictable structure you can use to engage students actively in a more teacher-directed lesson.

Scaffolds help students engage in specific kinds of thinking at critical moments in the text.

If this is a structure you use often, students will know to do this automatically.

Coaching readers is the ultimate responsive practice, offering students exactly what you see they need when they need it.

To keep readers engaged, plan to move predictably back and forth between a whole-class focus (where you're reading to students) and a partnership focus (where they are thinking together about the reading).

Read aloud is one of the best methods for teaching students what engaged reading looks and sounds like.

moves around to offer support. Some children start with a longer summary and Ms. Sayed says, "If you had to shorten that into a heading—a few words—what would it be?" Others come up with a topic and Ms. Sayed responds, "Yes, it's about kinds of dung beetles, but let's remember our strategy for moving from topic to idea. We can now say, 'So what about that?' to try to turn it into a phrase or sentence."

A room of readers will need different kinds of support.

After a couple of minutes, the class turns back to face Ms. Sayed for the last part of the book, where she pauses their listening a couple more times to invite them to think about the main idea and to practice figuring out the meaning of new words from context. She then transitions them to talk one last time for a quick discussion of what they read, "Readers, what do you think? Are dung beetles fascinating? Gross? Beautiful? Something else? Let's talk about it—and be sure to use information from the text to support your thinking!"

A read-aloud lesson should lead students to the rich thinking that comes from engaging with a powerful text. Learn more about how to support discussions in Chapter 11.

After a few minutes of conversation, Ms. Sayed ends with a quick recap: "Readers, the kind of thinking we did in this text is thinking you can do in any informational text you read. Look for context within a sentence to help you understand the meaning of unfamiliar vocabulary words. Pause your reading often to think about how the information fits together and what the section, part, or chapter is mostly about. These are important ways to monitor what you're understanding."

Restate the main goals of the lesson and strategies you guided students to use to make the teaching transferable to other texts.

Read-Aloud Lessons: A Planning Template

Literacy Goals:

- Learning vocabulary from context
- Synthesizing information to identify a main idea
- Monitors comprehension

Knowledge/ Vocabulary Goals:

- Life cycles and ecosystems and how organisms live in interdependent ways
- *Waste, dung, feces, poop, elytra, tunnel*

Teacher Materials:

- *Behold the Beautiful Dung Beetle*, by Cheryl Bardoe
- Notetaking forms

Student Materials:

- None

Establish a Focus (1 minute):

Connect to a study of life cycles and ecosystems and how plants and animals live in interdependent ways. We'll consider one creature and think about the ideas we have about it: fascinating, gross, beautiful?

Read Aloud and Engage (7–15 minutes):

Page #	What Will Students Do?	What Will You Say?
1	Turn and talk	*waste, dung, feces, poop* Reread context. Turn and Talk: How does the author help us figure out the meanings of these words?
3	Listen to think aloud	*elytra* Show how the definition is embedded in the sentence with an em-dash and the words *is called*.
6	Listen to a definition	*tunnel* (used as a verb) Use a kid-friendly definition: *dig*.
6	Use your fingers to make a mental list	"List the main ideas (different organisms) across your fingers."
6	Turn and talk	"Talk to your partner about how these organisms are connected."
9–12	Listen with a question in mind	"What is this new part mostly about?"
12	Listen to a think aloud	"I'm going to list some things we learned on these last few pages."
12	Turn and talk	"If you were to come up with a heading announcing what this part is *mostly* about, what would you write?"
End of Book	Turn and talk	"Are dung beetles fascinating? Gross? Beautiful? Something else?"

Clarify the Takeaways (1 minute):

Remind students to pause often to monitor comprehension using main idea strategies and to use context to figure out the meaning of any unfamiliar words.

An Overview: Read-Aloud Lessons

In elementary school, I remember sitting on the rug after lunch and recess, lights dimmed, as my teacher sat in a rocking chair and read us a chapter from *Charlotte's Web.* It was a beautiful time of day where we enjoyed a story and recentered after playing hard outside. This is certainly one kind of read aloud you may do with your students—a "story time" read aloud. But it differs in some key ways from the type of read aloud that's the focus of this chapter. Reading aloud to your students with an *instructional purpose* includes choosing texts with intention, purposefully planning places to stop and engage students in thinking strategically about the text, learning content and vocabulary, and modeling your own thinking and fluent reading. This type of read-aloud lesson, sometimes referred to as *dialogic reading* or *shared book reading* in the research, and often referred to as *interactive read aloud* or *instructional read aloud* in practitioner books and articles, involves active listening and participating—asking questions, adding information, prompting children to talk about what they are hearing in the text, and eliciting more sophisticated and elaborate responses from the children (Whitehurst et al., 1999). While any reading aloud to children can be beneficial, interactive and instructional read-aloud lessons (not to be confused with shared reading, see Chapter 7) offer additional benefits (see What Research Says, page 66).

What Research Says
About Read-Aloud Lessons

Interactive read-aloud lessons help readers to

➜ improve their language and literacy skills (Mol et al., 2008; Whitehurst et al., 1994; Whitehurst et al., 1999);

➜ develop an understanding of fluent reading as you read aloud with expression (Flood et al., 2005);

➜ develop comprehension as you offer students opportunities to apply strategies, check for understanding, and observe your thinking about the text. For example, one experimental study showed significant effects on students' ability to retell the story (Baker et al., 2020), while others demonstrated more detailed recounting and depth of understanding (Fisher et al., 2004; Hickman et al., 2004; Santoro et al., 2008);

➜ become more active in text-based discussions, constructing meaning of the text, and critiquing the ideas of their classmates (Beck et al., 2020);

➜ sharpen conversation skills as children have brief conversations with a partner and longer post-reading conversations with groups or the whole class (Worthy et al., 2012);

➜ get hooked on certain authors, topics, or series and increase motivation to read (Fisher et al., 2004; Gambrell et al., 1993; Ivey & Broaddus, 2001);

➜ celebrate examples of powerful writing, which will inspire and immerse students in exceptional writing craft when you guide children to notice and infer the authors' intentions (Beard, 1991; Fisher et al., 2004; Griffith, 2010);

➜ build community and strengthen relationships in the classroom as students learn from each other's ideas and share their own (Barrentine, 1996; Rizzuto & Steiner, 2022);

➜ expand oral language (Sulzby & Teale, 2003), improve vocabulary as students practice strategies for figuring out word meanings (Christ & Chu, 2018), and learn words through explicit teaching and exposure to rich vocabulary (Baker et al., 2020); and

➜ learn about themselves and their world (Bishop, 1990; Coelho, 2012; O'Neil, 2010; Rivera & Oliveira, 2021).

In a read-aloud lesson, you pause your reading to invite students to engage with the text and each other using your prompts and questions, share your own thinking, and model how to orchestrate a variety of strategies across a text—just as they'll need to do when they read independently. When you read aloud with the whole class, you will most often choose a text and strategies that align with curriculum and grade-level standards (as Ms. Sayed did in the Picture It vignette that opens this chapter). When you teach a read-aloud lesson to a small group, you will choose a text and strategies aligned with that group of students' individual goals. You might also plan a read-aloud lesson to pre-teach a text from your core curriculum to a small group who would find the text too challenging to read on their own. After the lesson, they can reread the text independently or with a partner.

Read-aloud lessons this rich and intentional are not only for young children— *all* students benefit from being read to and engaging with their teacher, peers, and a text during read aloud (Hurst & Griffity, 2015; Roessingh, 2020). And read-aloud lessons are not only for fiction—read aloud can and should happen across the day, in any subject area, with a variety of genres and text types. In fact, one study (Kraemer et al., 2012) found that first graders who listened to expository and informational texts scored significantly higher on comprehension tests, and most children in the study even preferred them over fiction.

As an added bonus, the strategies you offer to support students' thinking in a read-aloud lesson set them up to have rich, ready-to-go ideas they *want* to talk about. If you follow a whole-class or small-group read-aloud lesson with a discussion, students learn to use their ideas as they talk and you create a scaffold for great conversations they can have independently in partnerships or book clubs. See Chapter 11: Conversation Lessons for sample structures, tips, and video examples related to supporting powerful discussions.

Knowledge and Vocabulary Building
Within Read-Aloud Lessons

✿ Always read the texts ahead of time that you plan to read aloud to students. As you read, think, "What is this text expecting my students will already know? How does that match what my students likely *do* know?" Consider the supports you may want to offer in the form of think alouds and prompting (see pages 70–74) to help students activate the relevant prior knowledge they'll need to understand the text, and clarify knowledge and vocabulary goals you'll have for them during the lesson.

✿ Before reading aloud, identify and plan to highlight the vocabulary that's most important for students to understand the text conceptually (not every word they might not know) and/or Tier 2 vocabulary that they are likely to encounter again. (For more on word selection, see Chapter 5: Vocabulary Lessons, pages 134–135.)

✿ If the text offers context to infer the meanings of words you've selected, teach students strategies during the read aloud to figure them out (or model how you use such a strategy). If there is not contextual support, plan a kid-friendly definition (or synonym) ahead of time and jot it on a sticky note to leave on the page so you won't be forced to come up with a definition on the spot (Scott & Nagy, 1997; Stahl & Fairbanks, 1986; Wright, 2020). As you read, tuck this definition in as an aside when you come to the word ("Remember, a *tory* is a colonist who supported the British during the American Revolution"). Then, once students have more knowledge about the term or concept from the reading, plan to revisit important words after the read aloud with more depth (August et al., 2018; Silverman et al., 2013; Wasik et al., 2006). See Chapter 5: Vocabulary Lessons for more information.

✿ As you plan the texts to read aloud to students across time, consider building conceptually coherent text sets (see page 57) rather than reading about disconnected topics. As students encounter familiar words and concepts in increasingly complex texts, they will create semantic networks, linking information for deeper understanding and better retrieval (Cervetti et al., 2016; Lupo et al., 2019).

✿ Before you teach, craft knowledge-based questions (i.e., questions that ask students to explain, resolve discrepancies in knowledge, or recall key information) to deepen understanding (Scardamalia & Bereiter, 1992).

Planning: Read-Aloud Lessons

In a read-aloud lesson, you'll guide students to use (and watch as you model) a variety of strategies to understand and engage with the text. You'll need to select a meaningful text, carefully consider what goals (literacy, knowledge, and vocabulary) best align to that text, and plan for how to keep students actively engaged during the lesson.

Texts

The texts you read aloud should set students up to practice the reading strategies they need and have rich conversations, and do "double duty" by offering students opportunities to engage with content you're studying as a class. Whether you are searching for and finding your own texts to read aloud or choosing texts from your English language arts (ELA) or content studies curricular resources, here are some considerations to keep in mind:

* **Make sure the texts you read aloud align to what you're teaching.** Consider your curriculum plans, content studies, and the reading strategies you want to introduce and practice with students.

* **Choose texts that are inclusive, relevant, identity-affirming, and culturally responsive and sustaining.** Strike a balance between texts that offer students opportunities to see themselves, and those that offer them opportunities to learn about people, experiences, and topics that are new and different. Pay careful attention as well to problematic stereotypes, and avoid offering only one perspective on any given group (see more with Bishop, 1990; Ebarvia et al., 2020; España & Herrera, 2020; Hammond, 2015; Jones, 2020; Minor, 2018; Souto-Manning et al., 2018).

* **Read aloud texts with a grade-appropriate level of text complexity.** Since the read-aloud lesson is a structure that offers heavy teacher support and scaffolding, you can read texts that are more complex than what students are able to read without teacher support. Look for texts with rich and varied language, for example, or ones that introduce students to new themes, ideas, concepts, or perspectives.

* **Consider the length of each text you plan to read aloud.** You can read longer texts across a series of days; however, extremely long chapter books may end up taking so long that the lessons feel like they are dragging on and students won't have experience with other shared texts they can use for cross-text connections or analysis.

* **Preview texts for visual content and decide how you'll share that content with students.** For example, if you're reading aloud a picture book with illustrations, will you hold the book up for children to see before, after, or as you are reading each page of text? Also consider how much of the meaning is carried in the images, and if the answer is "a lot" (as in a graphic novel or a busy informational book), it might not be the best choice for a read-aloud lesson.

* **Make sure the texts you choose will be engaging to read aloud and to listen to.** Look for well-developed characters, interesting topics, or concepts that will move or amaze your students.

* **Aim for a variety of genres, text types and formats, lengths, topics, and more within a unit and across the year.**

Your curriculum probably suggests books and other texts, but there will be times you'll need to turn to trusted sources to find additional texts for read-aloud lessons or to replace texts from your core program that don't meet the above criteria. Check out annual awards (Newbery, Orbis Pictus, Caldecott, Asian Pacific American, Coretta Scott King, Lambda Literary, Stonewall Book, and so on) for reviewers' favorites. Consult trusted websites run by children's literature scholars and librarians, and follow them on social media (i.e., American Indians in Children's Literature curated by Debbie Reese, The Nerdy Book Club cofounded by Donalyn Miller and Colby Sharp, Colby Sharp's website, Booktoss by Laura Jimenez). And be sure to check in with your school and local librarians to find out their newest favorites or ask them to recommend texts that match what you're looking for in terms of content or format.

After carefully selecting a text, the next step is to read the text with the goals you have for your readers in mind and think about how you will need to support them to comprehend the text. Out of everything you *could* teach, decide which strategies you want to help students practice and which concepts and vocabulary you want to highlight during the lesson.

Think Aloud

Study the text you'll read aloud, think about what challenges it poses for readers, and plan scaffolds you'll offer to support them in understanding the content of the text. One of the ways that you will support readers during a read aloud is to model your own thinking, showing the processes or strategies you used to help you arrive at those thoughts.

Think alouds are very brief pauses where you'll use conversational, first-person narrative, acting as if you had the thought pop into your mind (though you likely prepared what you wanted to say in advance and wrote it down on a sticky note affixed in your book or in your lesson plan). Sometimes you might also ask questions that invite children to give a thumbs up or nod if they agree with you ("I'm going to . . . will you join me?" or "Are you thinking what I'm thinking?"), though you won't pause for them to respond verbally in that moment. Therefore, while think alouds can be a powerful way to model, they also can be used to have students practice the steps of a strategy quietly, thinking to themselves. They can also be helpful to call special attention to part of the text that you'll ask them to think or talk about later (see Table 3.1).

Table 3.1 Strategies and Think-Aloud Examples for Understanding Character Complexity

Strategies	Think-Aloud Examples
Pause at a point of conflict in the story. Notice how the character acts before, during, and after the conflict. Describe the character in a way that shows the character's complexity or their different sides.	▶ Hmm. I'm noticing a major problem for the character at this moment. She's acting in a way that's surprising. It's like she's showing us a new side to her that we've never seen before. ▶ Woah. This seems like a point of conflict for sure. Just look at how upset the main character is. I'm going to really pay close attention to how she acts going forward. Will you join me?
Notice a place where a secondary character is interacting with a main character. Think about how one's actions are impacting the other's thoughts, feelings, and actions. What ideas do you have about each of them and their relationship?	▶ It seems like [name] is really impacting [name] in this scene. I notice how she's acting differently than she did before. I'm going to stop here and think, because this seems important. Hmm . . . what words would I use to describe her? ▶ Oh! Here they are again, these two characters, _____ and _____, in the same scene. I'm going to think about how their actions impact each other.

Source: Adapted from *The Reading Strategies Book 2.0*, Serravallo (2023b).

Think alouds can also be used to support students with information or knowledge or to help them learn words they'll need to know to understand the text. For example, if you're reading aloud *I Am Farmer: Growing an*

Environmental Movement in Cameroon (Paul & Paul, 2019), you might pause at the mention of Cameroon on the first page and think aloud, "I noticed Cameroon on the world map we were looking at yesterday. Remember when we were looking at all of the continents? Cameroon is in the continent of Africa, on the west coast." Or later, when the book mentions the rainy season, you might share, "There is a whole season of rain! That must be great for the crops. Since this book is about a farmer, I bet that will be important."

Student Engagement

In addition to pauses for think alouds, you also want to plan to pause to have students engage with the text and with each other, practice strategies for understanding, and talk and write about the text. They might stop to talk, jot words or a sketch, or act out a part. Again, your prompts will align to strategies that help children understand the meaning of the text. Table 3.2 shows the same strategies that help students deepen their understanding of character complexity, but this time, the prompt language gets them thinking about the text and invites them to *do* something.

Table 3.2 Strategies and Prompt Examples That Invite Readers to Talk, Act, or Jot

Strategies	Prompt Examples
Pause at a point of conflict in the story. Notice how the character acts before, during, and after the conflict. Describe the character in a way that shows the character's complexity or their different sides.	▶ Are you noticing a new side to this character in this moment? Turn and discuss with your partner. ▶ Describe how the character acted before and during this moment. Are we seeing different sides to her? Stop and jot your thinking.
Notice a place where a secondary character is interacting with a main character. Think about how one's actions are impacting the other's thoughts, feelings, and actions. What ideas do you have about each of them and their relationship?	▶ Notice how they are interacting. Turn and describe the relationship between the two characters at this moment in the story. ▶ [Name a character and describe what they did.] Can you share your thinking with your partner about how that impacts the other character's thoughts, feelings, and actions?

Source: Adapted from *The Reading Strategies Book 2.0*, Serravallo (2023b).

With your literacy, knowledge, and vocabulary goals in mind, you might ask students to do the following during a read aloud:

* Listen as you think aloud.

* Turn and talk to a partner or small group. The best turn and talk prompts are open-ended and invite children to think, not merely recall literal information from the text. To quickly transition from listening to speaking to listening again, set partnerships up in advance and ask children to sit in the same meeting area spots each time you gather. You might also assign partners a name (i.e., Partner A and Partner B) and alternate which partner you prompt to go first to ensure both are participating throughout the lesson.

* Stop and jot (or sketch) in a notebook, on a graphic organizer, or on sticky notes. When students do this with your prompting and support in a read-aloud lesson, it creates a scaffold for meaningful note-taking and writing about reading that they can transfer to when they read independently. You can collect these quick jots to assess understanding and plan for follow-up teaching, and invite children to refer back to them for longer writing about reading, discussion, or cross-text analysis.

* Act out a moment in the text or something they imagine might happen next. This works well for stories and plays ("Imagine how the character is feeling here. Show me their facial expression") as well as for expository texts that are informational ("Pretend to be the praying mantis, about to capture its prey. Move like the praying mantis") or persuasive ("Partner B, you'll pretend to be an environmental activist arguing for changes in emissions policies. Partner A, you pretend to be the owner of a large manufacturing company. Discuss using information from the text").

Plan to pause once every few minutes to keep students engaged and interacting with the text without interrupting the flow of meaningful reading too much. You'll jot notes on your planning page, but you will likely also find it useful to flag spots in the text where you'll think aloud and prompts so you remember to pause while you're reading. I know I get into the flow and forget if I don't have notes to myself right there on the page.

Figure 3.1   An Example Read-Aloud Text Marked Up With Prompts

Plan the text you'll read aloud by marking spots where you'll pause and the prompts you'll use to guide students' practice. Use a simple code (such as *T&T* for *turn and talk*) and jot what you'll say to students to invite them to engage with the text and each other.

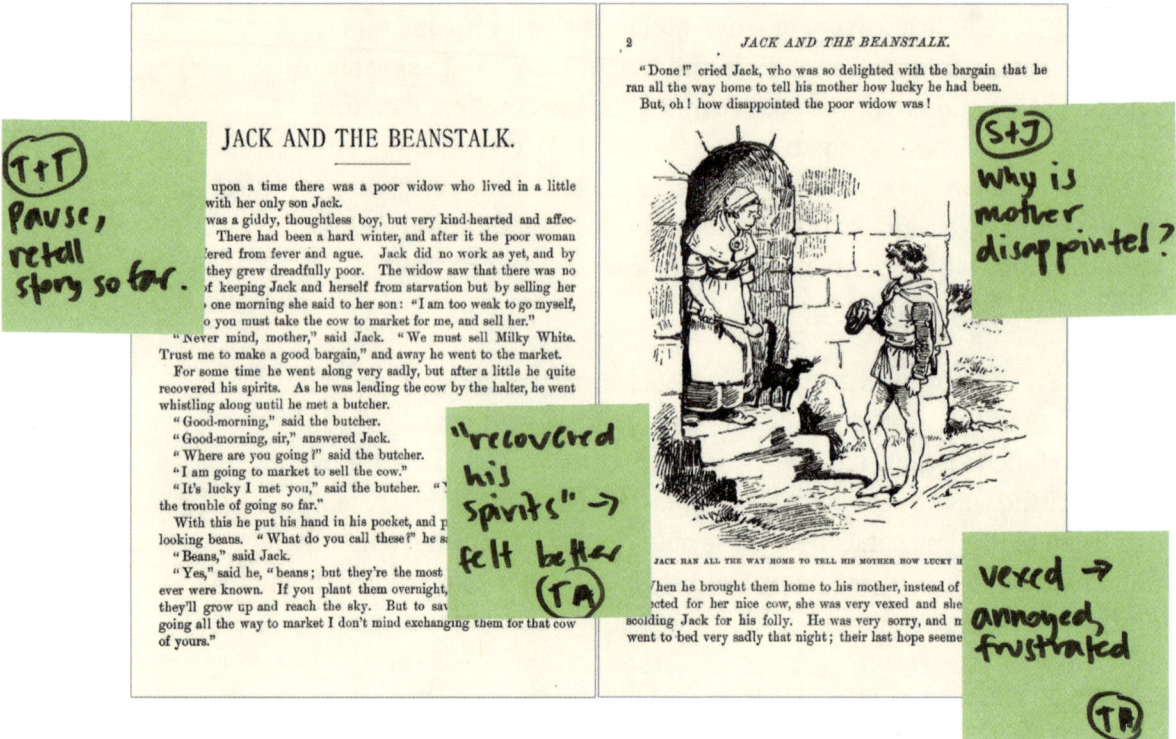

Structure and Timing: Read-Aloud Lessons

You can do a read-aloud lesson with the whole class or with a small group of students. Whole-class lessons are usually longer (+/–20 minutes), while small-group lessons are both shorter and focused on a smaller selection of text (+/–10 minutes). As you plan, remember that the total lesson time includes you reading aloud as well as any pauses you make to think aloud, define a vocabulary word, or have students actively practice or respond. You can also tag on a conversation at the end of a read-aloud lesson as children discuss the book in pairs, groups, or as a whole class (see Chapter 11: Conversation Lessons). Keep an eye on the time, and if the lesson you planned is running long or student engagement seems to be waning, end the lesson and return to the text and your plans at another time.

Read-aloud lessons go like this:

1. Establish a Focus
(1 minute)

Consider how you'll introduce the text to entice and interest your readers. Connect what you'll read about in this text to what they've learned elsewhere—this might be a content connection to social studies or science, it might be a connection to the type of reading work you're practicing (such as looking for themes in fables), or it could connect to something timely (such as a holiday or an upcoming field trip). Let students know why you chose this book for them and what they'll be learning and practicing as you read together.

2. Read Aloud and Engage
(7–15 minutes):

Read aloud the text (or a portion of a longer text) with expression and interest. Pause your reading at the places you've planned to think aloud or prompt students. Also remember that in a read-aloud lesson, you're the only one who is holding a copy of the text, so if there are illustrations, photographs, or text features, you might hold the book up or slide it under a document camera so students can see.

3. Clarify the Takeaways
(1 minute)

Offer a quick recap of some of what the students learned—about strategies, content, vocabulary—that they should remember and take with them to their independent reading, content studies, writing about reading, or conversations.

Responsive Teaching: Read-Aloud Lessons

You'll choose a text and plan ahead, but you won't know how your students will respond to your prompts and questions until the lesson is underway. Listen in and observe as students turn and talk or act, and take a peek at their stop-and-jots when you have them write about the reading. Based on what you hear or see, be ready to respond with support. You may need to switch gears and offer a strategy you hadn't planned to teach, do a quick demonstration or think aloud to support students' practice, or change your prompt or question. See Table 3.3 for examples.

Table 3.3 Example Language Frames, Responses, and Prompts to Teach Responsively During Read-Aloud Lessons

If You Hear or Observe . . .	Then You Might Say . . .
Students are quiet, fumbling, or frozen after a turn-and-talk or stop-and-jot prompt.	▶ Readers come back together, please. I think my prompt wasn't clear. [Rephrase prompt.] Does that help? Or should I reread so you can think about the text with that question in mind?
What students write or talk about in response to a prompt or question doesn't align well with the text.	▶ I'm noticing a bit of confusion based on what you're saying/writing. I'm going to reread so we can consider that question again.
Students react emotionally (laughing, gasping, showing expressions on their faces) during the reading.	▶ I can tell you all are thinking about this just like I am! ▶ I know, right? Terrifying! ▶ I was surprised about that, too. Let's keep reading to see what else we can learn.
Students could use support taking turns, or one student seems to dominate the conversation during turn and talks.	▶ I'm going to assign you to be Partner A and Partner B. [Point to each partnership so the assignments are clear.] This time, Partner A is going to go first and share their thought, and then Partner B is going to respond. Next time, we'll switch.

If You Hear or Observe . . .	Then You Might Say . . .
Students are writing furiously in response to a stop-and-jot prompt.	▶ I am going to get back to reading but I can see you have a lot to say. Take another moment to finish up your thought.
Students responded meaningfully to your prompt (during a turn and talk or stop and jot).	▶ Before I start reading again, I'd like to share what I heard/saw from [name].

Lesson in Action: Small-Group Read-Aloud Lesson, Fourth Grade, Social Studies

Prior to this lesson, as part of their social studies curriculum, the fourth graders in this class had role played as leaders of various types of government and learned some vocabulary and basics about the role of government. With this background knowledge, their co-teachers assigned an article from Newsela written at grade-level complexity; however, after doing a comprehension check, the teachers identified the group you see in the video as students who would benefit from revisiting the text with more support.

****Note that the entire lesson took eleven and a half minutes.** To respect copyright, we've edited out the majority of minutes where the actual text is read aloud, but you will be able to watch the teaching and the interactions between the students.

Read the lesson plan on the opposite page or online, watch the video (access it using the QR code), then come back to read the post-lesson reflection comments annotating the lesson plan.

Download the lesson plan and a blank template on the companion website https://companion.corwin.com/courses/2024_TRAD

Scan this code or go to https://qrs.ly/ygfg1qs to watch the video.

To read a QR code, you must have a smartphone or tablet with a camera. We recommend that you download a QR code reader app that is made specifically for your phone or tablet brand.

Video 3.1   Small-Group Read-Aloud Lesson, Fourth Grade, Social Studies

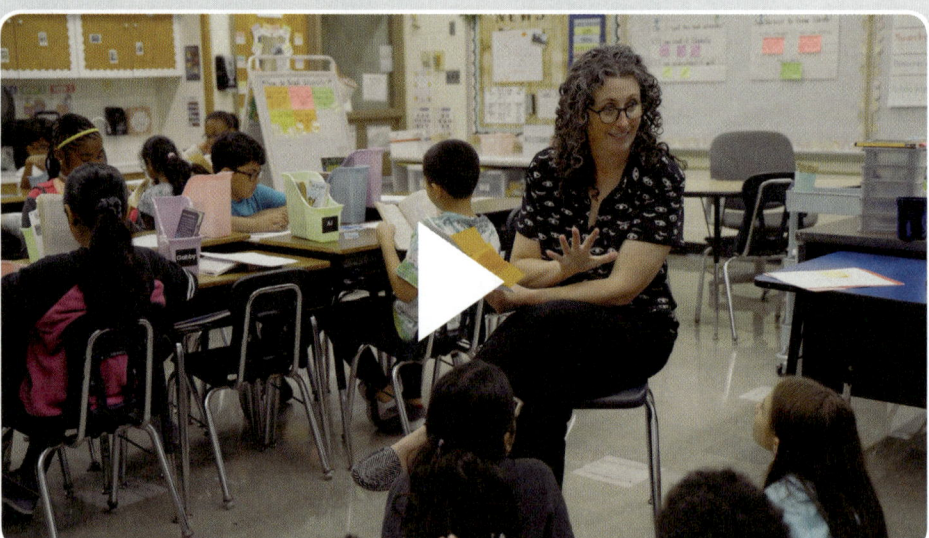

Read-Aloud Lessons: A Planning Template

Teacher Materials:
- "How Government Works: Comparing Governments" (USHistory.org, 2017)

Student Materials:
- None

Literacy Goals:
- Using headings to get ready to read, summarizing after each section

Knowledge/ Vocabulary Goals:
- Compare democratic and authoritarian forms of government and learn details about each.
- *Press, protest, military*

Establish a Focus (1 minute):

Connect to current study of different forms of government. The text is challenging, so we will slow down. Be ready to summarize.

Read Aloud and Engage (7–15 minutes):

Vocabulary and Strategy Practice for Comprehension and Conversation:

Page #	What Will Students Do?	What Will You Say?
1	Turn and talk, summarize	Let's recap. What do we know about government from what we've read so far?
1	Turn and talk	Why is voting important in a democracy ?
1	Think aloud	"Democracies rely on certain freedoms" What do you think the main topic of this next part will be? *Freedoms*—really listen for that.
1	Listen to think aloud	*Press* A multiple-meaning word—in this context, it doesn't mean to push on something. *Press* refers to reporting that people called *journalists* do. They write their reporting in newspapers and share it online or on television.
2	Turn and summarize	Did we learn about some freedoms? How many did we learn about? Show me with your fingers. List the freedoms you learned about in this section.
2	Think aloud	"Citizens must be active" What will we learn?
2	Listen to definition	*Protest* Quick definition: speak up when you disagree
2	Turn and talk	Going back to the heading, "Citizens must be active." What does that mean?
3	Compare and contrast	Compare authoritarian governments to democracies. Who has the power? What role do people have? What freedom(s) do people have?
3	Listen to definition	*Military* Quick definition: soldiers of a country.

Clarify the Takeaways (1 minute):

Remind students that informational texts are dense—we need to slow down, read headings to get ready to read a section, and pause often to check our understanding.

Lesson in Action: Whole-Class Read-Aloud Lesson, First Grade, English Language Arts

In the beginning of the school year, this first-grade class had worked a lot on developing phonemic awareness and phonics skills, and were beginning to read simple, controlled texts independently to help support their emerging decoding skills. Of course, it's important to balance that kind of reading with rich stories that offer them opportunities to infer, learn new vocabulary, learn content, and more. Read aloud also gives them opportunities to have conversations with their peers. I chose a beautiful, brief, award-winning picture book that lends itself to these goals and also tied in an essential question from their social studies unit—*What makes a community?*—so the class could revisit the book through that lens.

**Note that the entire lesson took about fourteen and a half minutes. To respect copyright, we've edited out the majority of minutes where the actual text is read aloud, but you will be able to watch the teaching and the interactions between the students.

Read the lesson plan on the opposite page or online, watch the video (access it using the QR code), then come back to read the post-lesson reflection comments annotating the lesson plan.

Video 3.2   Whole-Class Read-Aloud Lesson, First Grade, English Language Arts

Download the lesson plan and a blank template on the companion website https://companion.corwin.com/courses/2024_TRAD

Scan this code or go to https://qrs.ly/u8fg1qy to watch the video.

Notice I gave them a little prompting and wait time to get them thinking. This helped their brief conversation to be a bit more productive and focused.

As they talked, I listened in to one partnership and coached by offering open-ended prompts to keep them talking: "Can you say why you think that?"

I planned to pause after the word's second appearance to give students some time to figure out the meaning from context. At this point, I would offer a quick definition for any who hadn't figured it out.

I chose this word because of its ending. On later pages, the list of characters with various jobs that end with -er and -or offered me a chance to teach the children something about morphology in a first-grade-friendly way.

Even though I'd planned to highlight this, I had already stopped in that same spot to talk about how her feelings changed and tucked in the word *blue*. I decided that taking more time to unpack this word would create too long of a pause. I could always return to this word later in a vocabulary lesson.

I visited a different partnership each time to listen in and coach.

Notice how I encouraged children to elaborate: "What can we learn from that?" "Who can add on?" "Do you want to share?" Occasionally, I repeated some of what they said, but I tried not to evaluate the quality of their responses—though, at times, I was excited by their insights and couldn't hide my enthusiasm!

Read-Aloud Lessons: A Planning Template

Teacher Materials:
- *Thank You, Omu!* by Oge Mora

Student Materials:
- None

Literacy Goals:
- Inferring about character
- Figuring out vocabulary and figurative language from context
- Thinking about theme

Knowledge/ Vocabulary Goals:
- *wafted, delectable, vendor, blue* (multiple meaning—emotion)

Establish a Focus (1 minute):

Share title and author, awards, and what they mean. Invite children to think about whether they agree it's award-worthy.

Read Aloud and Engage (7–15 minutes):

Page #	What Will Students Do?	What Will You Say?
8	Turn and talk	What words can we use to describe how Omu is feeling?
9	Join in for hand gesture	*wafted* It's like floating. Make a hand gesture—show me what *wafted* looks like.
10	Listen to think aloud	*delectable* *Delectable* is really, really delicious.
11	Turn and talk	*vendor* Can we figure out from the page what a vendor is?
12	Listen to the teacher think aloud	*lawyer . . . dancer . . . singer . . . baker*" do you hear all the /er/s? That means it's someone who does those things—a singer sings, a dancer dances . . .
15	Turn and talk	Her feelings have changed, haven't they? She's sniffling. Look at the frown on her face. How's she feeling?
15	Listen to the teacher think aloud	*blue* [Point out that this is a multiple-meaning word—we know it as a color but here it means *sad*]
18	Listen to the teacher think aloud	"Her heart was filled with happiness and love" Does she regret it? I don't think so . . .
End of Book	Turn and talk Whole-class quick conversation	What does this book make us think about sharing?

Clarify the Takeaways (1 minute):

Remind students that we can understand and think about what is happening in the story. We can think about characters, how they feel, how those feelings change, and we can think about lessons.

Lesson in Action: Whole-Class Read-Aloud Lesson, Fifth Grade, Science

This fifth-grade science class had been learning about scientific method and had done one hands-on experiment to understand procedures scientists use to explore questions and come to discoveries. To help them understand that these procedures aren't merely something people use in school, I wanted to share the story of one scientist to help them apply their knowledge to a specific person.

**Note that the entire lesson took about sixteen minutes. To respect copyright, we've edited out the majority of minutes where the actual text is read aloud, but you will be able to watch the teaching and the interactions between the students.

Read the lesson plan on the opposite page or online, then watch the video (access it using the QR code), then come back to read the post-lesson reflection comments annotating the lesson plan.

Download the lesson plan and a blank template on the companion website https://companion .corwin.com/ courses/2024_TRAD

Scan this code or go to https://qrs .ly/i7fg1r2 to watch the video.

Video 3.3   Whole-Class Read-Aloud Lesson, Fifth Grade, Science

Read-Aloud Lessons: A Planning Template

Literacy Goals:
- Developing a habit of pausing to take notes and think
- Infer traits

Knowledge/Vocabulary Goals:
- Apply knowledge of scientific method to a specific story of one scientist (Charles Darwin)
- Reinforcing students' understanding of scientific method (question, research, hypothesis, experiment, data analysis, conclusion, and communication)
- *Casts, aerated, churns, groundbreaking*

Teacher Materials:
- *Darwin's Super Pooping Worm Spectacular* by Polly Owen
- Chart with steps of scientific process written out

Student Materials:
- Notebook
- Pen or pencil

Establish a Focus (1 minute):

Darwin is a famous scientist who made many important discoveries about animals, the natural world, and the development of life on earth. As we read about one of his fascinations today, let's think about the elements of the scientific method you can see in his work and what we can learn about being a scientist.

Read Aloud and Engage (7–15 minutes):

Page #	What Will Students Do?	What Will You Say?
A slimy . . .	Turn and talk	List some qualities of a scientist based on what you've learned so far about Darwin. Say, "Scientists are . . ."
Vibrations!	Turn and talk	Question, hypothesize, experiment, analyze data, draw conclusions . . . which of these did Darwin do? Give examples.
These lowly organized creatures . . .	Listen to a think aloud	Where is he here [gesture to process chart] when he's publishing his results?
	Listen to think aloud, practice repeating	*Casts* Let's use the science word to talk about poop. Repeat . . . What are you thinking now about scientists?
	Listen to think aloud	*Aerated, churns* *Aerated* means to put holes in the soil to allow air to get to them, which helps them grow. *Churn* means to turn over the soil.
Then up popped . . .	Turn and talk	I asked you to talk about the qualities of a scientist early on. Now that you've learned more, can you share what more you're thinking about scientists? What words would you use to describe him?
Every ones topped	Turn and talk	He faced some challenges. What lessons can we learn from this story as we continue to be scientists? You can say, "You should . . ."

Clarify the Takeaways (1 minute):

The scientific method is not only something we use in school—it's something scientists have been using for a long time! And like Darwin, asking questions, being curious, and seeking out answers can help you discover new things, too.

Spin It: Video Aloud

Consider using the read-aloud lesson structure with video and/or audio instead of printed text. For example, nature documentaries, movie trailers, Pixar shorts, interview segments, historical reenactments, and podcast episodes can make great texts to teach students using this lesson structure. Use the same process to choose a video and plan the lesson, jotting down time markers where you'll pause to offer prompts or think alouds as students view and listen to the text.

Keep in mind that a video text often contains more information (both audio and visual) for students to process than a printed text and may present that information more quickly than you'd experience it on the page, where you can slow your reading down as necessary. To support this processing, you might play a video clip twice—once with sound and once without—so students have a chance to notice details they might miss when they experience sound and image simultaneously.

Take It to Your Classroom

✓ Explore the texts your curriculum recommends, and evaluate them using the criteria you read about in this chapter. For replacements and supplements, browse any of the recommended websites, social media feeds, or award lists. Create a short stack of texts you plan to read over the next few weeks.

✓ Try planning a read aloud. Think about the strategies, content, and vocabulary you want students to learn, and jot prompts on sticky notes. You can also use the lesson planning template (available in the appendix and online) to support you.

✓ After teaching a lesson, reflect on your pacing and timing. Did the number of prompts slow down the reading too much? Was there too much time between opportunities for students to interact, talk, jot, or act? Was the text selection too long? Make adjustments based on these reflections.

✓ Try read alouds with other text types—movie clips, documentary excerpts, podcasts, and maybe even music videos. How would you compare the level of student engagement and thinking across text types?

Phonics and Spelling Lessons

Picture It: Introducing /sh/ to a Group of First Graders

"OK, everyone! Let's warm up," Ms. Walker begins. "I'll show spellings, you tell me . . ."

> Use the word *spellings* to mean "the letters that represent a sound."

The children respond, "Sounds!"

Ms. Walker uses index cards to display individual letters (*h, a, e, k, l*) and then double letters (*ll, ck, ff, ss*) that students have already been taught. When they hesitate, she supplies the sound: "Remember, *ck* together is /k/. What's the sound?" she asks as she points to the letters.

> Keep the review briskly paced. If students don't supply the correct answer, you can offer it and ask them to repeat it.

Students respond chorally, "/k/."

Then, she spreads the index cards on the table. "Which ones spell /s/?" she asks as children point to the *s* and *ss* cards. "Which ones spell /f/?" she asks. Students point to the *f* and *ff* cards.

> In each part of the lesson, students will work on the reciprocal skills of encoding and decoding.

"OK, let's practice some words with those spellings." She writes the word *sick* on her whiteboard. "Let's blend." Pointing under each letter, left to right, the children say the sounds slowly—/s/ /i/ /k/—then she sweeps quickly under the line and they say, *sick*. She repeats the procedure quickly with three more words. "You're really making sure you say each sound and then you blend the sounds together. Now, let's spell." She draws an Elkonin box on her whiteboard and says the word *will*. "Let's say the word slowly, hearing each sound: /w/ /i/ /l/. What's the first sound?" Students respond chorally, "/w/." She asks, "How do we spell it?" Students respond, and Ms. Walker writes *w* in

> These are review words, so shared practice makes sense (no demonstration is necessary). Offer support if you notice students hesitate or pronounce a word incorrectly.

> *Elkonin boxes* help children isolate individual sounds in words and match sounds to spellings.

Write out the explanation of the new concept in your lesson plan to make sure you have the wording right and that it's brief and clear.

the first box. She continues through the word, reminding them of the double-*l* at the end. She repeats the procedure with three more words.

"Now let's learn a new spelling. You know that sometimes you spell one sound using two letters. We've already learned about /l/ and double-*l*, /f/ and double-*f*, /s/ and double-*s*, and /k/ spelled *ck*. In all of those cases, one sound can sometimes be spelled by a single letter: *l, f, s, k*. Today, we'll learn about a sound we'll spell using two letters, but in this case, the two letters together spell a sound that's *different* from what either of the letters spells by itself: /sh/ is spelled with the letters *s* and *h* together. By themselves, we know that *s* spells /s/ and *h* spells /h/. But when *sh* are together, they spell /sh/. This sound and spelling can come at the beginning of the word, as with *ship* (she writes the word, sounding it out) or *shop* (writes the word, sounding it out). Let's spell another example where /sh/ is at the beginning—*shed*." The children say the word slowly, and Ms. Walker calls on them to help her spell the word; Ms. Walker writes it on the board. She then teaches them that /sh/ can also be at the end of the word—she models two words (*wish, dash*) and they write two other words together. Then they read the list of all the words they've written.

After a few teacher examples ("I do"), involve the children in shared practice ("we do").

You'll draw from a small set of activities for each part of the lesson. Teach children what their role is and what your role is in each activity so that over time, the practice is both efficient and engaging.

"Take out your whiteboards everyone. Let's do a word chain. Please spell the word *shin*." As students work to spell the word, Ms. Walker moves around the room, reminding them to say the word slowly, isolate each sound, and write what they hear. One student spells *s-i-n* and she reminds him that /s/ is spelled with *s*, but /sh/ needs two letters—*sh*. "What's the word you've written?" she asks once they all have it written correctly, and they all reply, "*Shin!*" "OK, now change one letter and spell *ship*." The children erase the last letter and write *p*. She continues with several more words, asking them to change vowels, endings, and beginnings and giving them practice with words with the *sh* spelling at the beginning and end of the words. They erase their boards and work to spell a few whole words, erasing the entire word each time—*rush, mush, shock, clash*.

With word chains, children isolate individual sounds as they consider which grapheme needs to change. Be sure to include words that allow practice with various placements of the grapheme (i.e., beginnings, endings, and, for older students, in one- and two-syllable words).

After spelling practice with the new concept, move into reading practice.

"Now I'm going to write a word, and you're going to read it. As I point under the word, say each sound, then blend them together."

She writes several words—*shell, she, flash, fresh, hush*—on her whiteboard and guides students to decode each word. After they read each word once, they go back and read them all again, starting at the end of the list and working their way back to the first word with more automaticity.

"OK, let's use our whiteboards again. Time for sentences." As Ms. Walker dictates several simple sentences, she asks children to draw a line for each word they will write, and then she coaches them individually as they write each sentence. She provides support when one student writes *box* as b-o-k-s, reminds another student how to spell *the*, and corrects a student's letter formation when they write an *s* backward. Some students need extra support with segmenting, so she says the word slowly with them and helps them isolate each sound. Others write with more fluency, and she prompts them to reread the sentence and check it before the group moves on to the next sentence.

> Be ready to provide corrective feedback so that students practice accurate spellings and reading.

> Although students are all learning the same concept in a lesson, you will tailor your coaching to individual needs.

"I brought a few books for us to read today. You'll get practice reading words with the *sh* spelling. Remember, when you see *sh* together, the letters spell one sound: /sh/." She has two copies of three different texts and gives one to each reader so they aren't reading the same book at the same time. The others are in the center of the table and the children know that when they finish one, they should reread it, and then start the next text. As students read, Ms. Walker moves around the table to coach. She reminds students of the strategies she sees they need: to read through a whole word, say each sound and then go back to blend the sounds together, and to reread a sentence to make sure it makes sense if they had to slow down to decode. After they each read, Ms. Walker has a quick conversation with them about what they read.

> Decodable texts that include the spelling from the lesson will help children immediately apply their new learning to connected text.

> To help each child have practice decoding, make sure they don't overhear their neighbor reading the same text.

> This is a great time to teach and prompt children with universally applicable decoding strategies.

She ends the lesson: "Remember, readers, that whenever you get to an unfamiliar word, you want to read it slowly and carefully, left to right, then read the word quickly, just as we practice when we read words by themselves and as we practiced today with these books. Also remember that when you see this spelling (she points to *sh*), those two letters work together to spell one sound—/sh/. So don't say /s/ and /h/ separately. When you see (she points to *sh*), say /sh/."

Phonics and Spelling Lessons: A Planning Template

Goals:

- /sh/ as new spelling
- Review single consonants and vowels and two-letter consonant patterns that spell one sound

Teacher Materials:

- Grapheme cards (*i, w, r, a, e, u, ll, ck, ff, ss, k, l, f*)
- Decodable texts: *Pug in the Shop, Tacos, Cat in the Box* (Daffodil Hill Press Books)

Student Materials:

- Individual whiteboards, markers, erasers

Warm-Up and Review (2 minutes):

- Review (visual/auditory): *i* (short *i*), *w, r, a* (short *a*), *e, u, ll, ck, ff, ss, k, l, f*
- (Display the letter and ask for a choral response. Place the letter on the table. When finished, say the sound, ask students to point to a letter.)
- Blend: *sick, pill, puck, struck*
- Segment: *slick, will, pick, strum*

Introduce a New Concept (2 minutes):

Review: two letters together can spell one sound (*ll, ff, ss*)

Today: two letters that spell one sound that's *different* from the sound either of the letters by themselves spells. *S* spells /s/ and h spells /h/, but *sh* together spell /sh/.

At the beginning of a word:

- (demo) *ship*
- (demo) *shop*
- (we do) *shin*
- (we do) *shock*

At the end of a word:

- (demo) *fish*
- (demo) *wish*
- (we do) *dash*
- (we do) *rush*

Spell Words/Word Work (3 minutes):

- Word chain: *shin → ship → shop → sock → sack → rack → rash → dash → cash*

Read Words (3 minutes):

Decode slowly, blend. Return to list to read more quickly.

shell, shed, flash, fresh, hush, smash

Write Connected Text (5 minutes):

- She will ship the box.
- Can we go to the shop?
- The snack is on the shelf.

Read Connected Text (10 minutes):

- *Pug in the Shop, Tacos, Cat in the Box*

Clarify the Takeaways (1 minute)

- Read carefully L to R, /sh/

Some Vocabulary About Phonics and Spelling

Alphabetic principle: There are predictable relationships between written letters and spoken sounds.

Authentic text: A text written without specific attention to the decodability of the words or following certain spelling patterns. Instead, it's a real-world text written to tell a story, inform, persuade, entertain, and so on.

Blending: A sub-skill of phonemic awareness, being able to take individual sounds and put them together to say a word. You can teach readers to blend continuously (i.e., *fffaaaann → fan*) or sequentially (i.e., /b/ /a/ /k/ → *back*) or successively (i.e., /b/ /br/ /brow/ /brown/). Continuous blending is likely to be most helpful for beginning readers; successive blending may be helpful for children who are blending longer words. Sequential blending challenges short-term memory but may be helpful for students still working to match graphemes to phonemes.

Decode: Applying knowledge of letter–sound correspondences to convert printed letters to spoken sounds; reading words.

Decodable text: A sentence, short text, or book that contains words with spelling patterns that match what a reader has learned.

Deep orthography: The match between sounds and spellings is not always simple or straightforward. English, for example, has approximately 44 phonemes with more than 200 ways to spell those phonemes. This means there are different spellings of the same vowel (/ī/, for example, can be spelled with *ie, y, igh*, or *i* in an open syllable), and there are different phonemes spelled with the same grapheme (for example, consider the different phonemes represented by the spelling *ow* in the words *brown* and *crow*).

Encode: Hearing spoken sounds and knowing what letters represent those sounds; spelling words.

Grapheme: Letter or letters that represent or spell a single speech sound (**phoneme**).

(Continued)

(Continued)

High-frequency word (HFW): A word that appears frequently in English. Lists such as Fry (1979) and Dolch (1936) include words organized from most common to least common. Many HFWs can be easily decodable (i.e., *if, can, to*) while others have irregular spellings (i.e., *the, from, have, of*). HFWs are sometimes confused with **sight words** though we do want children to learn to recognize HFWs and know them on sight.

Orthographic mapping: A process that happens in the brain when sounds, spellings, and meaning of a word are connected and stored for automatic future retrieval.

Phoneme: The smallest unit of sound in spoken language. The word *crack* has four phonemes although it's spelled with five letters (/c/ /r/ /a/ /k/).

Phonemic awareness: Understanding that spoken words are made up of individual sounds and being able to manipulate those sounds. Research has shown that phonemic awareness with letters is preferable to auditory-only exercises (National Reading Panel, 2000; Rehfeld et al., 2022).

Segmenting: A sub-skill of phonemic awareness, being able to isolate individual sounds (i.e., ship → /sh/ /i/ /p/).

Sight word: A word that a reader recognizes and can read on sight without needing to decode it. We want all words to become sight words so conscious attention is freed up for comprehension. Readers will be able to recognize words on sight after they orthographically map them. (Sight words are sometimes confused with **high-frequency words**.)

Spellings: Grapheme(s) representing sounds. One sound (phoneme) can have multiple spellings (i.e., /s/ can be spelled with *s* or *ss* or *c*), and one spelling can represent multiple sounds (i.e., consider the sounds the *o* spells in *clock, radio, to, oven, bacon, wolf,* and *one*).

Speech-to-print approach: Linking students' awareness of the phonemes in their spoken language with the different ways to spell those phonemes with graphemes.

Systematic instruction: Follows a scope and sequence to ensure skills build logically from simple to complex.

An Overview: Phonics and Spelling Lessons

In every phonics and spelling lesson, you'll review letter–sound correspondences you've previously taught, giving students opportunities to practice automatic retrieval; introduce a new concept that builds on prior learning; and support students as they practice reading and writing words in isolation, and in context with sentence dictation and decodable and authentic texts.

Children need to be able to connect written graphemes to phonemes in our spoken language to be able to decode and encode (spell) words. I've included spelling in a book about reading lessons because research has shown that spelling (or encoding) and decoding are closely related (Berninger et al., 2002; Ehri, 1997). Further, studies have shown that phonics lessons that include spelling, reading, and dictation are more effective than those without (Chall, 1967), that integrated decoding and encoding instruction yields higher reading achievement (Weisler & Mathes, 2011), and that spelling instruction positively impacts reading (Graham & Santangelo, 2014). Also, some recent research suggests that a speech-to-print approach to phonics instruction—beginning with sounds in children's spoken language and then connecting those sounds to spellings—can be a more logical and efficient approach (Wasowicz, 2021).

You can use the structures, routines, activities, and games in this chapter to teach any sound–spelling correspondence. However, to choose what you'll teach each day, you'll need to make sure your instruction is systematic: that it follows a logical scope and sequence that progresses from simple to complex, with new skills building on existing skills (Armbruster et al., 2001). For example, in the Picture It vignette, you may have noticed that the teacher began by reviewing double-letter spellings as well as other consonant and vowel sounds her students needed to know before they could understand the day's lesson—spelling /sh/ with *sh*. Commercially available phonics programs introduce letter–sound correspondences in slightly different orders. Research has not concluded that any single progression is superior to others, but it has shown that having a clear progression is important—not only for the year children spend in your class but also, ideally, schoolwide so that students are taught systematically across the grades (Ehri et al., 2001; Graaff et al., 2009). See the general progression in Table 4.1, but plan to search for and decide on a specific, detailed scope and sequence to use with your class.

Table 4.1   A General Phonics Progression

Concept	Examples
Consonant sounds and short-vowel sounds, VC (vowel-consonant) and CVC (consonant-vowel-consonant) words	*at, up, it, in, cat, rip, ten, box*
Double consonant pairs that spell one sound CVCC, CCVC	*will, less, rack, ship, with, strip*
Long vowels (VCe)	*bite, cake, home, mute, tape, eve*
Long vowels (CV) and vowel teams (common spellings)	*be, go, see, key, rain, play, vote, boat, doe*
r-controlled vowels and schwa	*sir, her, fur, car, circus, about, lesson*
Long vowels with vowel combinations (less-common spellings)	*eat, snow, happy, chief, either, eight, vein, great, they, buy, heist, though, open, toy, foil, now, out, bough*
Inflected endings (e.g., *-er, -ed, -ing*) and simpler multisyllabic words	*happier, happiest, running, wasted, going*
More complex multisyllabic words	*invisible, transportation, establish, calculator*

What Research Says
About Phonics and Spelling Lessons

➡ Phonics instruction supports automatic word recognition through orthographic mapping. Once students recognize words automatically, their mental energy is freed up to read with fluency and comprehension (Ehri, 2014, 2017, 2020; Share, 1995, 2008).

➡ As learners develop a knowledge of grapheme–phoneme correspondences and are facile with segmenting and blending, they will be able to apply this knowledge to new and novel words, even those you don't teach during phonics lessons (Share, 1995).

➡ Phonics instruction taught from the beginning (in Grades K–1) is most efficient (Ehri, 2004).

➡ When developing their phonics skills, students need ample opportunities to apply what they learn to connected text and to combine skills of decoding with self-monitoring their reading for meaning and making corrections. In one study, second graders in intervention showed significantly better growth in word identification, phonemic decoding, and fluency when taught to use context to self-monitor and self-correct (Denton et al., 2006).

➡ Individual students will need different amounts of phonics instruction. Teachers' observations of students and their evaluation of ongoing assessments should guide the amount and type of instruction students get (Snow & Juel, 2005; Tunmer & Arrow, 2013).

➡ As stated in the National Reading Panel (2000), "Phonics should not become the dominant component in a reading program, neither in the amount of time devoted to it nor in the significance attached" (p. 98). It is possible to overdo phonics instruction (Stanovich, 1993).

Knowledge and Vocabulary Building
Within Phonics and Spelling Lessons

✿ In a phonics lesson, children gain knowledge about the alphabetic principle. They learn that there are predictable relationships between spoken sounds and written letters.

✿ While vocabulary isn't the primary goal in a phonics and spelling lesson, it's likely that some of the words you include that fit the spelling pattern you're studying will have unfamiliar meanings. You can briefly define them for students so they can learn new word meanings as they decode, encode, and orthographically map the word (which includes knowing a word's meaning). For multilingual learners, you may need to define a higher percentage of words and sometimes provide picture supports.

✿ For more advanced readers, teaching etymology and morphology can support decoding and encoding (see also Chapter 5 for a deeper discussion).

Planning: Phonics and Spelling Lessons

If you do not have a phonics program, you can search online to find a scope and sequence and then use it to craft your own lessons from the suggestions in this chapter. That said, creating daily phonics lessons from scratch is a tremendous amount of work, so you may choose to adopt a program instead (University of Florida Literacy Institute [UFLI] Foundations, for example, is a solid research- and evidence-based program with a very affordable price point).

If you do have a phonics and spelling program, you might use the suggestions in this chapter to create additional lessons as you notice your students need them or modify existing lessons to better support your students or improve engagement. Some classes or groups, for example, will need to do more repetitions of a grapheme–phoneme correspondence than the program dictates. Or your program may include only phonics and reading, and you may use ideas in this chapter to incorporate spelling as well.

When you pull students into small groups for phonics and spelling instruction, your instruction should always be based on what students need. For example, some students will need more practice (a "higher instructional dosage") with what you've taught in whole-class lessons, so your small-group lessons will offer them either pre-teaching or review to give them the repetition they need. You also might find that some students need to back up in the scope and sequence (for example, a new student who came from a school without explicit phonics instruction). And then, you will almost certainly find that some students already know the spelling patterns you're introducing in whole-class lessons. In this case, you may choose to invite those students to read independently during the whole-class lesson and then meet with you in small groups to learn the concepts they are ready for.

Formative Assessments and Progress Monitoring

When you engage in formative assessment and regular progress monitoring, you can ensure you are teaching spelling and phonics skills that build on what your students already know; identify possible gaps for reteaching in small groups; decide whether to teach certain lessons with the whole class, in small groups, or a combination of the two; and know when it's time to move on to a new concept. Balance assessments of spelling (encoding) with word reading (decoding) for a more complete picture.

Spelling Inventory

A spelling inventory includes a list of words with increasingly complex spelling features. These are easy and quick to administer and give you valuable information about your students' abilities to encode, which usually lags behind their decoding with the same spelling patterns. To use the data, you will analyze correct and incorrect spellings for the features of the words children know and the features they are still learning (see Table 4.2). You can learn similar information by analyzing the misspellings in student writing. (For one example of this type of assessment, see Invernizzi et al., 2017.)

Table 4.2 A First Grader's Spelling Inventory and Teacher Evaluation

Spelling Inventory	Evaluation
1. FƏn 9. STIK 2. PeT 10. Chin 3. Dig 11. Dren 4. ROB 12. Bləᴅ 5. HOP 13. Koch 6. WəT 14. FrUt 7. GUM 15. ToD 8. SieD	**Knows:** ▸ consonants ▸ short vowels ▸ consonant blends **Needs:** ▸ digraphs (*sh, ch*) ▸ long vowels (*VCe, ai, ea, oa, ight, ew*)

The first grader was asked to spell *fan, pet, dig, rob, hope, wait, gum, sled, stick, shine, dream, blade, coach, fright, chewed*

Writing Sample

A writing sample can show what students know and need in terms of spelling instruction (see Table 4.3). To evaluate, list misspellings and match up the errors to your scope and sequence or another spelling assessment such as the spelling inventory. Note that a potential downside to using student writing samples is that they aren't controlled to sample every spelling pattern, and some students avoid using words they don't know how to spell, which can give you a skewed sense of their overall spelling abilities. However, from a short sample, you can still learn a lot about most students' spelling.

Table 4.3   A Second Grader's Writing Sample and an Evaluation of Her Spelling

Writing Sample	Evaluation
	Misspellings: ▶ siting (*sitting*) ▶ wigaling (*wiggling*) ▶ thot (*thought*) ▶ wigled (*wiggled*) ▶ aghin (*again*) ▶ exsited (*excited*) ▶ thair (*there*) ▶ mony (*money*) Knows: ▶ short vowels (*was, that, will*) ▶ consonants ▶ digraphs ▶ some long-vowels spellings (*y* for /ī/ in *myself*, *ay* for /ā/ in *today*) ▶ dipthongs (*ou* in *mouth*) ▶ inflected endings (*-ing* in *sitting* and *morning*) ▶ simpler multisyllabic words (*under, morning*) Needs: ▶ less-common vowel spellings (e.g., *ough* in *thought*, *ai* in *again*, *ey* in *money*) ▶ double consonants when adding *-ing* in short-vowel words ▶ more complex multisyllabic words (*wiggle → wiggling → wiggled*)

Alphabet and Letter–Sound Assessment

Letter–sound assessments ask students to say the name and/or sound(s) of the letter with automaticity. It's important to present the letters out of alphabetical order. The sample in Table 4.4 is excerpted from CORE Learning (2018).

Table 4.4   A Kindergartener's Alphabet and Letter–Sound Assessment

Alphabet and Letter–Sound Assessment	Evaluation
Alphabet Skills and Letter Sounds PART A **Letter names—uppercase** Say to the student: *Can you tell me the names of these letters?* If the student cannot name three or more consecutive letters, say: *Look at all of the letters and tell me which ones you do know.* D A N S X Z J L H T Y E C O M R P W K U G B F Q V I 2-6 /26 PART B **Letter names—lowercase** Say to the student: *Can you tell me the names of these letters?* If the student cannot name three or more consecutive letters, say: *Look at all of the letters and tell me which ones you do know.* b/ d̶ a n s x z j l h t y e c o m r p w k u g b✓ f q v i 25 /26 PART C **Consonant sounds** Say to the student: *Look at these letters. Can you tell me the sound each letter makes?* Be sure to ask if he or she knows of another sound for the letters *g* and *c*. If the sound given is correct, do not mark the Record Form. If it is incorrect, write the sound the student gives above each letter. If no sound is given, circle the letter. If the student cannot say the sound for three or more consecutive letters, say: *Look at all of the letters and tell me which sounds you do know.* d l n s x z j t y p /kuh/ c h m r k w /guh/ g b f q v 21 /21	Knows: ▶ all uppercase and most lowercase letter names (some *b/d* confusion) ▶ one sound for each consonant, hard *c* and *g* ▶ short-vowel sounds, long *o* Needs: ▶ adds vowel sounds to some consonants (i.e., saying "cuh" for *c*) ▶ soft *c* and *g* ▶ long vowels

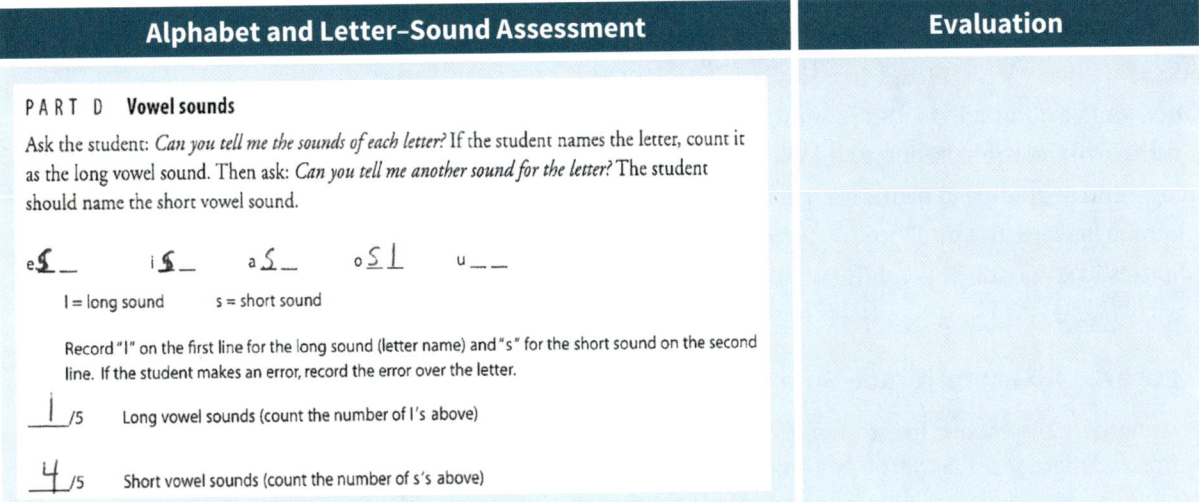

Source: © CORE, *Assessing Reading: Multiple Measures*, Revised 2nd Ed., 2018, Arena Press, pages 41–62. Used by permission of Consortium on Reaching Excellence In Education, Inc.

Phonics Survey

Word reading assessments, sometimes called *decoding inventories*, ask students to read real and nonsense words that fit with specific spelling patterns. Shorter versions of these assessments, focusing on the spelling pattern you're currently studying or have recently studied, will help you monitor students' progress (see Table 4.5; for example assessments, see Blevins, 2016; CORE Learning, 2018; Cunningham et al., 2023).

Table 4.5   A Kindergartner's Phonics Survey and Evaluation

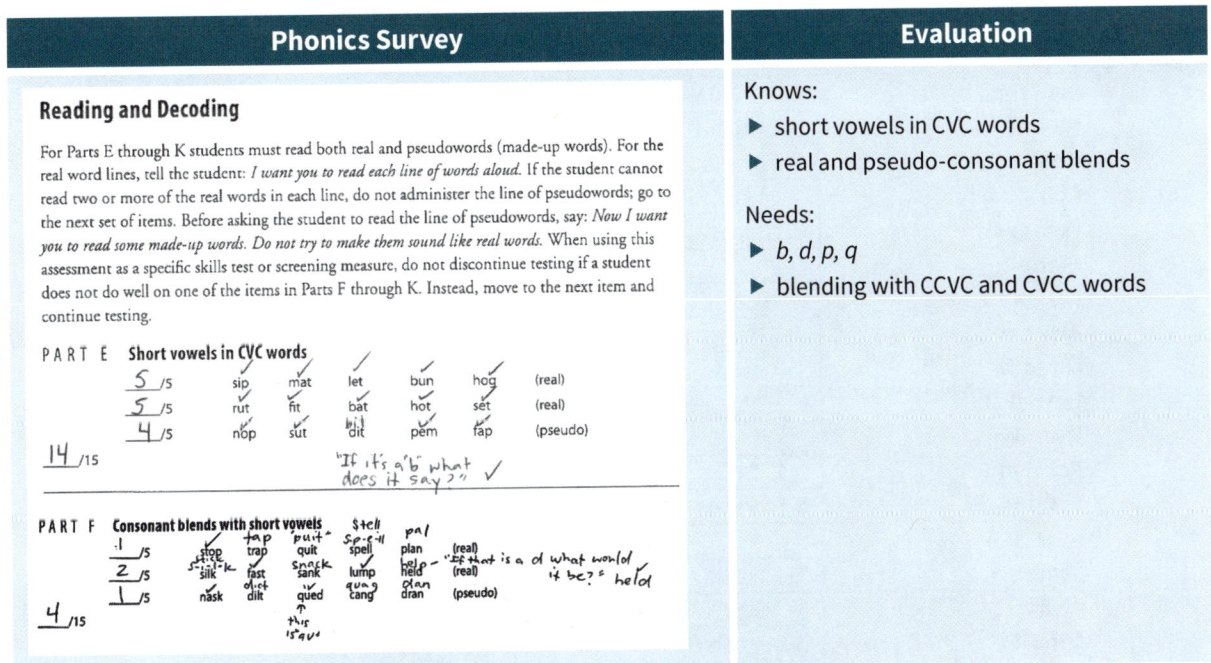

Source: Excerpted from © CORE, *Assessing Reading: Multiple Measures*, Revised 2nd Ed., 2018, Arena Press, pages 41–62. Used by permission of Consortium on Reaching Excellence In Education, Inc.

Assessment Summaries to Plan for the Whole Class and Small Groups

Once you've conducted letter–sound, phonics, and spelling assessments, you'll need a way to synthesize the information and look at it at a glance. This can help you to determine where in the scope and sequence to begin instruction for the whole class, identify which students need additional phonics lessons in small groups to help them catch up, and which students might have spelling and phonics knowledge beyond the whole-class lessons and might be excused.

Figure 4.1   Second-Grade Summary of Phonics and Spelling Assessments

The numbers correspond to the phonics scope and sequence (Column E). Students who need support with CVC words and digraphs (2, 3) will be one group and students who need support with consonant clusters (4, 5) are another group. The children who are in the long vowel and vowel combinations range are on pace with the whole-class lessons, so they don't need small-group instruction at this time. Students who have mastered all concepts in both reading and spelling can choose to participate in whole-class lessons if they'd like or can read independently at that time. So that's 12 kids below the level of scope and sequence pacing (small-group instruction plus whole-class instruction), 6 kids on level (whole-class instruction only), and 4–5 kids exceeding the class level (excused).

A Student Name	B September	C Notes	D	E	F
Ian C	2: CVC	Vowel review first		1 VC	
Malcolm C	12: Soft G&C			2 CVC	
Vladimir D	3: Digraphs			3 Digraphs	
Mandy F	12: Soft G&C			4 Floss	
Jane G	**			5 Chunks	
Laurel H	22: ou + ow			7 L Blends	
King H	3: Digraphs			8 R Blends	
Ervin J	12: Soft G&C			9 End Blends	
Celestino K	4: Floss	Encoding only		10 Open Long Vowels	
Rodrigo L	12: Soft G&C			11 Magic E	
Pietro L	2: CVC	Vowel review first		12 Soft g & c	
Cheyanne M	11: Magic E			13 ee & ea	
Aviva M	5: Chunks			14 ai & ay	
Olivia N	5: Chunks			15 oa & ow (o)	
Darrell O.	**			16 ild, ind, old, ost, igh	
Ryan O	**			17 ue, ui, ew	
Rosalyn P	2: CVC	Vowel review first		18 ar, or	
Sofia R.	3: Digraphs			19 er, ir, ur,	
Kurt S.	**	Encoding only on Floss		20 oo & oo	
Jaycee S.	5: Chunks			21 tch & dge	
Claire T	11: Magic E			22 ou & ow	
Otha T	3: Digraphs			23 oi & oy	
Isabela W	4: Floss	Encoding only		24 au & aw	
				** Mastered all Skills	

Figure 4.2 First-Grade Class-at-a-Glance Summary of Phonics and Spelling Assessments

A first-grade teacher's class-at-a-glance summary of a phonics (decoding, D) and spelling (encoding, E) assessment. In the first column, she lists the number of uppercase (U) and lowercase (L) letters and the number of sounds (S) each student knows. The numbers under each column are out of 10. The scope and sequence aligned to her phonics program is along the top. Based on these results, where would you start in the scope and sequence for whole-class lessons? Who needs support in a small group to help them catch up?

Name	Letters and Sounds	VC		CVC		Digraphs		Short Vowels with Floss Rule		Chunks		Short Vowels with S Blends		Short Vowels with L Blends		Short Vowels with R Blends		Short Vowels with Ending Blends		Long Open Vowels	
		D	E	D	E	D	E	D	E	D	E	D	E	D	E	D	E	D	E	D	E
Alia	26U 26L 26S	9	5	7	3	1	1														
Aaron	26U 26L 26S	7	2																		
Brigitta	20U 17L	0	0																		
Davide	26U 26L 26S	8	4	7	3	7	5	8	3	8	2	8	2	9	1	9	0	6	1	7	0
Marcia	26U 26L 26S	9	2	7	5	0															
Isabelle	15U 14L 4S	0	0																		
Kady	26U 24L 25S	1	0																		
Luca	26U 26L 26S	6	2																		
Elizabeth	26U 26L 26S	10	5	9	5	2															
Jayson	26U 26L 26S	10	5	7	4	6															
Dominic	26U 26L 26S	8	5	10	5	5															
Alexi	25U 25L 21S	4	3																		
Scotty	26U 26L 26S	7	2																		
Tom	26U 26L 26S	9	5	8	5	9	2	5													
Olive	26U 26L 26S	10	5	7	5	7															
Jamaal	26U 26L 26S	8	5		8	5	0	0													
Jayden	26U 26L 26S	6	2																		
Sophia	16U 13L	1	0																		

Tools and Materials

You'll be able to lead a variety of effective phonics and spelling activities with a small set of simple materials.

Movable Letters/Word Work Mat

Figure 4.3   Magnetic Letters

For beginning readers, you'll need individual, movable letters that are a uniform color so students will distinguish them based on the letter shapes rather than the colors.

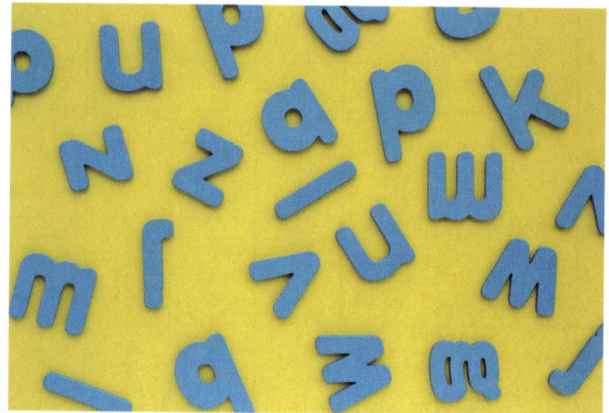

Istockphoto/Василий Авраменко

Figure 4.4   Word Work Mat

As students progress and learn common consonant and vowel combinations, you can add new cards to this mat (**sh**, **th**, **ea**, **ee**, etc.).

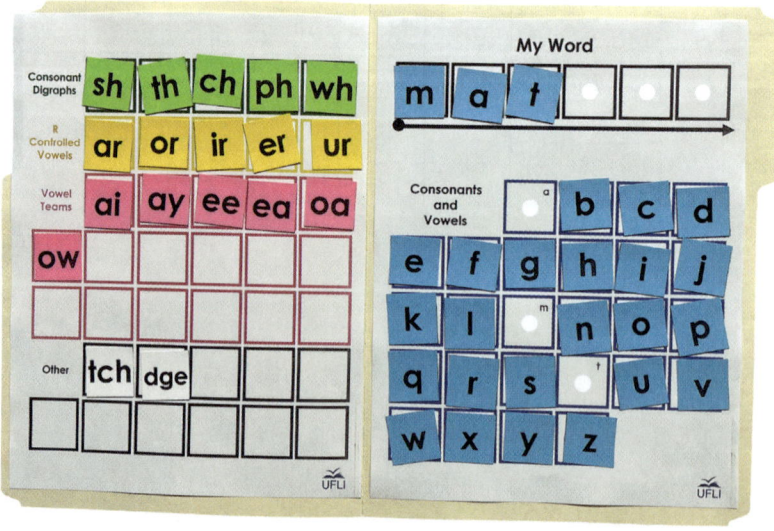

Source: Contesse (2024).

Figure 4.5   Digital Word Work Mat

You can also find digital versions of a word work mat, such as this one from UFLI Foundations.

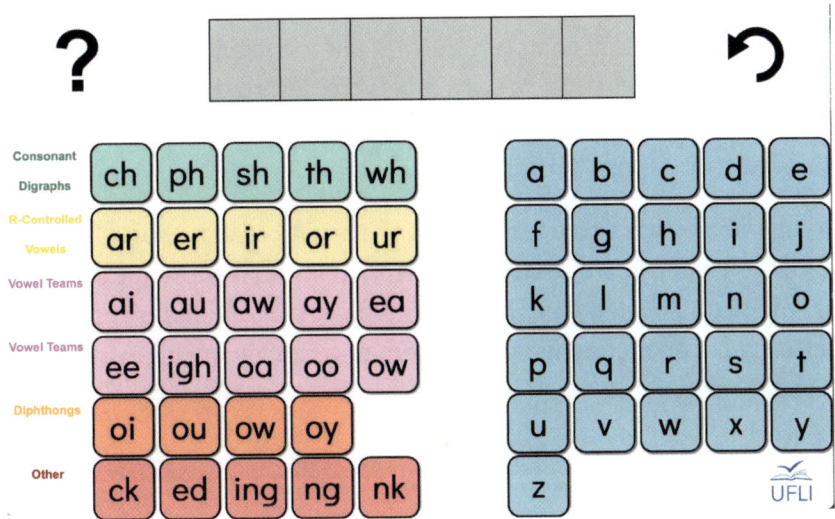

Source: Contesse (2024).

Whiteboards, Markers, and Erasers

Students should have opportunities to write during each lesson, so they will each need their own set of materials.

You will also write graphemes and words for children to read and/or demonstrate writing for children during the lesson, so it will be helpful to have a large whiteboard for display. Alternatively, you could present graphemes and words on slide decks or have a digital display where you type letters, words, or sentences and practice reading them.

Words on Cards or Slips of Paper

If you plan to do word sorting activities, before the lesson you'll need to write the words you'll sort on individual cards or slips of paper. Alternatively, an easy Google search will take you to word sorts (related to the spelling pattern you're teaching) that you can print and cut out in advance. You can also use the website Phinder to search for words, sorted by frequency, that match the grapheme(s) and phoneme(s) you're teaching or reviewing (www.devinkearns.com/phinder).

You might create a filing system to save these cut-out word sorts from year to year or you can ask children to cut them up for homework and bring them back in an envelope. Or, if you want to avoid individual slips of paper altogether, you can dictate words for them to write under columns on whiteboards or paper.

Figure 4.6   Movable Words for Sorting

Word sorts give students practice reading words that fit the spelling pattern you're studying, isolating the focus sound(s), and sorting based on categories.

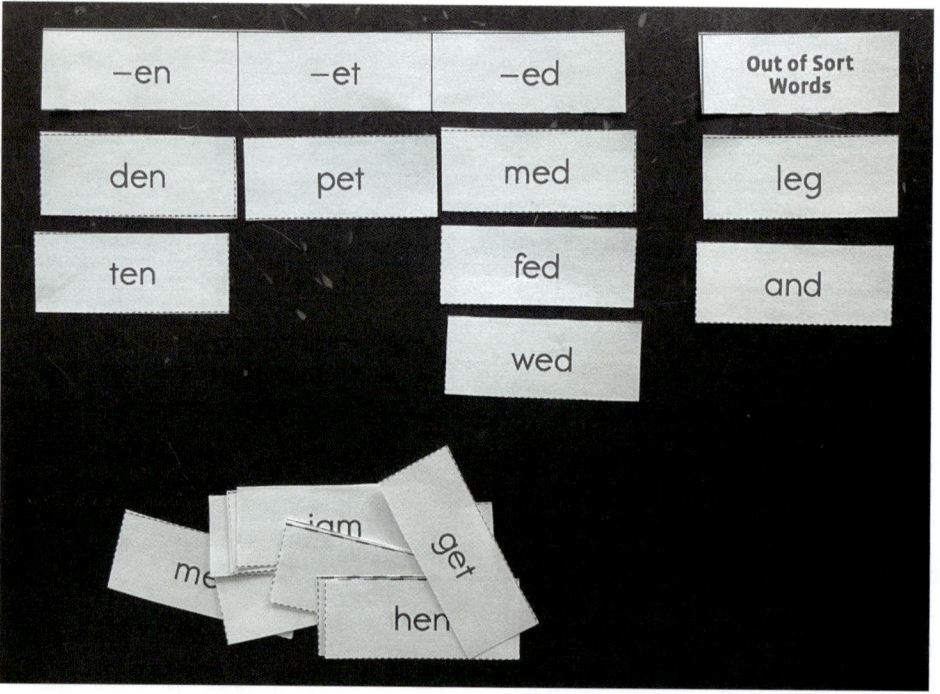

Student Engagement

Phonics and spelling lessons typically last about 20–25 minutes, so you'll need to plan strategically and with intention to keep children actively engaged and attentive throughout. To maximize engagement, give students many opportunities to practice and respond, and provide many opportunities for feedback during the lesson, keep the following in mind (Archer & Hughes, 2011; Carnine, 1976):

Pacing: Keep lessons moving quickly without downtime as you move through activities and transition from one part of the lesson to the next.

Signals: Establish consistent nonverbal prompts that students recognize and you use from lesson to lesson, such as sweeping your finger under a word to indicate to students that they should blend the sounds, or pointing to yourself when you'll model and to them when they should repeat you.

Echo response: Model an action, spelling, or pronunciation, and then prompt children to repeat or echo what you say or do, step by step. ("I'm going to say each sound and slide the letter down as I say the sounds: /s/ (slide down the *s*). Your turn. Slide down the letter for /s/, /a/ (slide down the *a*). Your turn. Slide down the letter for /a/ and /t/ (slide down the *t*). Your turn. Slide down the letter for /t/. SSsssaaaaatttt. *Sat*. Your turn. Read your word.")

Choral response: Prompt students to respond in unison or read together in one voice after you direct them to do so. ("Let's read through this list of words together, in one voice. *Thin, thick, think, three*.")

Written response: On individual whiteboards, have students practice writing words, then hold up their boards. ("Say the word slowly, hearing each sound, and write down the letter or letters to represent each sound.") Alternatively, children can make words on metal trays with magnetic letters or on word work mats (see Figures 4.3, 4.4, and 4.5).

Turn and Talk: Students are prompted to quickly turn and share a response with a peer. You can cue the listening partner to give feedback, such as a thumbs up if they agree, or to respond with a different answer if they disagree. Turn and talks should be brief.

Should Lessons Include Teaching Articulatory Gestures?

Some phonics programs recommend teachers model the shape of the mouth and placement of lips, teeth, and tongue (for example, pointing out to children that when you say the sound /m/ your lips are closed tight, but when you say the sound /th/, your tongue is between your teeth, etc.). Some encourage children to have individual handheld mirrors to notice their mouth shapes as they speak different sounds. Often, these programs also recommend that teachers include a "sound wall," with each sound represented by an illustration or photograph of the mouth when speaking the sound with the written sound (i.e., /ē/ as in *tea*). This type of sound wall differs from a sound–spelling wall recommended by speech-to-print proponents such as John Walker (the creator of Sounds-Write), where a sound is represented by an anchor picture (no mouth shape) such as an acorn for /ā/, with various spellings (*a* as in *baby*, *a_e* as in *cake*, *ai* as in *rain*, *ay* as in *play*, *ei* as in *reindeer*, *eigh* as in *weight*, *ea* as in *steak*, and *ey* as in *they*) beneath the picture.

I chose not to include the teaching of articulatory gestures as a regular part of each lesson (see Structure and Timing section, pages 116–117) because the research at this point is mixed, and I couldn't find evidence of this practice being used in general education classrooms. One study compared students whose phonemic awareness instruction did and did not include instruction with articulatory gestures and found that the two groups did not differ on spelling or nonsense-word reading ability, though the group who received articulatory gesture training had a slight advantage over the other with real-word reading seven days later. However, the study points out that the group also received more phonemic awareness practice, which might account for this difference (Boyer & Ehri, 2011). This finding is consistent with prior studies (Castiglioni-Spalten & Ehri, 2003; Wise et al., 1999). Students with severe reading disabilities (such as dyslexia) or with specific speech and language needs may benefit from direct attention to articulatory gestures, however (Alexander et al., 1991; Torgesen et al., 2001). There is also some evidence to suggest that the inclusion of a multisensory approach increases engagement in lessons and is valuable for that reason alone (Boyer & Ehri, 2011).

Adding this component will add extra time to your lesson. You may choose to include it for whole-class lessons under the rationale of "It couldn't hurt!", or you might decide to use it for students with reading disabilities, and/or you may choose to include it in cases where students seem to need additional support or ways to engage with the material (as evidenced by the number of repetitions they need to learn new concepts or by their observable level of engagement during lessons). Keep an eye on the research as it continues to evolve; I expect we will have new findings on this in the coming years.

Activities and Games

Phonics and spelling lessons have a predictable structure, and you can choose different activities and games (such as the examples listed on this page through 112) to teach, guide, and reinforce students' learning in each part of the lesson. Note that this is far from an exhaustive list of every possible activity, so when you and your students are comfortable with these and are craving something new, you might search online for some other ideas that fit with the goals of each lesson part. Activity *selection* is key—there isn't time to do every activity in every lesson. Rather, plan to vary the activities you select over time to keep lessons novel and offer students practice with slightly different applications of skills. The first time you use an activity, be sure to teach children their role and your role so they understand expectations and you can keep the pacing brisk.

Review and Warm-Up

Visual Drill: Display a card with a grapheme and ask students for a quick choral response with the phoneme(s) (sound). For example, if you display *ck*, children should say /k/.

Auditory Drill: Say a phoneme (sound) and ask children to identify or produce the grapheme(s) (letter[s]) that students learned can represent that sound. For example, if you say /k/, children might write or find letter tiles for the graphemes *c, k*, and *ck*.

Blending Drill: Say separate sounds (/s/ /i/ /p/) and ask students to blend them together to read the word (*sip*). You can display letters (written, with magnetic letters, or with letter cards) and slide a finger under the letters as students blend the sounds together.

Segmenting Drill: Say a word (*soap*) and ask students to separate the sounds (/s/ /ō/ /p/). You can display magnetic letters or letter tiles and then move the letters as you say each sound. You might use Elkonin boxes to help students make spelling–sound connections (see Figure 4.7).

Figure 4.7   Elkonin box

Elkonin boxes are a helpful tool to support students in isolating individual phonemes and connecting the graphemes used to spell each phoneme.

Spell Words/Word Work

Word building or writing: Dictate a word and ask children to spell it (using magnetic letters, letter tiles, a word work mat, or by writing the word). For more support and scaffolding, you can say the word slowly, helping students hear each individual sound (fffffiiiiiiisssssssttt or /f/ /i/ /s/ /t/) and/or reduce the number of letters or tiles they have to choose from. For less support, say the word and give students the challenge to say it slowly to themselves, isolate each sound, and spell each sound with a letter(s), using the entire word-building board. In a study of instruction with struggling beginning readers, students who used a combination of writing and manipulative letters to make words outperformed those who used only one component (Lane et al., 2009).

Word sorts: You can ask children either to sort words that are already written on separate sheets or cards or to write words in different categories. If you use pre-written words, students will read the words, paying attention to the sound–spelling pattern, and then sort them into categories (see Figure 4.6). They can figure out the categories by discovering the pattern (sometimes referred to as an "open sort"), or you can tell them the categories and then ask them to sort the words ("closed sort"). The sets of words should have consistent differences that help students understand a spelling pattern (for example, the four possible spellings for /ē/: e, ea, ee, or eCe). If you ask children to write words, have them set up their paper or whiteboard with the categories, then dictate each word. Ask them to decide which category it goes in, and write it using that spelling pattern (see Figure 4.8).

Figure 4.8   Handwritten Word Sort

After hearing a word dictated, the student considers what box to write the word in, and practices spelling it.

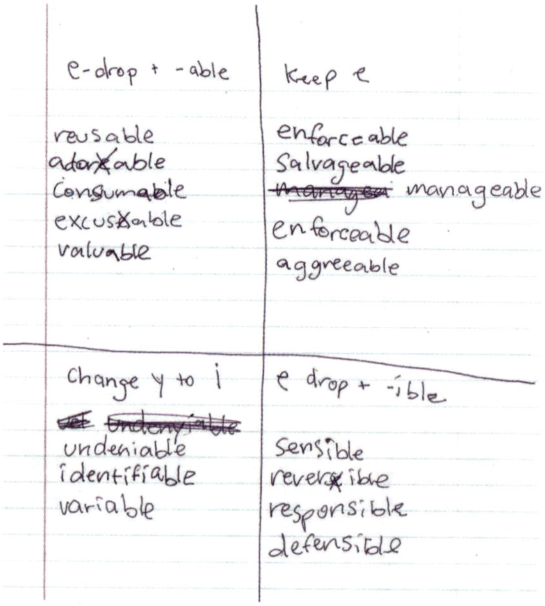

Word chains: Dictate a word and have students spell it using magnetic letters or letter tiles or by writing the word. Then, prompt them to substitute, insert, or delete letters to review sound spellings. For example, for *sat →* *sang → rang → ring*, you might say, "Write (or make) the word *sat*. Change *sat* to *sang*. Change *sang* to *rang*. Change *rang* to *ring*," and so on. After each new prompt, expect to coach children to slow down, hear sounds, reread what they've written, make corrections, and so on.

Read Words

Word chains: This is similar to the word chain activity you'll use for writing (see above), except that in this portion of the lesson, you are doing all the writing, making changes, and manipulating the letters, and students are reading the new words as you make for them. For example, for *sat → sang* *→ rang*, you might display *sat* and ask them to read the word. Then say, "I'm going to change the /t/ to /ng/. What new word have I spelled? Now I'll change the /s/ to /r/. What's the new word?" and so on.

Partner games: Generate a list of 36 words (try using Phinder online) that use the spelling pattern you're studying and organize the words into a 6 × 6 grid. The same grid of words can be used for a variety of games and activities.

bite	stride	dive	mile	hive	drive
fine	dine	lime	hike	glide	bike
dime	wipe	wide	crime	pride	shine
hide	slide	pine	five	side	line
kite	ride	bride	pipe	mine	slime
life	stripe	ripe	vine	slide	splke

Figure 4.9a   Roll and Read

Head each column with the numbers one through six and hand out dice. With a partner, students take turns rolling the dice, reading a word under the corresponding column, and coloring in the box once they've read it correctly. Whoever reads the final word in a row gets a point. The one with the most points wins.

bite	stride	dive	mile	hive	drive
fine	dine	lime	hike	glide	bike
dime	wipe	wide	crime	pride	shine
hide	slide	pine	five	side	line
kite	ride	bride	pipe	mine	slime
life	stripe	ripe	vine	slide	spike

Figure 4.9b   Four in a Row

Take turns reading and then coloring in the box wlth the word (or cover it with a chip), trying to get four in a row. You can play it in a similar way to Connect Four™ if your students know that game, starting from the bottom of each column. The first one to four (horizontally, vertically, or diagonally) wins. (The student using green will get four in a row diagonally once they read *pipe* and *five*.)

Figure 4.9c   Maze Reading

Start at the upper left-hand "start" corner and take turns reading a word in a box touching any word's box you've already read, coloring or covering as you go. The first to make it to the "finish" at the bottom right-hand corner wins.

START!					
bite	stride	dive	mile	hive	drive
fine	dine	lime	hike	glide	bike
dime	wipe	wide	crime	pride	shine
hide	slide	pine	five	side	line
kite	ride	bride	pipe	mine	slime
life	stripe	ripe	vine	slide	spike
					FINISH!

Figure 4.9d   Spin and Cover Up

Spin a spinner with the numbers one through three, and read the number of words corresponding to the number on the spinner; for each correct word, color it in. Once the entire page is colored in, count how many you each colored. The student with the most colored squares wins.

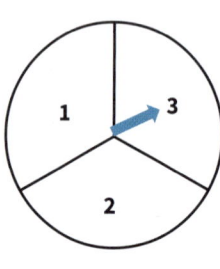

bite	stride	dive	mile	hive	drive
fine	dine	lime	hike	glide	bike
dime	wipe	wide	crime	pride	shine
hide	slide	pine	five	side	line
kite	ride	bride	pipe	mine	slime
life	stripe	ripe	vine	slide	spike

Decoding drill: Provide students with a word (written on a card, slide deck, or a whiteboard). Ask them to read through the word, continuously blending each sound or syllable, and then return to read through the word more quickly.

Sight word drill: Provide students with words (written on a card, slide deck, or a whiteboard) they should know on sight because they have already practiced decoding them in previous lessons. Ask them to read them chorally.

Write Connected Text

Dictation: Say a sentence, enunciating each word clearly. Have children repeat the sentence out loud. For beginning writers, you may have them plan their sentence by writing a line for each word to reinforce spaces between words, then repeat words as necessary to help them remember what they will write. Provide more scaffolding by modeling how to stretch out the word or by isolating each sound as they spell it. Offer more independence by encouraging children to say the word slowly to themselves to hear the sounds before writing it.

Read Connected Text

Decodable texts: Decodable texts are especially important for beginning readers who don't yet have a lot of phonics knowledge and need practice applying their newly learned skills. One study found that decodable texts helped readers read more independently and accurately and more easily apply their phonics knowledge (Mesmer, 2005). In texts that are less controlled, beginning readers may have no choice but to figure out unfamiliar words with spelling patterns beyond their knowledge by inferring from context and/or using pictures—practices that won't cement the learning from the phonics lesson. It's important to note that what makes a book "decodable" is relative: It depends upon whether the spellings in the book match what the reader has learned. Eventually, all books are decodable.

When looking for decodable texts, make sure the series is aligned to your phonics program's scope and sequence so you can easily select the right text to go with each lesson. Also, make sure the texts offer students an opportunity to talk or think about something meaningful and that the texts sound like authentic language—not nonsensical tongue twisters. Children should be thinking and monitoring for meaning and self-correcting, not simply decoding words. I like Fly Leaf Publishing and Daffodil Hill Press Books, and there are many other high-quality series available that fit these important characteristics.

During the phonics and spelling lesson, provide students with decodable texts they can read either chorally (display the text and have the whole group or class read it together), in partnerships (chorally or by taking turns reading sentences), or independently (students can whisper read to themselves as you move around the group to provide feedback). After reading and rereading, engage children in a brief discussion, have them sketch a picture about what they read, or ask them comprehension questions to check understanding.

Multiple criterion texts: Texts that are written to give students exposure to and practice with high-frequency words, are controlled for decodability to align to what students are learning in phonics and spelling lessons, and are meaningful and possibly even content-rich have been shown in some studies to have the potential to be more effective than authentic literature for developing (but not advanced) decoders (Cheatham et al., 2014). For examples, see TextProject.org.

Authentic texts: English is a morphophonemic language, meaning some of the logic of spelling can be based on word roots and word meanings, not only on phonics. Consider, for example, /ā/ spelled *e-t* in *ballet*, which comes from French, or the spelling *s-i-g-n*, pronounced differently in the words *sign* and *signature*. In fact, while about 50 percent of English words can be spelled or pronounced by predictable sound–symbol relationships alone, another 34 percent vary by less predictable sound–spelling combination. This means that while phonics teaching is essential, students also need to develop a "set for variability" (Steacy et al., 2019)—they need to learn that they must approach words with flexibility, trying alternate feasible pronunciations based on their phonics and vocabulary knowledge until they reach the correct word. If all of the texts students read are overly controlled, they will not have opportunities to practice this flexibility. Supporting this idea, one recent study compared the use of decodable texts, authentic texts, or a combination of both with elementary-aged students with reading difficulties and found that including both types was most beneficial for students' word recognition abilities (Pugh et al., 2023).

No matter the type of text a student is reading, help them practice flexibility by offering feedback that reminds them to use what they know from phonics, as well as other strategies, to monitor, correct, and read with accuracy.

High-Frequency Words

High-frequency words (HFWs) are critical for students to know to be able to successfully read connected text, so it's important to have a plan for how you'll teach these words and that you teach them in a way that helps students orthographically map. Of course, most HFW lists (i.e., Fry, Dolch) are organized according to frequency, not spelling pattern.

One efficient approach is to identify HFWs with spelling patterns that align to your lesson objective and include them in your lesson activities and in the connected texts you'll have students read or the sentences you'll dictate. For example, when you're learning words with short vowels (VC, CVC), include words such as *at*, *in*, *got*, *yes*, and *did*. You may also choose, during a phonics lesson, to introduce words that are irregularly spelled (i.e., *does*), or a HFW students will need to know with a spelling generalization they haven't yet learned (i.e., *the*). In these cases, as you do with other words, first help them hear the individual sounds and identify which spellings connect to each sound. Then discuss the part(s) of the word with a predictable spelling and the part(s) with an unusual, unfamiliar, unexpected, or irregular spelling. For example, for children who have not yet learned about the schwa sound, the /th/ (voiced) in the word *the* is predictable (as in *that, those, this, than*) but the *e* spelling the schwa is not (yet!). However, having children connect the two sounds to the spellings *th* and *e* will help them to remember it. Elkonin boxes (see Figure 4.7) can be helpful here.

Keep in mind that phonics lessons are not the only time you can introduce HFWs. See, for example, how I introduce a couple of words at the beginning of the shared-reading lesson with first graders (Video 7.1, Chapter 7). You can also bring spelling practice of HFWs into interactive writing lessons (Serravallo, 2021).

Structure and Timing: Phonics and Spelling Lessons

The structure of the lesson in this chapter is adapted from a variety of sources: CORE Learning's six-step phonics lesson (2018), Blevins's lesson elements as described in *A Fresh Look at Phonics* (2016), lessons as described by Lindsay (2023) in *Reading Above the Fray*, the routines and procedures in a *UFLI Foundations* lesson (Lane & Contesse, 2022), and *Making Sense of Phonics* by Beck and Beck (2013). The lesson design is also influenced by the emerging research about a speech-to-print approach to phonics instruction. I agree with authors John Walker (Sounds-Write), Jan Wascowicz (Spell-Links), and others that introducing new patterns by connecting spellings to spoken language makes a lot of sense, so you'll notice I recommend starting with sounds, moving to spellings, then moving to reading words in each portion of the lesson as students are learning new letter–sound correspondences. Though the order, timing, and procedures of the lessons in each of the previously mentioned resources differs slightly, they all have a few elements in common: In every lesson, students will have some practice with phonemic awareness, some practice connecting phonemes and graphemes as they encode (spell) and decode (read), and an opportunity to practice reading and writing words in context. You will find each of these elements in my suggested lesson sequence:

1. Warm-Up and Review
(2 minutes)

Review sound–spelling correspondences from prior lessons and practice blending and segmenting—the two phonemic awareness skills most closely tied to reading and spelling ability.

2. Introduce a New Concept
(2 minutes)

Explicitly teach a new spelling. Provide examples of the spelling by sounding out words displayed on a card, moving graphemes into Elkonin boxes as you say the sounds, and/or writing the letter(s) on a whiteboard as you say the sounds. Involve children in sounding out and writing a few words with you.

3. Spell Words/Word Work
(3 minutes)

Students spell words by writing them, make words with magnetic letters or letter tiles, engage in a word chaining activity, and/or sort words based on patterns (see page 110). Remember to include HFWs that fit the spelling pattern you're studying in your word lists.

4. Read Words
(3 minutes)

Support students as they sound out words with the lesson's new spelling pattern or other words you've previously taught that they need to review. After reading through the words slowly, working to blend each sound, return to the list so students can read them with more automaticity. Remember to include HFWs that fit the spelling pattern you're studying in your word lists. Students can also play games with partners to practice reading words with automaticity (see pages 111–112).

5. Write Connected Text
(5 minutes)

Dictate one to three sentences that include words with spelling patterns you've taught, including the new pattern introduced in this lesson.

6. Read Connected Text
(10 minutes)

Offer students an opportunity to read connected text (decodable, multiple criterion, and/or authentic) where they will encounter the new spelling pattern and will have an opportunity to review spelling patterns you've previously taught. You can read chorally, set up children to read with partners, or ask them to read independently as you coach. Students may reread the text several times during this portion of the lesson. You may also have a brief discussion as a group after reading (if students are all reading the same text), ask some questions to check for comprehension (if they are reading different texts), or ask them to sketch a picture that shows what they read about (if the text isn't illustrated).

7. Clarify the Takeaways
(1 minute)

Remind students of decoding strategies you may have reinforced during the connected text reading (i.e., reading through the word left to right, rereading to make sure it makes sense, blending through the word, and so on). Also, repeat the new spelling–sound pattern from the lesson.

Responsive Teaching: Phonics and Spelling Lessons

Before a phonics or spelling lesson, you'll plan which sound–spelling patterns to review, what you'll introduce, what words students will practice reading and spelling in isolation, what connected text they'll read, and what sentence(s) you'll dictate for them to write. During the lesson, you'll need to be ready to respond when students need a redirection, some corrective feedback, and/or positive reinforcement (see Table 4.6 for examples). You can also note students' level of independence with the lesson to decide whether to pick up the pace or slow down and offer more practice.

Table 4.6   Example Language Frames, Responses, and Prompts to Teach Responsively During Phonics and Spelling Lessons

If You Hear or Observe . . .	Then You Might Say . . .
Students mumble through words rather than decoding them.	▶ Let's say each sound, sliding it into the next one (continuous blending). ▶ Say the first sound. Now say the first and next. Now say the first, next, and the one after that (successive blending).
Students seem very wiggly, are looking away from the words or text, aren't responding to your prompts, or aren't participating in writing.	▶ Let's pick up the pace. ▶ I can see some of you are losing focus. Is the lesson moving too slowly or should I back up and give you more help? ▶ Let's take a quick movement break before we get into the next part. ▶ Let's do this last one and then we'll save the rest of the lesson for later.
Students generate a plausible but incorrect spelling for a word you dictated.	▶ You are right that one way to spell the sound _____ is with the letter(s) _____. In this word, that sound is spelled _____.
Students make an error with a previously taught spelling.	▶ Remember, _____ is pronounced _____. Listen to me read it. Now you read it. ▶ Remember, _____ is spelled _____. Try to spell the word again. ▶ The sound is _____. What's the sound?

If You Hear or Observe . . .	Then You Might Say . . .
Students need support in hearing all the sounds in a word to spell them.	▶ I'm going to say the word slowly. Listen: _____. Now you say the word slowly. What's the first sound in the word? How can you spell that sound?
Students need help reading a word with an unfamiliar or irregular spelling.	▶ Let me read/spell the word for you to show you how the sounds are spelled. [Touch each letter as you say the corresponding sound or isolate each sound as you write the corresponding letter(s).]
Student partially decodes (attends to some but not all letters).	▶ You read some of the word. Let's go back to the beginning and read the word from left to right, saying each sound as we slide a finger under the word.
Student reads or spells correctly.	▶ You remembered the spelling for that sound. ▶ Yes, _____ spells _____.
A student's pronunciation or spelling of a word (i.e., *color* [United States] versus *colour* [United Kingdom]) differs from yours or that of other students because of dialect, regional accent, country of origin, and so on.	▶ It's so interesting that in one language we can have different sounds for that spelling. ▶ These are both acceptable spellings for that word. In this country, you'll see the spelling _____.

Lesson in Action: Small-Group Phonics and Spelling Lesson, First Grade, /o/

In the beginning of first grade, some students in this class were still working on blending, segmenting, and spelling CVC words, as well as remembering consonant and short-vowel sounds. Other students were independently reading books with a couple of sentences per page. Their teacher identified a small group of children who needed a review of a concept the whole class had already covered (short *o*). In addition to reviewing this short *o*, I planned for a lot of interleaved practice, revisiting prior concepts such as consonant sounds and spellings, and practicing segmenting and blending. The whole lesson took about 25 minutes and we ran out of time for reading connected text; in the future, I would split a full lesson into two 12–15-minute partial lessons to better hold the students' attention and engagement and ensure we get to all lesson components across the two.

Read the lesson plan on the opposite page or online, then watch the video (access it using the QR code), then come back to read the post-lesson reflection comments annotating the lesson plan.

Download the lesson plan and blank template on the companion website https://companion .corwin.com/ courses/2024_TRAD

Scan this code or go to https://qrs .ly/3sfg1r4 to watch the video.

Video 4.1   Small-Group Phonics and Spelling Lesson, First Grade, /o/

Phonics and Spelling Lessons: A Planning Template

Teacher Materials:

- Grapheme cards (*i, a, m, s, t, p, f, g, h, n, k, x, j,* r)
- Decodable texts: *Max and Cat, Too Big, Jon and Sis* (also have short *e* titles on hand for early finishers)

Student Materials:

- Individual whiteboards, markers, erasers

Goal:

- Short *o*

Warm Up and Review (2 minutes):

(Display, choral response. Place on table. When finished, say the sound, and ask students to point to the letter.)

- Review (visual/auditory):
  i (short *i*), *a* (short *a*), *m, s, t, p, f, g, h, n, k, x, j,* r
- Blend: *rat, hit, mat*
- Segment: *pig, hip, sat*

Introduce a New Concept (2 minutes):

Introduce sound /o/ as in *otter*. Repeat, isolate sound. Show *o* spelling.

- Beginning of the word: *otter* or *on* or *ox*.
- Middle of a word, as in *mom* or *not*.

Spell words.

- (demo) *fog*
- (we do) *on*
- (we do) *job*
- (demo) *mom*
- (we do) *got*

Read (decode slowly, return and read more quickly)

- (demo) *dot*
- (we do) *hop*
- (demo) *on*
- (we do) *box*

Spell Words/Word Work (3 minutes):

- Word chain: *not → lot → pot → hot → hat → mat → map → mop*

Read Words (3 minutes):

Word sort: Read the word slowly, then sort it under the category it belongs to (*o* or *a* in the middle).

cod	jot	rag	mad	bat
cot	got	pat	wag	
dog	fog	max	bag	

Write Connected Text (5 minutes):

- He can jog.
- Bob got me a pot.
- The dog sat on the bag.

Read Connected Text (10 minutes):

Short *o*:

- *Max and Cat*
- *Too Big*
- *Jon and Sis*

Clarify the Takeaways (1 minute)

Repeat /o/ as in *otter*.

Annotations:

I always intend to say, "How do I spell that sound?" but sometimes I slip and say, "What letter makes that sound?"

One thing I need to be careful of is to hold the sound, not repeat the sound. For example, I notice when sounding out "pig" I repeated /i/, /i/, /i/. It would have been better to just hold the sound /iiiiii/. Sometimes when children to to spell, they repeat the sound and end up writing a letter multiple times.

I used a picture anchor because I wasn't sure if they knew the animal.

When we use words that fit the spelling pattern that students don't yet know, I embed quick definitions.

I noticed some confusion with m and n, so I helped them to say the sound and notice the difference in mouth positions (though I don't call this out). I need to include words with m and n in the next lesson.

I did a lot of redirecting to get them to look back at the board, not at me.

Noticing some of the challenges these three students had next time I will offer the letters we need to make the words so they are working from a limited choice.

Rewatching this, I think I should have included visual anchors (otter and apple) to support their sorting.

I decided to stop the lesson because their attention was waning. I can repeat this lesson with new words and have them read the connected text in that lesson.

I noticed the students needed support with the concept of letter versus word and needed a lot of support overall to write the sentence so I stopped after one. In the next lesson, I will model a sentence for them first and then have them practice.

When she said that the letter i spells /ē/, I connected what she knows (spelling in Spanish) to what she's learning (spelling in English).

Lesson in Action: Whole-Class Phonics and Spelling Lesson, Second Grade, VCe Review

While I find the emerging research into a speech-to-print approach to phonics compelling, I want to note that this lesson followed the class's scope and sequence, where all VCe spellings are reviewed in one lesson. This runs counter to a speech-to-print approach (which may have, for example, reviewed long o and various spellings for long o in one lesson), but as a guest teacher, I felt it was important to stick to the established scope and sequence. I did, however, alternate between encoding and decoding, starting with encoding when possible, which is a practice aligned to a speech-to-print approach.

Read the lesson plan on the opposite page or online, then watch the video (access it using the QR code), then come back to read the post-lesson reflection comments annotating the lesson plan.

Download the lesson plan and blank template on the companion website https://companion.corwin.com/courses/2024_TRAD

Video 4.2   Whole-Class Phonics and Spelling Lesson, Second Grade, VCe Review

Scan this code or go to https://qrs.ly/t9fg1r8 to watch the video.

I tucked in definitions when I thought students might not know a word's meaning. To support orthographic mapping, readers need to connect the sound to the meaning to the letters. Also, this is a great way to support vocabulary development while working on phonics and spelling!

The way I explained this to the children wasn't exactly as I have it written here. I talked about long and short vowels and the "magic e." Some would say that that terminology is unnecessary. Also, I included all the vowels because this was the beginning of a second-grade review rather than an introduction.

I modified this plan after I got to the classroom and saw that one of the children's names was Jake. I also ended up using fewer of these words than planned to keep the pace brisk and the engagement high.

Notice that I was able to easily scan and identify children who needed feedback and coaching.

Notice I was coaching not only their spelling but also other conventions of writing, such as leaving finger spaces, capital letters, and punctuation at the end.

I noticed that although some students needed support spelling words with VCe patterns, almost all of them were able to easily read the words. That makes sense in a review lesson, as students often need support with spelling for a bit longer than reading a particular sound–spelling correspondence.

Phonics and Spelling Lessons: A Planning Template

Goal:
- Review long vowels with a VCe spelling pattern

Teacher Materials:
- Slide deck
- Decodable text: *Blake Bakes a Cake*

Student Materials:
- Individual whiteboards
- Markers
- Erasers

Warm Up and Review (2 minutes):
- Review (visual/auditory—on slide deck): vowels, digraphs, *ck, ff, ll, ss, zz, s*
- Blend: *thick, stub, quick, whack*
- Segment: *kick, stunk, shin*

Introduce a New Concept (2 minutes):
Today, we are going to work on spelling and reading words that have the sounds *a, e, i, o,* and *u* in them. One of the ways to spell these sounds is to use the vowel letter *a, e, i, o,* and *u,* then a consonant, and then an *e.* The *e* at the end is silent.
Read Words (all shared practice, review)
- *acorn,* isolate /ā/.
  - *make, fame*
- *ice,* isolate /ī/.
  - *bike, mine*
- *open,* isolate /ō/.
  - *joke, stone*
- *eagle,* isolate /ē/.
  - *eve, theme*
- *spoon,* isolate /o͞o/.
  - *flute, tune*
- *unicorn,* isolate /yu/.
  - *cube, mute*

Write Words:
- (demo) *shin → shine*
- (we do) *glob → globe*
- (we do) *not → note*
- (we do) *tub → tube*

Spell Words/Word Work (3 minutes):
Word chain: *make → cake → came → lame → lime → slime → slide → ride → rode → mode*

Read Words (3 minutes):
cute, time, same, here, phone

Write Connected Text (5 minutes):
- We will rise and shine!
- I see he made a cake.

Read Connected Text (10 minutes):
- *Blake Bakes a Cake*
- Read in partners, then illustrate.

Clarify the Takeaways (1 minute):
- One way to change a short vowel to long Is to add e to the end of the word.

Take It to Your Classroom

✓ Conduct assessments mentioned in this chapter to get a sense of your students' spelling and decoding abilities. Study them to make a plan for whether you'll teach the whole class the same sequence of lessons, split the class into two groups, or work with some children in small groups but most of the class as one large group. Because of the time it takes to teach phonics lessons, what you decide may also depend on whether you have a co-teacher or an aide and the total amount of time it would take to teach several phonics and spelling lessons in one day.

✓ Make a plan with your colleagues for which scope and sequence of phonics and spelling you'll use across Grades K–2.

✓ Once you've planned your first lessons, remember that you'll need to teach children their roles and responsibilities for each of the activity types and games.

✓ Keep an eye on your pacing and your students' level of engagement. If engagement is waning, decide if you need to split a lesson and teach it across two days or find ways to quicken the pace to keep students' attention.

Individual students will need different amounts of phonics instruction. Teachers' observations of students and their evaluation of ongoing assessments should guide the amount and type of instruction students get.

Picture It: Second Graders Expand Their Vocabulary With a Morphology Lesson

"Second graders," Ms. Washington begins, "We enjoyed the story *Crown: An Ode to the Fresh Cut* (2017) by Derrick Barnes. I want to return to one of the words we encountered when reading—*rearrange*—to understand it more deeply and to explore what other words we know or can learn that are related to this word." Ms. Washington writes the word *rearrange* on the whiteboard and asks students to read it out loud.

> Carefully select a word students encountered in a meaningful context that has potential for deeper learning and extension.

"Alright. So this word, *rearrange,* is from the sentence, 'You might just smash that geography exam tomorrow and rearrange the entire principal's honor roll' (unpaginated). We talked about how in this context, the word means that he'd change the order of the list. Maybe the people at the top would move to the bottom. Most likely, he'd move himself to the top of the list! *Rearrange* is a verb which means to organize into a different order. You might rearrange *things*, such as books on a bookshelf. You might rearrange *parts*, such as puzzle pieces you're trying to fit together. Your grown-up might rearrange your *plans* for the weekend after your soccer game is rained out or your friend cancels their birthday party because they got sick."

> Remind readers of the context in which they first encountered the word.

> Give a definition.

> After defining the word, offer additional uses of the word.

"I'm wondering, Can you rearrange items in your cupboard in your kitchen?" After students respond, she follows up with, "Why?" Then, she asks, "Can you rearrange the trees in the park?" They giggle and say no. She asks, "Why not?" Next, she asks them to think of something they have *rearranged* or that they might *rearrange*, and directs them to turn and talk to a neighbor.

> After providing students with multiple uses in context, have them apply the word to new contexts. This helps them go from being able to recognize or understand the word to being able to use it.

As students try to use the words *rearrange* or *rearranged* in a sentence, Ms. Washington moves around to listen in, assessing their usage and offering positive or corrective feedback. She calls the class back together and shares a few examples where students used the word accurately. "Now, can we think of some synonyms and antonyms for the word *rearrange*? What words mean something similar and what words mean the opposite?" Ms. Washington elicits ideas from the class and adds them, and a sentence context, to a Frayer model diagram (see Figure 5.1).

Figure 5.1   Frayer Model for *Rearrange*

This Frayer model diagram was created with students during the lesson.

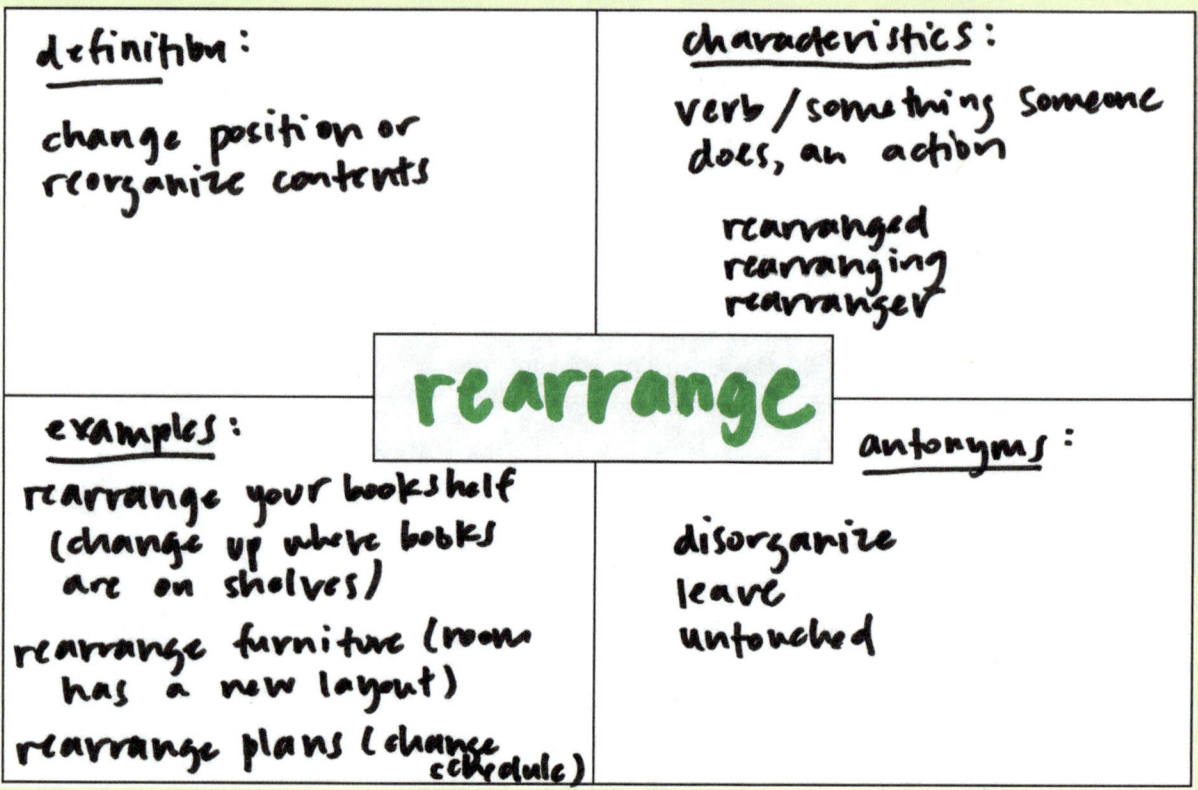

After making sure students understand the word *rearrange*, Ms. Washington moves on to an extension—a morphology lesson that will pique curiosity about words, help them learn generalizable knowledge about how words work, and reinforce their understanding of various affixes. "Now, let's underline the base . . ."

A student raises his hand and when Ms. Washington nods, he supplies, "*Arrange.*"

"And box the affix. Spell it for me?"

Everyone calls out, "*r-e.*"

> Encourage spelling affixes rather than pronouncing them, since pronunciation of affixes can sometimes change. Your focus in morphology lessons is on the meaning-based units; spelling is consistent when considering meaning.

Part 2: Lesson Structures

"What other words do you know that have the base word *arrange*?" The students supply the words *rearranging, arranged, rearranged, arranging,* and *arranges* and Ms. Washington adds them to the board.

Monique raises her hand, "How about *unarranged*?"

Ms. Washington asks the class, "What do we think? Is *unarranged* a word? What would it mean?" They talk about how the prefix *un* means *not*, so *unarranged* would be to take something that was in order and put it out of order, or it could mean that it wasn't planned. She adds the word to the board. Ms. Washington offers a few others that students didn't generate and invites them to discuss what each word means, based on what they know the base and affixes mean: *arrangeable, arranger.*

Ms. Washington reveals a word matrix for *arrange* with prefixes and suffixes and with word sums beneath it (see Figure 5.2). "Excellent work today, everyone! Look at all the words we made from the base word *arrange*. You could do this because you know what each of the affixes mean. Remember, you'll see these prefixes and suffixes attached to other bases, too. I'll add this matrix to our bulletin board and I want you to remember that anytime you're reading and come upon a longer word with some of these prefixes and suffixes that you know, you can break the word apart, think about the meaning of each part, and put the word back together to help you figure out its meaning—even when I'm not there to help you!"

> Sometimes students will create a word with affixes and bases that is not a real word, or is a word, you don't know or aren't sure about. These are great opportunities to discuss what it would mean and cement their understandings of morphology. These "nonwords" might also encourage wordplay when writing.

> Think of the matrix as a summary of the lesson, something you can offer once students have generated multiple words that they know using the base.

> Students learn many new words by adding affixes to the base word in the lesson, but they also learn about how to approach any unfamiliar word that contains bases and affixes.

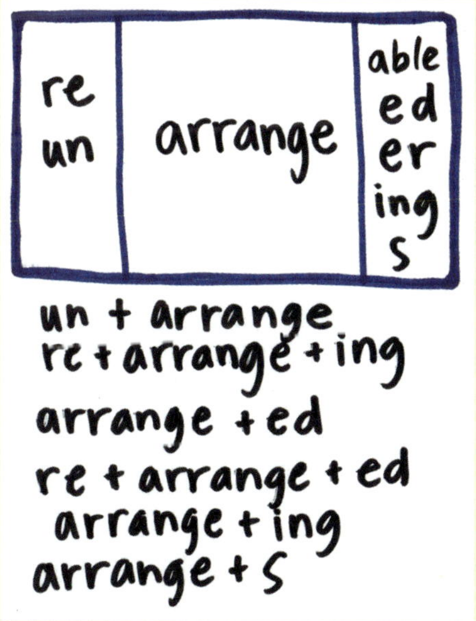

Figure 5.2   Word Matrix for *Arrange*

Word matrix for ***arrange*** with prefixes and suffixes.

Vocabulary Lessons: A Planning Template

Goals:

- *rearrange*, word matrix with base *arrange*

Teacher Materials:

- Blank Frayer model template
- Whiteboard
- Word matrix (*arrange* and affixes)
- Note-taking forms

Student Materials:

- None

Introduce and Explain: (3–5 minutes)

Focus Word:

rearrange

Initial Context:

"You might just smash that geography exam tomorrow and *rearrange* the entire principal's honor roll" (*Ode to the Fresh Cut* by Derrick Barnes)

Examples:

- Rearrange things (clothes in dresser)
- Rearrange parts (puzzle)
- Rearrange plans (weekend)

Synonyms/Antonyms: n/a

Parts of Speech: verb

Visual: n/a

Apply (3 minutes):

Choose:

Yes/No/Why Questions:
Can you rearrange items in your cupboard in your kitchen? Why?

Can you rearrange the trees in the park?

Word in Context:
Think of something you have *rearranged* or that you might *rearrange*. Turn and talk.

Sentence Completion:

Synonyms/Antonyms:

Elicit, add to Frayer

Extend (5 minutes):

Circle One:

word sums

(word matrix)

word web

concept map

rearrange

unarranged

arranged

arranging

arranges

Clarify the Takeaways (1 minute):

Show word matrix, review how knowing bases and affixes can help with many words.

An Overview: Vocabulary Lessons

A robust research base confirms that developing students' vocabulary is critical (see What Research Says, page 132). Therefore, you'll find a callout in each chapter of this book with ideas to embed vocabulary and knowledge building into every lesson type. Across the day, for example, students will learn strategies for figuring out meanings of words from context. They'll learn words as they encounter them in the varied reading diet of books they read themselves, with you, with peers, and those you read aloud to them. They will learn words through their content studies in math, science, and social studies. And they will learn words through the rich and varied vocabulary you use as you speak (Wanzek et al., 2023). In short, you'll be teaching vocabulary all day long.

This chapter, however, focuses on lessons that directly teach students about words and how words work and, when used regularly, can help students learn hundreds of words a year. In a vocabulary lesson, you'll revisit a word students previously encountered in meaningful context (a "focus word"), help them deeply process that word, and extend the learning by connecting that word to other conceptually related words or exploring morphology and etymology (Beck, McKeown, & Omanson, 1987; Kame'enui et al., 1982; McKeown, 2019; National Reading Panel, 2000; Stahl & Fairbanks, 1986).

What Research Says
About Vocabulary Knowledge and Instruction

➡ Reading comprehension is empirically linked to a reader's ability to know and understand the words in the text, from primary grades through adulthood (Beck et al., 2013; Kenneth & Kieffer, 2017; Mancilla-Martines & McClain, 2020; Stanovich, 1986; Watts-Taffe et al., 2017).

➡ Vocabulary is linked to general and conceptual knowledge development, and research has established a reciprocal relationship between the two (Baumann et al., 2002; Cervetti et al., 2016; Cromley & Azevedo, 2007; Wagner & Ridgewell, 2009; Wright & Gotwals, 2017; Wright et al., 2022).

➡ Explicit instruction in roots and affixes helps readers understand words with those same roots and affixes, and awareness of roots and affixes can help readers figure out word meanings when reading independently (Crosson & McKeown, 2016; Goodwin & Ahn, 2013).

➡ In addition to explicitly teaching new words, students also need strategies for learning word meanings on their own (Lubliner & Smetana, 2005). Read more about embedding strategies for figuring out word meanings (such as from context) in Chapters 3, 6, 7, and 8.

➡ Some researchers have argued that the number of words readers need to learn is so enormous (compared to what they can feasibly learn each year), that direct instruction of individual words alone is not enough (Anderson & Nagy, 1992). However, by teaching some words and then exploring the word roots and/or creating concept maps to other words, you can extend the learning and better support students with the number of words they need to learn (Biemiller, 2001; Stahl & Shiel, 1992), especially when you couple this with reading from a variety of texts on a range of topics (Anderson & Nagy, 1992).

➡ Most words are learned through context: by listening to others talk, reading books, trying new hobbies, exploring content areas (math, science, social studies) in school, watching television and movies, and more (Baumann et al., 2003; Duff et al., 2015; Hayes & Ahrens, 1988; Krashen, 2004; Miller, 1999; Nagy et al., 1987; Wright & Cervetti, 2017; Wright 2020). Students learn words that are useful for communicating something or understanding something.

Some Vocabulary About Vocabulary

Affix: Prefix (attached before a base) or suffix (attached after a base). Several affixes can be added to any base. When teaching, spell—don't pronounce—the affixes to keep the focus on the spelling and meaning; note that pronunciation of affixes can vary (*lumped*, *rented*; *educate*, *collegiate*).

Bound base: Needs an affix added to make it a word (i.e., *struct*)

Etymology: A study of the origin of words and how meanings have changed throughout history

Free base: Can stand alone as its own word (i.e., *tree*, *port*)

Morpheme: A word or part of a word that is meaningful and cannot be further divided (i.e., words such as *eat* or *dive*; bases such as *spect* or *duce*; and affixes such as *-er*, *anti-*, *un-*, and *-ness*)

Morphology: The study of morphemes

Morphological awareness: Awareness that words are made up of morphemes

Planning: Vocabulary Lessons

Make sure every vocabulary lesson helps children learn both the focus word(s) and multiple other words that are related to that word either conceptually or morphologically. Choose focus words that are worth exploring, and make a plan for how you'll teach both that word and extend the learning to a network of other words.

Choosing Focus Words

Many of the focus words you select for vocabulary lessons will come from texts you read to or with students (e.g., during read-aloud lessons, close-reading lessons, shared-reading lessons, and so on). Children's literature is filled with interesting words worthy of deeper study and endless opportunities to teach children how to use contextual clues to figure out those words. In fact, analyses of words used in children's literature have found that the vocabulary is more sophisticated than the words adults use in everyday conversation (Hayes & Ahrens, 1988). And as you read in Chapter 2, when you curate conceptually coherent text sets related to your content studies, students will encounter a related set of important words across a variety of contexts, building a deeper knowledge of concepts that will help them to learn more words (Cervetti et al., 2016). As an added bonus, words from these text sets often lend themselves well to concept mapping, a possible component of the vocabulary lesson.

You'll also find many opportunities to revisit words students may have first encountered in your science, social studies, and math lessons; hands-on explorations; videos; field trips; immersive experiences; problem-based learning experiences; and so on.

In truth, the problem won't be finding words to explore, it'll be choosing which words to focus on based on all the possibilities. Most often, you'll want to select words for vocabulary lessons by considering their utility, prevalence, and instructional potential to extend students' word learning. The best words to study are words that

* students need to know to understand the concepts in a text (or content study),

* may appear frequently and therefore are important to know,

* are words that students will have an opportunity to use,

* offer an opportunity for students to learn some generalizable principles about meaningful word parts (morphology instruction),

* have multiple meanings, and

* students can connect to other words (semantic mapping).

The three tiers of vocabulary by Beck and colleagues (see Figure 5.3) endure as a helpful framework for understanding the kinds of words readers are likely to encounter across different disciplines, the etymology of those words, and which ones are most instructionally valuable (Beck, McKeown, & Omanson, 1987; Beck, McKeown, & Kucan, 2013).

Figure 5.3   Three Tiers of Vocabulary

This vocabulary framework can help you select worthwhile words for vocabulary lessons.

	Key Information	Examples
Tier 1 Most children do not need instruction in these words.	• Often Anglo-Saxon in origin • Unlikely to be challenging (from a meaning perspective) for children who are fluent English speakers • Most (~80 percent) words fall into this category and are not typically the words that differentiate children with strong or weak comprehension (Cunningham & Stanovich, 1998; Hayes & Ahrens, 1988)	*does, of, one, two, run, see, book*
Tier 2 These words are valuable to teach.	• Many, but not all, come from Latin and have a bound base that must be combined with one or more affixes (i.e., *circum-* and *ob-* and *trans-*) • Uncommon in everyday conversation • Nation and Nation (2001) and Coxhead (2000) refer to these as *academic words*, and they estimate they make up about 10 percent of the words in academic texts	*fortunate, industrious, humorous, valiant, exhaust*
Tier 3 Teach these words in conjunction with specialized subject matter.	• Specialized words that are subject specific; for example, words you see in science or the arts • Typically Greek in origin • Nation and Nation (2001) refer to these as *technical words* • Frequency of these words is low and specific to the discipline	*respiration, perimeter, amendment, protagonist, typhoon, hue*

Source: Adapted from *Bringing Words to Life* (Beck, McKeown, & Kucan, 2013).

Online Tools and Word Lists to Support Selection

Academic Word Finder (https://tools.achievethecore.org/academic-word-finder/): Cut and paste a digital copy of your text and select your grade level, and this tool will identify Tier 2 words for you to consider teaching to your students.

Word Sift (https://wordsift.org/): Cut and paste your text and this online tool will create a word cloud (showing which words are most repeated in the text) and pull out key sentences that contain those common words. It also creates a word web from key terms in the passage to show the connections between words in the text. It provides images and videos to support some of the key vocabulary.

Coxhead Academic Word List (https://www.wgtn.ac.nz/lals/resources/academicwordlist): Created by Averil Coxhead, this is a list of the 570 words that are most common in academic writing but less common in everyday speech. Words are organized into 10 lists, ranked from most common to least, grouped with related words (for example, for the word *prohibit*, you'll find a list including *prohibited, prohibiting, prohibition, prohibitions, prohibitive, prohibits*).

Explaining

You'll need to plan the language you'll use to offer a clear definition of the focus word and a context for its use and to think ahead about other helpful information you might share: examples and non-examples, synonyms and antonyms, the part of speech, and possibly a visual representation of the word (see Table 5.1). You'll spend a couple of minutes on this part of the lesson.

Table 5.1   Sample Procedure and Language for Teaching a Focus Word: *Indignant*

Offer examples and non-examples	"When you're *indignant*, you feel or show anger about something that you find unfair. You could be *indignant* because some kids in class got extra credit and you didn't. You wouldn't be indignant about your dog having an accident on the carpet—you might be frustrated or annoyed or even angry, but there's nothing particularly unfair about it. But you could make an *indignant* plea to your siblings that it shouldn't always be you who cleans it up—they need to take a turn!"
Provide (and maybe elicit from students) synonyms and antonyms	Synonyms: *furious, heated, irate, incensed* Antonyms: *calm, peaceful, pleased*
Teach the part of speech	"*Indignant* is an adjective; it describes how someone is feeling."
Illustrate the word with visual representations	Display a photo of a child with arms crossed, scowling face, and a thought bubble above their head that says, "Not fair!"

If the word is a multiple-meaning word, review any other meanings students might know for the word (i.e., *bark*—of a tree, the sound a dog makes, etc.). You might also share the words that can collocate with that word—for example, if the target word is *rain*, you might describe it as *gentle* or *heavy* but not *mean* or *bulky*.

Applying: Deep Processing

To really learn a new word, we have to know more than its definition: We need to know how to use the word, what words it relates to, the concept(s) it represents, and what the word does not mean. One true test of whether someone knows a word is if they can use that word, correctly, in their own speech and/or writing. To get there, you'll need to plan opportunities for students to deeply process the word (Beck & McKeown, 1991; McKeown, 1993; McKeown & Beck, 2014; Rupley et al., 1999; Wright et al., 2021). You'll choose a couple of the activities in Table 5.2 when teaching a word, spending a couple of minutes on this part of the lesson.

Table 5.2   Sample Activities and Language to Use When Planning for Deep Processing of a Word's Meaning

Check understanding with yes/no/why questions	▶ Could you be *indignant* after someone suggested you made a mistake? Why? ▶ If you wrote to your town about knocking down the only playground in your community, would your letter be an *indignant* letter? Why?
Substitute the word into a sentence	What word would you substitute for the word *indignant*? ▶ "She gave an angry speech in front of the courtroom when she felt she was being treated unfairly."
Think of an original context for the word	Ask students a *who, what, where, when,* or *why* question: ▶ What would make you *indignant*? ▶ When was a time you were *indignant*? ▶ Why was the character in the story we read *indignant*?
Rate the degree	On a scale of 1 to 5: ▶ How *indignant* would you be if your plants needed water? ▶ . . . if everyone got dessert after dinner except you? ▶ . . . if you got a problem wrong on your math test? ▶ . . . if you saw someone bullying a younger child?
Complete the sentence	Finish this sentence: ▶ "I was *indignant* when . . ." ▶ "I knew he was *indignant* because . . ."

After engaging children in deep processing, you might use the Frayer model (Figure 5.4) to capture key contextual information—synonyms, antonyms, characteristics, and context (Frayer et al., 1969). It's best if you cocreate this with students, asking them what information to add that would be most helpful for them to remember the word and its meaning.

Figure 5.4   Frayer Model for *Indignant*

definition: Anger based on something that's unworthy or unfair	characteristics: adjective (noun → indignation)
examples: If a teacher gives out free extra credit to some but not all, you'd be indignant outraged, furious, angry	antonyms: delighted agreeable pleased amenable

indignant

Extending

Word learning involves creating a network of connections, understanding how each word relates to other words. In this portion of the lesson, you can choose to explore morphology or semantic/conceptual connections between words. Think about what extension with the focus word makes the most sense.

Figure 5.5   Shades of Meaning

You can supply words or elicit words from students that have a similar meaning, and sort the words on a continuum from most extreme to least extreme, then display them using color gradients.

HAPPY	SAD	TIRED	SCARED
delighted	upset	sleepy	afraid
thrilled	forlorn	drained	terrified
elated	miserable	exhausted	panicked
over-the-moon	heartbroken	wrecked	petrified
ecstatic	downtrodden	debilitated	horror-stricken

Figure 5.6   Which One Doesn't Belong

Present students with a set of words that have some connection and one outlier, then ask students to discuss the connections between the ones that go together: Why do they connect? What's the variation in their meaning? Which has the weakest connection to the others? Why? This challenges students' abilities to see patterns and connections across words.

Figure 5.7   Connections

A free online game through *The New York Times* called Connections (https://www.nytimes.com/games/connections) is a fun challenge for older students. The game offers sixteen words and players group them into four groups of four based on (usually meaning-based) categories. You could adapt this game by using your own set of words, writing the words on movable sticky notes, and encouraging students to sort and discuss possible ways the words can be grouped.

Saxophone	Shirt	vest	harp
Pegasus	blouse	beret	trumpet
Sombrero	cap	piano	frock
goblin	fedora	dragon	unicorn

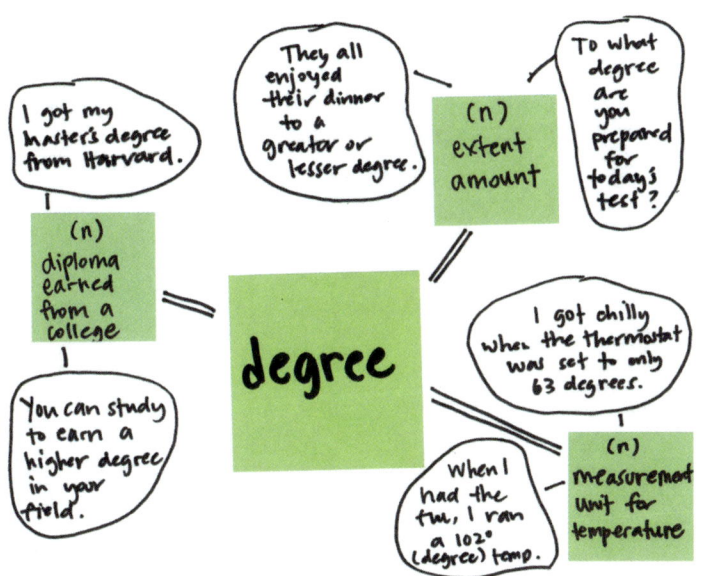

Figure 5.8   Semantic Map

You might choose a word that has multiple meanings and that you are using across subject areas, then create a semantic map with definitions, examples of context (sentences where the word appears), and or/photos and illustrations.

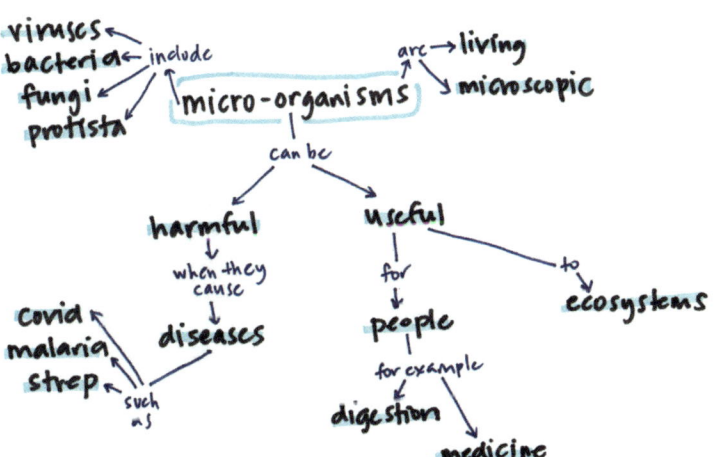

Figure 5.9   Concept Map

You could extend the learning about a word semantically by creating a concept map that shows the relationships between a content-specific word (from a unit of study) and various other words students have learned as they have built their vocabulary over time.

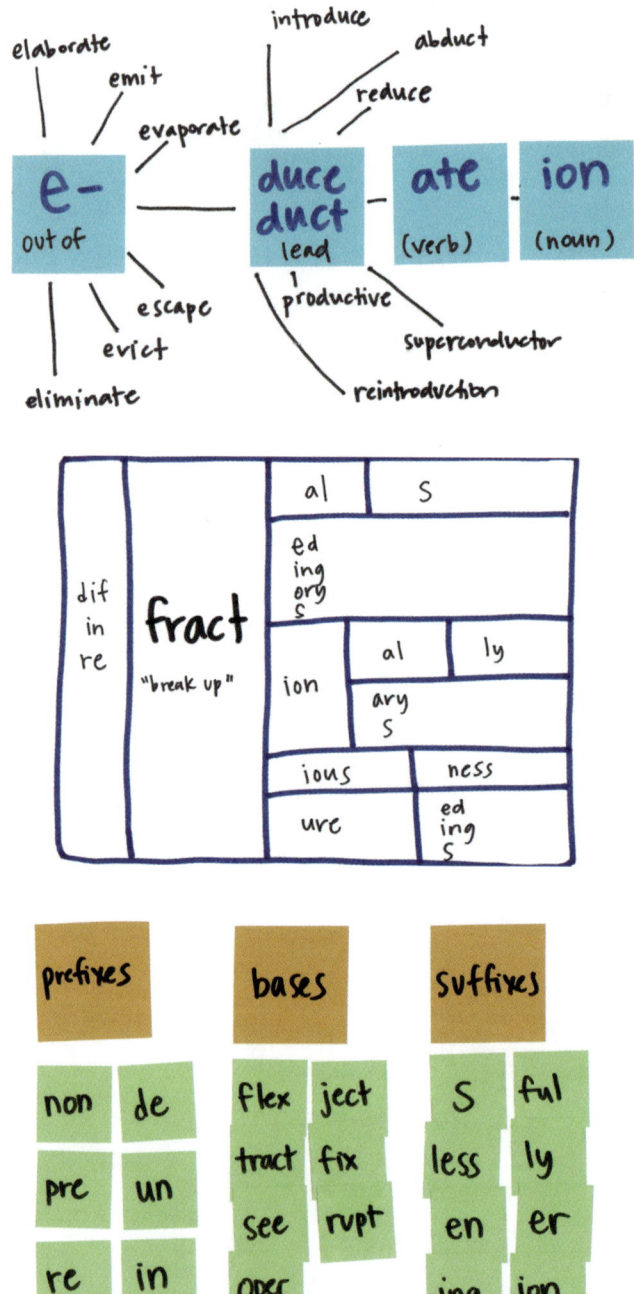

Figure 5.10   Word Web

To explore morphological extensions, you might create a word web with students. Break the focus word into its morphological parts and brainstorm other words they know that share the same affix or base.

Figure 5.11   Word Matrix

Create word webs or word matrixes during a lesson as you explore meaning-based units. After creating the word matrix with students, display it on a vocabulary wall for students to refer to.

Figure 5.12   Vocabulary Board

To capture morphological learning over time, consider creating a bulletin board with bases and affixes your students have learned across the year.

You might find or create an already-completed graphic (semantic web, word matrix, or Frayer model) as you're planning and even add it to your plans for your own reference, but during a lesson, always create it *with* your students by asking them questions and leading them through a problem-solving approach to trigger deeper focus and processing (Bowers et al., 2010). Your questions should help students generate words, consider whether the words they've supplied are real words, and think about word meanings and words in relationship to other words. Remember that in a vocabulary lesson, you're teaching students about words but you're also teaching them to be curious about words—a habit of mind that can apply to future investigations, including ones they may do on their own when reading independently.

Online Tools for Vocabulary Lesson Planning

There are many free online tools to speed up your planning:

√ **Etymonline.com:** Look up any affix or word for a definition and history of the word. For longer words, you can view the history and meaning of each word part (for example, look up *unsuspecting* and get information about *un-*, *sus*, *pect*, and *-ing*).

√ **Vocabulary.com:** More than a dictionary, this site offers a variety of different contexts for a word—some made up for the site and others pulled from literature. They also offer a list of morphologically related words in a word family graphic, synonyms, and parts of speech. Basically, the site provides everything you need for the Apply and Extend portions of the vocabulary lesson!

√ **Visualthesaurus.com:** Enter a word on this site and it creates a word web, sorting the words and their definitions into parts of speech.

√ **Neilramsden.co.uk:** Enter your own word sums (i.e., *un+sus+pect+inq*, *sus+pect*, *sus+pect+cd*) and this site will generate a word matrix for you.

√ **Textproject.org:** Developed by researcher Elfreida Heibert, this site is a treasure trove of resources for teachers and includes complete texts, extensive word lists, and many word maps.

Structure and Timing: Vocabulary Lessons

Vocabulary lessons are brief (about 10 minutes total). You'll revisit a focus word, help students deeply process that one word, and then extend the learning by connecting that word to others morphologically and/or semantically. At the end of the lesson, students should have had opportunities to think about many words and the connections between them and should deeply understand the focus word.

Vocabulary lessons go like this:

1. Introduce and Explain
(2 minutes)

Remind students of a focus word that they previously encountered in context from a book or content study. Explain the meaning of the word by providing a clear definition, examples of the word in context, synonyms, antonyms, a visual image, and the part of speech.

2. Apply
(3 minutes)

Support deep processing of the word. Ask students to, for example, share other synonyms or antonyms of the word and/or put the word in novel contexts. For example, you might place the word in various sentences and ask students yes/no questions about whether the usage makes sense. You might also ask students to turn and talk, describing how the word relates to other words you supply and/or their own experiences. Consider creating a Frayer model to capture students' understandings of the word. Clarify misconceptions and misunderstandings as needed. (See the Responsive Teaching section on page 145 for more.)

3. Extend
(5 minutes)

Use the focus word and extend the learning by exploring morphology or semantic/concept mapping. During this portion of the lesson, elicit suggestions from students and guide them in an exploration of the words they generate. For example, when extending with morphology, as students add affixes to the base, ask them to define what the whole word means, given what they know about each word part and referencing past work they've done with affixes when appropriate. Clarify misconceptions and misunderstandings as needed. (See the Responsive Teaching section on page 145 for more.)

4. Clarify the Takeaways
(1 minute)

Reiterate the meaning of the focus word, key understandings about semantic mapping or morphology exploration, and/or how students can apply what they learned when they are reading on their own.

Responsive Teaching: Vocabulary Lessons

Research has shown that engaging students in explorations of vocabulary (rather than giving them a list of words and definitions) is the best way to make the learning stick (Beck & McKeown, 2007; Nash & Snowling, 2006; Stahl & Nagy, 2005; Steele & Mills, 2011). Though you'll have some ideas of what you're trying to elicit from students, exploration is also open-ended, so you'll need to be ready to respond to your students' comments, suggestions, and questions.

Table 5.3 Example Language Frames, Responses, and Prompts to Teach Responsively During Vocabulary Lessons

If You Hear or Observe . . .	Then You Might Say . . .
A student offers an incorrect definition, synonym, or antonym.	▶ That word is close, but the difference between that word and our initial word is _____. So, it's not quite a synonym. ▶ Remember, an antonym needs to mean the opposite. ▶ Let me share the context again and try the definition one more time.
The student uses a word incorrectly in context, misunderstanding the meaning.	▶ Remember, the word means _____. Let me give you another example of how I might use it in a sentence, and then you can try to compose another sentence. ▶ The way you used the word, it would mean _____. The word actually means _____. Can you try to come up with a new sentence? ▶ Use this sentence starter to help: "The mother spoke about her child with *admiration* when . . ."
The student uses a word incorrectly, using the wrong part of speech.	▶ The word means _____ and is a [part of speech]. Let me give you a sentence and you tell me if I've used the word correctly. ▶ Your use of the word is not quite right. The word is a verb, an action word. It names what someone would do. Can you try again?
During the Extend part of the lesson, the student correctly offers a morphologically related word.	▶ Yes! That's a word. ▶ Let's make sure we understand what this word means. What does [affix] mean? What does [root] mean? So, what would it mean together?
During the Extend part of the lesson, the student offers a morphologically related word that is not a real word.	▶ Let's think about each of these word parts. Put together, what would this word mean? ▶ I can see how that could be a word, but it's not—you've invented a new word!

Lesson in Action: Whole-Class Vocabulary Lesson, Fifth Grade, Science

The week before planning and filming the lesson, I asked the fifth graders' science teacher to share her plans for the upcoming unit on mixtures and solutions. She showed me a very long glossary and I was struck by how many terms students would need to learn and use in the unit, so I tried to find connections between the words based on morphology or etymology. Knowing that Tier 3 domain-specific vocabulary is less common, I wanted to plan a lesson that got them thinking about meaningful word parts that would help them in this domain-specific context and beyond. I also wanted to help them understand the multiple meanings of the word *solution*, as it is used quite differently in English language arts, math, and science.

Read the lesson plan on the opposite page or online, watch the video (access it using the QR code), then come back to read the post-lesson reflection comments annotating the lesson plan.

Download the lesson plan or blank template on the companion website https://companion.corwin.com/courses/2024_TRAD

Scan this code or go to https://qrs.ly/jbfg1ra to watch the video.

Video 5.1   Whole-Class Vocabulary Lesson, Fifth Grade, Science

Exploring *polysemy* (words with multiple meanings) and teaching children to inhibit the word meaning unrelated to current context supports executive skills and comprehension.

This little bit of etymology will help them with words in this unit but may also pique their interest in how words with parts that are spelled the same often have common meaning-based roots.

Each of these could have been framed as a turn and talk, but I found this class so delightfully conversational that it seemed natural to talk teacher-to-student for this part of the lesson (and it also kept the pace brisk).

When the student offered a synonym for a math context, I acknowledged it as correct in one context and redirected everyone to think about *solution* in the context of science. This builds helpful flexibility for multiple-meaning words.

There is no good reason that I left this off—I just forgot it! If we had considered it quickly as we did *solvent* and *solute*, I could have talked about the affix *-able*. But it's okay; we can do another lesson in a few days to add this word and others to the chart.

When we talked about this word and someone contributed *dissect* and *disassemble*, I pointed out that they share the same affix but I wish I'd talked about their meanings to better clarify the meaning of *dis-*.

They weren't offering the words I'd wanted to focus on for *solv-* and *solu-* in a science context, so I suggested this word for us to discuss.

Vocabulary Lessons: A Planning Template

Goals:
- *solution*, word sums with *sol*

Teacher Materials:
- Whiteboard
- Chart paper to create concept map

Student Materials:
- None

Introduce and Explain: (2 minutes):

Focus Word:

solution

Initial Context:

"A *solution* is all about solving or dissolving. If you find an answer to a question, both the answer and how you got there is the *solution*. If you dissolve a solid into a liquid, you've created a different kind of *solution*.

Examples/Non-examples:

Solution, solve, dissolve. Do you hear a word part in all of those that are the same?

Other (Etymology): The Latin root *solver* means *to loosen*; this is the root for both *solve* and *solute*

Examples of the Word in Context:

- When you mix sugar, water, and lemon juice, you make a solution called lemonade.
- When you figure out a complex math problem, you figure out the solution—you loosen up the confusion to get to an answer.

Apply (3 minutes):

Choose:

Yes/No/Why Questions:

- Can you make a solution of salt and water? What happens?
- Can you make a solution of pencils and pens? Why not?

Word in Context:

Sentence Completion:

Synonyms/Antonyms:

- Synonyms: *mix, melt, blend*
- Antonyms: *separate, remove*

Other:

Extend (5 minutes):

Circle One:

(word sums)
word matrix
word web
concept map
Generate a list of words with *sol* words (*solve, solu*).

Solvent (noun): liquid that dissolves a solid, liquid, or gas

Dissolve (verb): liquefy, melt into a fluid; disintegrate chemically into a solution by immersion into a liquid or gas

Resolve (verb): find a solution to a problem, solve again

Generate a list of words with *solu*

Solute: the dissolved matter in a solution; the component of a solution that changes its state. In sugar water, the solute is the sugar because it changes from solid to liquid. The water is not a solute.

Solution: a mixture of two or more substances

Soluble: Sugar is *soluble*; it dissolves easily in water. You can also use the word to describe a problem that can be solved easily.

Clarify the Takeaways (1 minute):

We will be exploring these words (and others) that have *solu-* and *solv-* in this unit. Knowing what that base means and seeing it attached to prefixes such as *re-* and *dis-* and suffixes such as *-able* can help us to learn and remember what those words mean.

Lesson in Action: Small-Group Vocabulary Lesson, Second Grade, Social Studies

I pulled this small group of multilingual learners after a whole-class shared-reading lesson (see Video 7.2 in Chapter 7) to give them more practice with some words they need to understand to participate in discussions about their social studies curriculum. I chose concept mapping to help them see the connections and subcategories of the many words we encountered in the shared text and to help them learn more words they'll need to know for future texts and conversations.

Read the lesson plan on the opposite page or online, watch the video (access it using the QR code), then come back to read the post-lesson reflection comments annotating the lesson plan.

Download the lesson plan or blank template on the companion website https://companion .corwin.com/ courses/2024_TRAD

Video 5.2   Small-Group Vocabulary Lesson, Second Grade, Social Studies

Scan this code or go to https://qrs .ly/3nfg1rb to watch the video.

Vocabulary Lessons: A Planning Template

Goals:
- Deepen understanding of *urban* and *rural* and create a concept map of other useful words related to this study.

Teacher Materials:
- Whiteboard
- Chart paper to create concept map

Student Materials:
- None

Introduce and Explain: (2 minutes):

Focus Word:

urban

Initial Context:

"Many people live in urban areas." *Urban* is an adjective (a describing word) that means *city*.

Additional examples of the word in context:
- Urban planners figure out where to put parks, roads, and buildings so everyone can live comfortably. It's a job you can have.
- Urban gardens are small lots of land, sometimes sandwiched in between two buildings, where the community grows food.
- Urban animals are animals that live in the city—for example, we might see pigeons, squirrels, or raccoons.

Apply (3 minutes):

Choose:

Yes/No/Why Questions: Do you think there is such a thing as urban art?

Word in Context:

Sentence Completion: "In urban areas, we see . . ." (give students a stem and have them finish the sentence in pairs).

Synonyms/Antonyms:
- Synonyms: *city, populated*
- Antonyms: *country, rural*

Extend (5 minutes):

Circle One:

word sums
word matrix
word web
concept map

Generate a list of words that relate to antonyms *urban* and *rural* and words that relate to both. Prompt as necessary: "What kinds of buildings are in each setting? What kinds of transportation do people use? Where do people live? What might we see there? How would we describe what life is like?"

public transportation
subway
apartment
populated
rural
farmland
country
nature
livestock
mountains and hills (sometimes)
house
quiet
urban
skyscraper

Clarify the Takeaways (1 minute):
- Where would you rather live? Use words from the concept map.
- You will need to use these words throughout the unit, and we will see them again! I'll display the chart and you can refer to it as we talk about urban and rural communities.

Notice I used my hands to gesture as I talked about *buildings* and an *empty lot*.

The children were eager to offer their input, and as multilingual learners, opportunities to use expressive language are always valuable. So I decided, if they wanted to talk . . . talk!

Even after we'd read the word "urban" several times and I defined it for them, someone still asked what it means. This confirms that this group really needed the opportunity to revisit terms.

This sentence stem offered them a chance to practice some of the words we'd already talked about, and it also allowed me to introduce some new words and assess their understanding so far. When one child suggested that we'd see a *farm* in an urban area, I clarified the difference between a *garden* and a *farm*.

I decided to introduce them to this word and teach them a basic definition of it, though most of the words in this lesson came from students.

Notice how he was working to find the word *hill* and we all paused to help him by making the hand gesture he was using to communicate and thinking, "What would we call that?"

I wish I'd had something visual on hand to refer to during the lesson.

The students used very few words on the chart and will need more exposure to them and opportunities to use them.

Take It to Your Classroom

✓ With vocabulary in mind, take a look through some of the texts you plan to use in your instruction in the next week. Make a list of words that are Tier 2 or 3 words and are both useful and have potential to teach students more about words.

✓ Look at your plans for content studies over the next week and make a list of the words students will need to know to understand and engage with the content. Make a plan for which of those words you'll teach using the processes outlined in this chapter.

✓ Explore the online tools to support your planning (see page 143) to find context, synonyms, antonyms, definitions, and mapping options for the word(s) you selected to help you plan your lesson.

✓ Reread the Vocabulary and Knowledge boxes across Chapters 3, 4, and 6–11 and consider how the suggestions in those chapters, together with the suggestions in this chapter, can support your students' vocabulary learning.

Select words for vocabulary lessons by considering their utility, prevalence, and instructional potential to extend students' word learning.

Focus Lessons

Picture It: A Small Group of Fourth Graders Learns a Strategy to Support Their Reading Engagement

A group of four students joins Ms. Dozier on the rug. The rest of the class is settled, reading independently and working in texts on tasks aligned to their reading goals. She begins, "I pulled you four together today because you all have shared that you want help reading with more focus and engagement. You've all reflected and realized that you get distracted often or find that your eyes are going over the words, but you aren't really thinking about what you're reading. I'm going to share a strategy with you that you can all try."

> It's important to teach strategies aligned to a purpose. Start the lesson clarifying *why* you're teaching the strategy you've chosen.

> Based on assessment, you'll plan ahead to teach a single strategy.

Because the strategy she's chosen will work in any text, she has a short story she uses often for demonstration and the students each have their own self-selected novels for practice. As she introduces the strategy, she explains both when it's helpful to apply it as well as how to apply it. "When you find yourself distracted or disengaged— and by the way this happens to *all* readers at one point or another—it can help to slow down and really focus on visualizing the story. You can imagine yourself there, in the scene, with the characters. You can ask yourself questions to check in with your mental picture: What do I see? Hear? Feel?" She references a chart she had quickly prepared in advance of the lesson (Figure 6.1).

> Decide what text you will use to demonstrate the strategy and what text(s) students will use to practice.

> To keep your teaching lean and efficient, think ahead about how you will explain the strategy.

> Consider creating some sort of visual support to help students remember the strategy.

Figure 6.1 Anchor Chart

An anchor chart helps students focus and reminds them of the steps of the lesson.

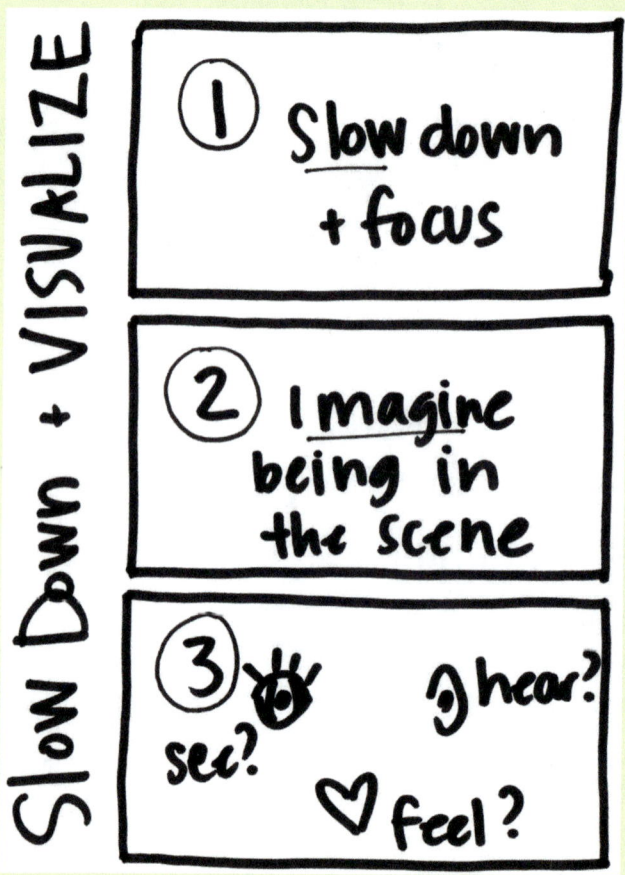

Ms. Dozier gives a quick example with her own text. She demonstrates how she pauses after reading a sentence or two and thinks aloud, asking herself the questions she shared to prompt her thinking. Then, she turns it over to the students. She asks them to open their books, pick up their reading where they left off, and try this slower-than-usual pace using the question prompts to help them visualize their stories. She moves around the group, coaching individual readers as they practice. She prompts them with questions ("What do you see at this point in the scene?"), offers compliments ("Yes, you described the scene in a way that I can picture it, too!"), and leads with directives ("Now say what you'd hear in that scene at that moment.").

After checking in with each student at least once—and one student who needed a bit more support twice—she pulls the group back together. "Readers, I realize that right now, sitting with me here in

> Before the lesson, decide how you will demonstrate the strategy: what you will read, where you will pause, and what you will think aloud about.

> When students begin to practice, your teaching becomes responsive— more like coaching—as you listen, observe, and decide in the moment what to say to best support each student with the strategy.

this group, you might not have had one of those distracted, unfocused moments, but I hope practicing this strategy with your friends and me helped you get the feel for it. Now it's up to you. As you continue reading on your own, remember to catch yourself if you become distracted or your mind wanders, back up to the last thing you remember reading and understanding, and reengage. As you reengage, use this strategy to slow down, intentionally visualize, and see if it helps get you back into the story. I'll check in with you soon to see how it's going." She hands them each a sticky note with a picture of the eye, ear, and heart on it (Figure 6.2) to support them as they use the strategy while they read independently.

> Most strategies worth learning take time to learn. The goal of a focus lesson is to introduce a strategy and set students on their way to using it effectively.

> Follow-up is the key to making sure the strategies you teach support students as readers beyond the lesson.

Figure 6.2   Individual student reminder cards

Leave students with a visible reminder of the strategy they learned. Ms. Dozier prepared these in advance of the lesson, but, depending on the age of your students, you could also have them create their own at the end of the lesson.

Focus Lessons: A Planning Template

Literacy Goal(s):

- Engagement, visualizing

Knowledge/ Vocabulary Goals:

- N/A

Teacher Materials:

- *A Dog's Life* by Ann Martin (2009)
- Strategy chart
- Student-facing sticky notes
- Note-taking forms

Student Materials:

- Self-selected books

Establish a Focus (30 seconds):

Remind students of their goal (staying focused and engaged)

Teach (1–4 minutes):

Strategy: Try to experience all the author is describing by using your senses. Read a little, then pause. Think, "What do I see? Hear? Feel?"

Think aloud from p. 91 of *A Dog's Life*, first three sentences of the first full paragraph

Coach (2–5 minutes):

- Refer to the chart
- Students practice independently with books

Clarify the Takeaways (1 minute):

Give students sticky notes to remember the strategy.

An Overview: Focus Lessons

Focus lessons are individual, group, or whole-class lessons where you teach a single strategy that is aligned to grade-level standards or curriculum, is tied to student needs based on your assessment, is something students need to be able to do to read a text you're studying together, or some combination of all three. This lesson type allows you to introduce a strategy using explicit teaching and a "to–with–by" gradual release model while making it clear to students that the purpose of the strategy is to have a goal-aligned how-to strategy ready to go in times of need.

Regardless of the group size, you'll frame the lesson by clarifying the purpose for the strategy, naming it and demonstrating it, explaining or giving an example through direct instruction so students understand it, and then offering students a chance to practice the strategy with some differentiated and targeted feedback and coaching.

Focus lessons are extremely versatile: You can teach students a strategy for any reading goal, from engagement (as in the Picture It vignette at the start of the chapter), to supporting skills for improving word reading accuracy, to comprehension, to writing about reading, and more. These lessons also work well in any grade level from pre-K to high school. You could even use this lesson structure across the curriculum in writing, math, studio art—whenever!

What Research Says
About Focus Lessons

Although this specific lesson structure does not appear in the literature, qualities of instruction that are key to focus lessons have been studied and found to be effective.

➜ Focus lessons give students the opportunity for repeated practice, allowing them to practice a skill under varied circumstances in one lesson with one strategy (Larsen-Freeman, 2012).

➜ They offer students support with one instructional focus at a time, a practice that reduces cognitive load (Peng et al., 2023; Schnotz & Kürschner, 2007; Torcasio & Sweller, 2010).

➜ You'll teach with direct, explicit instruction with clear, step-by-step how-tos and guided practice, with the aim of having students transfer these to independent practice (Anderson et al., 1979; Carlisle, Kelcey et al., 2011; Swanson, 1999).

➜ The feedback in focus lessons is tied to the strategy students recently learned, keeping the lesson objective clear and giving students repeated practice with support (Hattie & Clarke, 2019; Hattie & Timperley, 2007; Wisniewski et al., 2019).

➜ Feedback is tied directly to students' goals and can be immediate, supporting skill acquisition (Hattie & Clarke, 2019; Hattie & Timperley, 2007).

➜ Lessons focused on one skill at a time can be more effective than multiple-skill, comprehensive approaches in intervention settings (Hall & Burns, 2018; Peng et al., 2023; Vaughn et al., 2010).

➜ When done in small groups, focus lessons can yield significant gains as they allow for increased focus and feedback responsive to students' needs (Amendum, Li, & Creamer, 2009; Foorman & Torgesen, 2001; Wasik, 2008).

Focus lessons can also be taught with any group size—from one student to the entire class—though the pacing and timing of the lesson components, the amount of individualized feedback you'll give, and the length of your demonstration will vary slightly with each (see Table 6.1).

Table 6.1

Focus lessons are sometimes referred to by different names, but they all follow the same structure (for more, see Serravallo 2018, 2019).

A Focus Lesson Can Also Be Called a . . .	When It's With . . .	And Will Be Unique in These Ways . . .
coaching conference	one student	You'll teach the strategy quickly and spend most of the time coaching.
strategy lesson	a small group of learners who have the same need	After you teach the strategy, each student practices independently while you move around the group to provide individualized prompting, feedback, and support aligned to the strategy.
mini-lesson	the whole class or most of the class	You'll spend more time demonstrating. All students will have a chance to practice, but you won't provide as much individualized support to each student.

You can use focus lessons to introduce a new strategy or to reteach a strategy students need more practice with. You might set students up for success by pre-teaching a strategy in a small group before introducing it to the whole class, or let students try out a single strategy before they practice it in orchestration with other strategies in a read-aloud or shared-reading lesson (see Chapters 3 and 7, respectively).

If the strategy you are teaching in a focus lesson is new for the individual, group, or class, you might find that by the end of the lesson, some students are *approximating* its use but are not yet *automatic* with it, and that's OK. After some time practicing with you, they can continue practicing alone or with peers, and you can revisit the strategy in another lesson to give them the additional practice they might need. Other times, no doubt, you'll find that one quick focus lesson is all students need to start independently applying a strategy right away.

Knowledge and Vocabulary Building
Within Focus Lessons

☼ You can use the focus lesson structure to teach students strategies that help them figure out the meanings of vocabulary words—from being word conscious and curious, to using different kinds of context to seeking support from outside sources (such as a dictionary), to using their knowledge of morphology (Baumann et al., 2002; Beck et al., 1982; Crosson & McKeown, 2016; Duke et al., 2021; Ericsson & Kintsch, 1995; Goodwin & Ahn, 2013; Lubliner & Smetana, 2005; Pressley & Allington, 2014; Sampson et al., 1982; Scott et al., 2012.; Serravallo, 2023b; Wright & Cervetti, 2017).

☼ Knowledge is critical for comprehension, and students will need strategies that help them activate relevant knowledge before, during, and after reading and synthesize the knowledge they have with new information in a text (Kintsch, 2005; Peng et al., 2023; Pressley 2002a, 2002b). For example, if you prompt students to activate their prior knowledge, it is possible that without helpful strategies, they may think of irrelevant knowledge, which will challenge and complicate comprehension (Williams, 1991). In focus lessons, you can offer direct instruction that shows students how to think about what they already know about a topic, add to what they know as they read by linking relevant information, build knowledge by reading across a set of texts with the same topic, and/or reflect after reading to articulate their new learning.

☼ Carefully consider your text selection—both what you'll use to demonstrate and what students will practice with—as the texts may offer opportunities for vocabulary development and knowledge building together with the strategy focus of the lesson.

Planning: Focus Lessons

As with all lessons, once you've landed on a goal (from assessment, curricular objectives, and/or text demands), you'll need to decide who will be part of your lesson: the whole class, a group of readers with a similar need, or an individual who could use targeted support. You'll then need to decide what strategy to teach to support that goal, what text you will use to teach the strategy, and what text(s) students will use to practice.

Articulating a Strategy

A focus lesson centers around one strategy. Think of the goal or skill as the *what* of the lesson and the strategy as the *how to.* Your demonstration or explanation and the guided practice you lead will be focused on the steps of the strategy, so be sure your teaching language makes sense to you and your students.

When crafting strategies, you can rely on your own experience and reflect on what you do (step by step) to accomplish a goal. Notice that the examples in Table 6.2, though supporting very different goals, have a series of steps you can follow. This level of explicitness and clarity provides an important scaffold for readers.

Table 6.2   Examples of Goals and Skills Versus Strategies

What? (Goal or Skill)	How? (Strategy)
Monitoring comprehension	Read a sentence. Pause and think, "Did I understand what I read?" If it clicked ("Got it!"), keep reading. If it clunked ("Hmm . . ."), go back and reread before moving on.
Improving listening during conversation	Listen to what the person before you said. Say back what you understood in your own words ("So what you're saying is . . ."). Decide if you agree or disagree. Add your own thought that connects to the others' ideas.
Decoding multisyllabic words	Cover the word with your finger. Slide to reveal the first part of the word. Read the first part. Slide it to reveal the next part. Read the second part. Keep going all the way through the word. Then go back to the beginning, blending the sounds together.
Synthesizing information from the main text and text features	Look at the diagram. Read the text on that page. Think to yourself, "What does the diagram show that the author also explains in the text? What new information is in either the diagram or the main text?"

Source: Adapted from *The Reading Strategies Book 2.0*, Serravallo (2023b).

Texts for Demonstration

As you read in Chapter 2, you have a choice of how you'll teach the strategy (see pages 46–47): Will you demonstrate, give an example and explain, involve the students in shared practice, or engage them in guided inquiry? Your decision will be based on how much support you think students need to be able to understand the strategy before trying it themselves.

No matter which method you choose, you'll likely need a text to work with in a focus lesson, often an excerpt of something students are already familiar with. Over time, you will probably curate a core set of texts in a variety of genres that you and your students know well and that are well-suited to demonstrate a range of strategies. You won't need many; strategies that are well-crafted should be applicable to a wide range of texts, sometimes even texts in different genres.

Texts for Student Engagement

You will also need to consider what text(s) students will use to practice the strategy during the lesson.

If you offer time for students to read independently, they might practice the strategy in whatever text they are currently reading. In fact, research has shown that independent reading is most beneficial when it's scaffolded (see, for example, Reutzel et al., 2008). One way to provide scaffolding is to ensure students have targeted goals to focus on during independent reading time, teach them strategies to practice that support their goals using focus lessons, and hold them accountable for continued practice beyond the lesson.

Other times, the objective of a focus lesson might be inspired by a particular text and its challenges, and you'll decide students will all practice with this same text. For example, if you notice students are struggling with the busyness of their textbook pages, they'll bring that textbook to the group and you can offer them a strategy that will help with the pages they are reading now *and* the ones they'll read next week.

Sometimes, when the strategy you want to teach will require that the text has certain elements or features, you might decide to preselect the text(s) students will use for practice or ask students to bring a specific text when they meet with you. For example, when I taught a group of third graders how to put the moral of a fable into their own words, I found some short fables with the moral clearly stated at the end. When I worked with a group of sixth graders who needed practice using the glossary definition of a word together with context, I asked them to bring their science textbook, which I knew had a glossary.

Always keep the readability of the texts students will use to practice in mind. A focus lesson doesn't provide the same support as lessons where everyone will be reading the same text, such as a close-reading lesson (see Chapter 8), shared-reading lesson (see Chapter 7), or read-aloud lesson (Chapter 3). In a focus lesson, they need a text with an appropriate level of complexity so they can focus their attention on practicing the strategy.

Visual Anchors

There are two types of visual anchors you might plan for—one to share with the group and refer to during the lesson (Figure 6.1) and another to give to students at the end of the lesson (Figure 6.2). You can create either or both when you plan or make them on the spot with students (though you still may want to think about the content in advance). There are pros and cons to each approach. When students help create a visual, it might make their learning stick more and it will save you prep time, but it will take more time during the lesson. Whether you create a visual reminder in advance or in the company of students, keep it simple and clear, use as few words as possible, and use icons, steps, keywords, and/or examples so it is easy for students to refer to independently.

Structure and Timing: Focus Lessons

Focus lessons include the "I do" (modeling and demonstration), "we do" (shared practice and coaching), and "you do" (independent practice) of gradual release (Archer & Hughes, 2011; Pearson & Gallagher, 1983), all within a 3- to 10-minute time frame. One-on-one lessons usually last about 3–5 minutes, and small-group and whole-class lessons are generally longer, around 7–10 minutes (see Figure 6.3).

As you read earlier, in a focus lesson with the whole class, you'll spend more time demonstrating or explaining, with only a quick practice to get students started trying the strategy. When you are teaching a focus lesson to an individual or a small group, you'll give students more time to practice so you can offer feedback to each student.

Figure 6.3   Pacing of the Focus Lesson According to Group Size

The balance of time in each lesson component varies based on the size of the group.

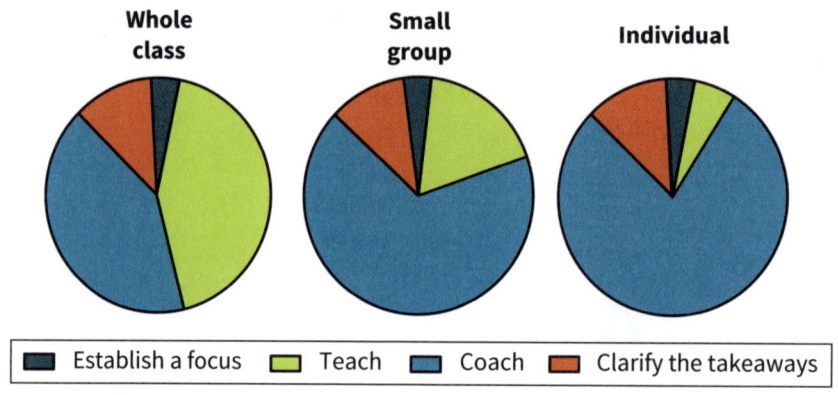

Focus lessons go like this:

1. Establish a Focus
(30 minutes)

Gather students in a comfortable meeting area for the whole class, at a small table for a group, or meet a student at their desk for a conference. Tell the students why you've pulled them together and why you chose the strategy you did.

2. Teach
(1–4 minutes)

Share a strategy. It can be helpful to have the steps of the strategy visible (on a chart, piece of paper, or whiteboard) to refer to as you teach. Next, you can choose how much support children need to be able to understand the strategy and begin practicing. You might offer a short explanation, provide a demonstration, show an example, engage the children in guided inquiry, and/or practice together in a shared text.

3. Coach
(2–5 minutes)

In a whole-class lesson, you'll set all students up to practice and you'll circulate, checking in with a few students or pairs. With small groups and individuals, you'll spend most of the time on this important part of the lesson. Ask students to begin practicing the strategy and then move among them, offering feedback and prompts aligned to the strategy as needed. In a coaching conference with an individual student, you can offer repeated prompts, questions, and quick examples. In small groups, you'll move around and offer support to individual students while the others practice applying the strategy independently.

4. Clarify the Takeaways
(1 minute)

After a few minutes of practice, clarify what you want students to take back to their independent work as readers. Repeat the steps of the strategy and remind students of when it might be helpful to use it. Share any visual reminders you've prepared (for example, notes about the strategy on a sticky note they can affix to their book's cover), or you can prompt students to create a quick written reminder for themselves.

Responsive Teaching: Focus Lessons

While you've carefully planned ahead for the focus lesson, during the "we do" and "I do" portions of each lesson, you'll get important feedback from students—What are they able to do that you want to reinforce? Where do they still need support? What confusions do they have? If you pay attention to this feedback, you'll find lots of opportunities for responsive teaching.

When I first wrote about small-group focus lessons (or *strategy lessons*), I used the analogy of a plate spinner to describe the teacher's role during the Coach portion of the lesson (Serravallo, 2010). After getting all of the plates spinning (practicing the strategy), you'll notice a plate is wobbling (a student could benefit from a prompt or redirection). You can then work with that student one-on-one, briefly, until they are back "spinning" again, then move on to another student in the group. This pace of spending 30–60 seconds supporting one student at a time with feedback also gives the other students in the group time to approximate and attempt with you nearby to help as needed.

In a focus lesson, responses that support students as they practice will most often be strategy specific. For example, if you're teaching students to use within-sentence context to figure out the meaning of new words, you might show them how key phrases such as *this is called*, *known as*, or *which means* and punctuation such as em-dashes and parentheses often signal that a definition is right there in the sentence. Then, when they practice, match your prompts to your teaching:

* "Do you see any punctuation that sets you up to read a definition?"

* "Are there key words or phrases within the sentence to let you know there's a definition?"

* "Yes! You're using the punctuation to find the definition."

Table 6.3 shares some general language frames and types of responses you might try based on typical observations during strategy practice.

Table 6.3   Example Language Frames, Responses, and Prompts to Teach Responsively During Focus Lessons

If You Hear or Observe . . .	Then You Might Say . . .
A student is forgetting to try a step of the strategy.	▶ You're doing [step] and [step]. Don't forget about [step]. ▶ Remember to [step].
A student is using the strategy well and with independence.	▶ Yes! It seems like this strategy is helping you. You're remembering to [repeat strategy].
A student has had an opportunity to practice but is still approximating and needs support.	▶ This was a great first try with this strategy. I'm going to leave you with the written steps of the strategy so you can practice on your own. I'll meet with you again soon to give you more support.
During a whole-class lesson, students are quiet or stuck during the coaching/practice part of the lesson.	▶ Readers, it looks like most of you are stuck. I'm going to give you another example/demonstration to see if that helps make the strategy clearer.

Lesson in Action: Individual Focus Lesson (Conference), Sixth Grade, Social Studies

Balthazar volunteered for this conference—his teacher asked who needed some extra support understanding the main ideas in a text they'd been assigned to read for social studies, and he spoke up. The text was definitely challenging—both in its content and in the density of information. I chose a strategy to help him synthesize and summarize the key information, a critical skill for comprehending and learning from expository texts.

Read the lesson plan on the opposite page or online, watch the video (access it using the QR code), then come back to read the post-lesson reflection comments annotating the lesson plan.

Download the lesson plan and a blank template on the companion website https://companion .corwin.com/ courses/2024_TRAD

Scan the code or go to https://qrs.ly/ bdfg1rg to watch the video.

Video 6.1   Individual Focus Lesson (Conference), Sixth Grade, Social Studies

Focus Lessons: A Planning Template

Literacy Goal(s):
- Understanding main ideas and details in a complex text

Knowledge/ Vocabulary Goals:
- Understanding causes, different perspectives, and beginnings of the Seven Years' War

Teacher Materials:
- Visual on a sticky note

Student Materials:
- "Conflicting Claims" article from social studies

Establish a Focus (30 seconds):

The text you've been assigned is dense and challenging; I'm going to offer a strategy to help you.

Teach (1–4 minutes):

Strategy: Read the heading, then read the information in the section. Go back to the heading and try to turn the heading into a statement that captures what the section is mostly about. Think to yourself, "What's the *what* and the *so what*?"

Explain the strategy

Coach (2–5 minutes):
- Guide practice with the "Conflicting Claims" section
- Guide practice with "The Ohio Valley" section
  - What's the most important info that relates to the heading?
  - What's the *what*?
  - What's the *so what*?
  - What's the most important idea to understand about the Ohio Valley related to this war?

Clarify the Takeaways (1 minute):

Continue pausing after each section to turn the heading into a main idea statement as a way to check understanding and synthesize information in each section.

> I like to prepare a sticky note ahead of time—sort of like a mini anchor chart for the lesson—that we can refer to again and again.

> As he tried to state a main idea, I listened for the elements—was he including all the information? Was he saying it concisely?

> Because I had him practice twice, this conference was a bit longer than usual. I did this because I wasn't sure if he'd be able to go from "what" to "so what" independently after only one time. And I was right! He once again gave a long summary and needed coaching to make it concise.

> I decided to modify the steps of the strategy to more closely match what he was doing and what I was able to coach him to do. The last step—saying it concisely—is certainly the most challenging for him, but I wanted to honor his process of saying a longer summary first.

Lesson in Action: Whole-Class Focus Lesson (Mini-lesson), Fourth Grade, Science

I found a text that was aligned to the class's science unit (rocks and fossils) and taught them how to slow down and annotate the text—a strategy that will serve them in science, social studies, English language arts, and beyond! Often in content areas, students all read the same text, which means the reading will most certainly be more challenging for some. This strategy, and ones like it, belong in all content area classrooms.

Read the lesson plan on the opposite page or online, watch the video (access it using the QR code), then come back to read the post-lesson reflection comments annotating the lesson plan.

Download the lesson plan and a blank template on the companion website https://companion.corwin.com/courses/2024_TRAD

Video 6.2   Whole-Class Focus Lesson (Mini-lesson), Fourth Grade, Science

Scan the code or go to https://qrs.ly/g7fg1rj to watch the video.

Focus Lessons: A Planning Template

Literacy Goal(s):
- Annotating

Knowledge/Vocabulary Goals:
- Fossils, how fossils are formed, types of fossils
- *Annotating*—taking notes in the margin (word, phrase, sketch)

Teacher Materials:
- Fossil text (enlarged or projected)

Student Materials:
- Fossil text, clipboard, pen or pencil

Establish a Focus (30 seconds):

Introduce a strategy for handling more complex texts.

Teach (1–4 minutes):

Strategy: Annotation slows us down to check for understanding. Notes help us when we want to do something with our reading, such as write about it or talk about it. To annotate, read a chunk—a paragraph or, if they are short, maybe two. Pause and ask, "What was the main idea of what I read? What was it mostly about?" In the margin, jot a word or phrase or draw a quick sketch.

- Model reading, thinking aloud, taking notes in the margin after the first paragraph
- Model reading the second paragraph, take notes as a sketch after the second paragraph

Coach (2–5 minutes):

Students practice on the third paragraph of the same text.

- What was that part mostly about?
- Look for a repeated word.
- What can you write or sketch to remember that part?
- Reread. Check that what you wrote matches the main idea of that part.
- Share.

Clarify the Takeaways (1 minute):

Remember that as you continue to read, slow down to annotate. Jot a quick word, phrase, or sketch in the margin.

I don't always do two demonstrations, but each of these was short and, together, they allowed me to show two different options for annotating.

While I had prepared these prompts to coach students as they practiced, by scanning their papers, I could see that nobody was stuck; so instead, I chose to voice some of what I was seeing as a way to prompt them. For example, I said, "I see someone putting it in her own words . . ."

I decided to call on children to share who could offer different examples, so I scanned to find someone who used words and someone else who used images.

The whole lesson lasted only five and a half minutes, but notice how many times I repeated the steps of the strategy. This repetition is intentional; it helps them transfer what they practiced to the rest of this text and other texts.

Lesson in Action: Small-Group Focus Lesson (Strategy Lesson), First Grade, English Language Arts

The two children in this video needed support with smoothing out their reading—their teacher and I saw this need when they read decodable texts in phonics lessons, when they participated in shared reading, and when we listened to them read independently. The simple strategy I taught them will help them across all of those contexts.

Read the lesson plan on the opposite page or online, watch the video (access it using the QR code), then come back to read the post-lesson reflection comments annotating the lesson plan.

Video 6.3 Small-Group Focus Lesson (Strategy Lesson), First Grade, English Language Arts

Download the lesson plan and a blank template on the companion website https://companion .corwin.com/ courses/2024_TRAD

Scan the code or go to https://qrs.ly/ a3fg1rm to watch the video.

Focus Lessons: A Planning Template

Literacy Goal:
- Fluency (phrasing)

Knowledge/ Vocabulary Goals:
- N/A

Teacher Materials:
- Chart

Student Materials:
- Independent reading books

Establish a Focus (30 seconds):
Reading words accurately, ready for the next step to smooth out reading

Teach (1–4 minutes):
Strategy: Instead of reading word by word, try to scoop up a few words at a time. Read all the words in one scoop together before pausing. Then scoop up the next few words.
- Use the chart to model reading a sentence word by word, then model scooping.
- Students practice with me on another sentence on the chart.

Coach (2–5 minutes):
As students practice independently in their books, move between them and coach one-on-one.

Possible prompts:
- What words will you scoop together?
- That sounded like you went word by word; try it again by scooping.
- Let me show you where to pause (add scoops or slashes), and you read the words.
- Repeat after me. (Read in phrases and have the student read the same words you read.)
- That sounded smooth!

Clarify the Takeaways (1 minute):
Give students a small card to use to remember the strategy.

Here, I was following the "I do, we do, you do" of gradual release. Notice that after a minute and a half, they were already working in their own books. Though some students may need more shared practice before trying it on their own, I could see these readers were ready to try the work in their own books.

Notice I moved quickly between the two students, giving them one-on-one feedback. A few times, I offered some support to help them read the words accurately so they could focus their attention on fluency.

Though I had all of these prompts ready, I didn't use them all and I didn't always use them verbatim.

I was careful to offer positive reinforcement whenever possible because knowing when they are meeting the expectation is just as important as getting corrective feedback.

Spin It: Student-Led Focus Lessons

Students develop expertise as they work on their own goals and learn strategies over time. A great way for them to showcase their learning and celebrate accomplishing goals is to teach their peers what they now know and are able to do.

When students regularly participate in teacher-led conferences and small-group focus lessons, they often pick up the structure and teaching moves of these lessons and make great teachers themselves. I've seen students as young as second grade teach quite well with little or no support, though older students often take to it more easily.

During student-led focus lessons, you may choose to sit nearby and offer the student-teacher tips as they teach. For example, you might nudge them to move from their explanation to student practice, encourage them to offer readers help as they practice, or remind them to speak up or hold their work up so other students can see and hear.

Figure 6.4

Students in Jean Rex's third-grade class participate in a student-led focus lesson about summarizing using plot structure.

With a sign-up system, students can indicate both what they are able to teach and what they'd like to learn about (see Figure 6.5). You might also encourage a student to lead a group when you know other students might benefit from it: "Sasha, I know you worked on synthesizing text features and the text to figure out a main idea, and Jasper and Miko could really benefit from learning about it, too. Would you be up for teaching them?"

Figure 6.5 Sign-Up for Strategy Groups

Once students become an "expert," they can offer to teach lessons on strategies they've mastered; peers sign up to show their interest.

Once children are comfortable leading lessons and participating in lessons led by their peers, you'll multiply the number of experts in the room! This idea also has the potential to develop a supportive classroom community, especially when you make sure *all* students have opportunities to lead and teach, even those for whom reading is more challenging.

Take It to Your Classroom

✓ If you're new to teaching focus lessons and coaching as students practice a strategy, you might try one-on-one focus lessons (coaching conferences) first. In these lessons, you'll practice many of the same teaching moves you'll need for a group, but your attention will be on one student versus multiple students, making it easier to think through and execute effective responsive instruction.

✓ It can take some practice to get focus lessons tight and well-paced. If you're new to this teaching, consider setting the stopwatch on your phone to keep an eye on the time. If a lesson went on for too long, try to figure out why. Did you demonstrate too many times? Did your demonstration last too long? Did you engage in a lot of back-and-forth with students where a quick turn and talk or independent practice might have been more efficient? Once you understand how the timing got away from you, you can be more intentional about it in the next lesson.

✓ Look at the texts you've used recently to demonstrate strategies. Could these same texts be used in other lessons? Working to curate a small set of texts you can use again and again can simplify your planning time and speed up the lesson as students focus more easily on the strategy you're demonstrating because they already know the text.

Focus lessons include the "I do" (modeling and demonstration), "we do" (shared practice and coaching), and "you do" (independent practice) of gradual release, all within a 3- to 10-minute time frame.

Shared-Reading Lessons

7

Picture It: Second Graders Practice Fluency and Comprehension With Poetry

"Good morning, second graders," Mr. Lew begins as his students settle into their spots in the meeting area. "I brought two poems for us to read today. First, we'll warm up with one of our favorites—'April Rain Song' by Langston Hughes—and then I can't wait to share a new poem by Douglas Florian."

> Revisiting familiar texts helps students get the feel for fluent reading and what it sounds like.

Mr. Lew slips a copy of "April Rain Song" under the document camera and zooms in so the words are easy for all the children to see from the screen, even from the back row. "Let's read in one voice. I'll sweep my pointer under the line to keep us together." After they finish the last line "And I love the rain . . . ," Mr. Lew gives them some feedback: "Readers, you really kept pace with each other, reading in a smooth voice. I could feel the rhythm of the first three lines beginning with 'Let the rain . . .' and noticed a change in rhythm with the next three lines beginning with 'The rain . . .' I'm wondering if we can add some emotion to our voices as we read it one more time. Think about what his words are saying. One more time in one voice, with feeling."

> Students must all be able to see the same text in shared reading because you will be interacting directly with it as you teach.

> You won't plan ahead for feedback like this—you'll respond to what you see and hear.

> You will find lots of opportunities in shared reading to show students how comprehension is tied to fluency.

He removes the poem from the document camera. "That was a great warm-up. Now we will read a poem about the beautiful monarch butterfly. I know we've studied a bit about the butterfly life cycle in science, and this poet gives us some true information but is also clever and I'd even say funny. Let me read the poem to you once and as I read, please follow along—join if you wish—and see if you can

> With careful text selection, you can make many interdisciplinary connections during shared reading.

If the text you are using is new to you or if it's been a while since you've read it, be sure to study it closely and think carefully about its meaning during your planning so your model reading captures that meaning clearly.

You can draw students' attention directly to the text in shared reading, showing and telling at the same time as you teach.

With echo reading, you'll model fluent, meaningful, engaged reading and ask students to immediately match their own reading to yours.

The pointer keeps the class together as they read chorally, of course, but it also supports students for whom the text may be a bit of a stretch to match the print to their oral reading.

Because rereading (to build fluency) is a staple of shared reading, short, engaging texts work best for these lessons.

visualize the images the author is describing with his words." Mr. Lew reads the poem aloud and the children laugh as he reads the last lines: "Swallows that swallow him / frequently puke."

He then returns to some of the key vocabulary in the poem to support their comprehension. He talks about the word *monarch* and points out that the author uses *prince* and *king* and *duke* metaphorically to compare the butterfly to royalty. He points out the mention of blackbirds and swallows and asks the children to turn and talk about why there might be birds (predators!) in a poem about butterflies. He points out the word *migration* and the line "past nations he wings" and makes sure the children understand that migration is a great journey, and that in this line, *wings* is an action synonymous with flying.

After this talk about words, Mr. Lew invites the students to read with him. "Readers, I'm going to read the first four lines and ask you to read them after I do." Mr. Lew models expressive reading, keeping rhythm with the A-B-C-B rhyme pattern. As the children echo, he slides his pointer under the words. He continues on, modeling four lines at a time, supporting them as they echo read. The poem is short, taking only a few minutes to read this way. He next invites them to read together chorally, as they did with their warm-up of "April Rain Song," reminding them to read both smoothly and to think about the author's words to communicate emotion.

Mr. Lew closes the lesson with a reminder: "Readers, as you return to your own reading, remember the rhythm and smoothness—and emotion—we brought out with our voices as we read these two poems and see if you can read your poems and stories with the same expression."

Shared-Reading Lessons: A Planning Template

Literacy Goals:

- Fluency (phrasing, prosody), vocabulary, inferring

Knowledge/Vocabulary Goals:

- butterfly food web (predator/prey) and life cycle of a monarch butterfly (migratory)
- *monarch, wings* (verb), *migration, duke*

Teacher Materials:

- *Warm-up text:* "April Rain Song," by Langston Hughes
- *New text:* "Monarch Butterfly" by Douglas Florian
- Pointer
- Document camera
- Notetaking forms

Student Materials:

- None

Establish a Focus (1 minute):

- Remind students that we've been working on fluency and reading smoothly. Try adding emotion in as we read, connected to what the words say.
- Connect to our study of animal life cycles in science.

Warm-Up (3 minutes):

What Will Students Do?	What Will You Say?
Choral read (first read), "April Rain Song"	"Let's read in one voice. I'll sweep my pointer under the line to keep us together."
Choral read (second read), "April Rain Song"	TBD

Read and Teach (5–10 minutes):

Which Pages or Lines?	What Will Students Do?	What Will You Say?
Whole poem (first read), "Monarch Butterfly"	Listen to me read it aloud	"See if you can visualize the images the author is describing with his words."
Lines 2–4	Listen to a think aloud	"Note how the author's word choices *prince, king,* and *duke* connect to the idea of a *monarch* butterfly."
Lines 7 and 9	Turn and talk	"Why do you think there are birds in a poem about butterflies?"
Line 10	Listen to a kid-friendly definition	*Migration*: a great journey
Whole poem (second read)	Echo read, four lines at a time	"Read after me."
Whole poem (third read)	Choral read	"Let's read it now together."

Clarify the Takeaways (1 minute):

Make sure your reading of any text is smooth, expressive, and full of emotion.

An Overview: Shared-Reading Lessons

When Holdaway (1979) and, later, Parkes (2000) first wrote about shared reading, they described a practice designed to replicate the experience of a child sitting with a parent and engaging in a joint reading activity. Over time, the teaching approach has evolved to incorporate insights from the last several decades of research into effective practices. A shared-reading lesson is now much more interactive and often includes repeated reading, choral and echo reading, intentional strategy instruction, and responsive feedback and prompting. As a result, shared reading is a powerful tool for supporting students' reading development.

In shared-reading lessons, all of your students' eyes will be on the same physical copy of text (a big book, a poem or song on a chart, or a text you display on a screen) throughout the lesson. You'll alternate between demonstration (modeling fluent reading, thinking aloud about meaning, articulating steps you use to decode words, thinking aloud about print and book concepts, and so on) and guiding practice (asking students to read aloud while you offer feedback, prompting them to turn and talk in response to your questions, and so on). Students will reread often, working toward more fluent and accurate reading with each repetition.

What Research Says
About Shared-Reading Lessons

➡ Shared-reading lessons support word recognition of orthographic representations and, in turn, promote word recognition, spelling, and meaning (Shakory et al., 2021; Wegener et al., 2018).

➡ Shared-reading lessons improve alphabet knowledge and print recognition in even the youngest students. One study found that HeadStart students who were assigned to a print-focused shared-reading group outperformed the picture-focused reading group in overall scores on post-treatment assessments (Justice & Ezell, 2002).

➡ Students' reading prosody (an aspect of fluency) improves when lessons include modeling, choral reading, guided practice, and feedback (Paige, 2011; Quadri et al., 2023; Rowen et al., 2015).

➡ Studies of younger readers who engaged in echo reading (Turner, 2010) and older readers who used choral and echo reading (Landreth & Young, 2021) had significant comprehension improvements.

➡ Shared-reading lessons build confidence and pride among readers of various oral reading levels (Paige, 2011).

Comparing Shared Reading, Close Reading, and Read Aloud

In some ways, shared-reading lessons are similar to read-aloud lessons. Both require you to carefully select the texts and plan with standards and students' needs in mind. In both lesson types, you'll challenge students with more complex texts than they can read independently. Also, in both read-aloud and shared-reading lessons, you model expressive, fluent reading; you pause to prompt discussions; and you support comprehension. However, there are also key differences. One main difference is that in shared reading, students can see the text, allowing them to follow along and join in the reading. This often means the pace of shared reading is a bit slower than during a read-aloud lesson as during shared reading students track the text with both their eyes and their voices. (For more on read-aloud lessons, see Chapter 3.)

Shared-reading lessons can also seem similar to close-reading lessons, as one option for close-reading lessons is to focus students' attention on one physical copy of text and they may engage in choral reading. However, close reading (Chapter 8) typically focuses on deeper analytic reading whereas shared reading tends to focus on accuracy, fluency, and basic comprehension.

When used as a whole-class structure, you can plan shared-reading lessons to align with your curriculum and grade-level standards and to support the transfer of foundational skills (such as decoding skills you may have taught in phonics lessons) to continuous text. You might also plan for shared-reading lessons when students are required to read texts (from core reading programs or content study textbooks) that are too demanding for them to read independently without support (Kuhn, 2020).

When you choose a shared-reading lesson for small groups, you can pull students together based on their skill needs and select appropriate texts and strategies to address those needs with additional precision. When you preview a text with a smaller group of students in mind, you can anticipate what support they will need and plan the shared-reading experience accordingly.

Knowledge and Vocabulary Building
Within Shared-Reading Lessons

⚙ To build important background knowledge and teach students how to activate relevant knowledge, you might choose texts for shared reading that are aligned to the topics and concepts you're studying in content areas. You could use a short excerpt from a textbook or a longer trade book that you're reading to the students or find a complementary short text. With a document camera, projecting the text for all your students to see is easy—any text can become a shared-reading text!

⚙ Because you are all looking at the same text during a shared-reading lesson, you can really show students how to figure out vocabulary from information on the page by physically pointing to features such as definitions embedded within the sentence, words whose meanings are supported by text features such as illustrations, and words that show up multiple times across a text where rereading them in context can help you develop a cumulative understanding of the word.

⚙ If a text you are using with beginning readers to support decoding or foundational skills has limited vocabulary and/or content, plan to use richer and more varied vocabulary in your discussion about the text. For example, if the character in a simple story seems sad, you might use the words *forlorn*, *miserable*, or *brokenhearted* to describe them. As you prompt children to talk about the text, you might prompt them with academic vocabulary—instead of saying *turn and talk*, for example, you might say *turn and describe*, *turn and explain*, or *turn and define*.

Planning: Shared-Reading Lessons

You can plan your shared-reading lessons to help students orchestrate many skills and strategies as they read connected text, or you can decide to revisit the same text across several days, focusing your instruction on a different skill each day (see Table 7.1 and 7.2).

Table 7.1 Sample Four-Day Shared-Reading Schedule

One option is to read and reread different texts; each lesson with a new text has multiple objectives.

Day 1:	Day 2:	Day 3:	Day 4:
Reread a familiar text (Text A) as a warm-up, focusing on fluency. Read a new text (Text B), focusing on decoding, monitoring comprehension, and fluency.	Reread Text B as a warm-up, focusing on fluency. Read a new text (Text C), focusing on decoding and figuring out vocabulary using context. Reread for fluency.	Reread Text A and Text B as warm-ups. Reread Text C for fluency and pause for quick pair discussions—practicing retelling and basic inference.	Reread Text C as a warm-up. Read a new text (Text D), practicing decoding and fluency. Reread at the end.

Part 2: Lesson Structures

Table 7.2 Sample Four-Day Shared-Reading Schedule

Another option is to revisit the same text(s) across a series of days with a different focus each day.

Day 1:	Day 2:	Day 3:	Day 4:
Reread a familiar text from a prior week as a warm-up. Read a new text (Text A), focusing on accurate word reading—applying decoding strategies and phonics knowledge.	Reread a familiar text from a prior week (different from Day 1) as a warm-up. Revisit Text A, focusing on fluent reading and choral reading with feedback.	Reread a familiar text from a prior week (different from Day 1 and Day 2) as a warm-up. Revisit Text A, focusing on inferring about character feelings and reading with expression (prosody).	—

I have found that the first version—introducing new texts each day—tends to be most engaging for the students I have taught, but you can see what works best for you and your students. Regardless of which schedule you choose, you'll need to select an appropriate text to read with students (or use one your curriculum provides) and then decide which skills the text demands of readers and which strategies you will highlight.

Texts

One of the key considerations in implementing shared-reading lessons is using texts that are well-suited for this instructional approach.

First, go for brevity. Short texts will keep the lesson focused, well-paced, and engaging. Poems, songs, nursery rhymes, and picture books with concise text are great options. Alternatively, you can choose an excerpt from a longer text to maintain students' interest and attention, or plan to read portions of a longer text across several days.

Second, consider complexity. The text should pose a slight challenge to students, encouraging them to stretch their reading abilities; letting them encounter unfamiliar words, concepts, or text structures; or giving them an opportunity to apply newly introduced phonics concepts that they are not yet applying automatically.

Of course, you should consider your instructional objectives. If your goal is to integrate accuracy strategies or apply phonics knowledge, a decodable or multiple criteria text (see page 113) may work best to ensure students have opportunities to practice decoding words with the spelling patterns they are learning. If your goal is to help students develop their phrasing and fluency, rhythmic texts such as poems and songs provide excellent support. To show students how to integrate text features as they explore topics in content area studies, informational texts related to the subject matter may be your best choice.

You might also support reading and writing connections by using texts the class has written together during shared or interactive writing lessons. Students will feel a sense of ownership and familiarity with these texts, enhancing their engagement and comprehension. (For more on shared and interactive writing, see Serravallo, 2021.)

Finally, remember that all students need to be able to see the text, so make sure the print of any text you choose is large and easily visible to all students—even those in the back of the group need to be able to read the text clearly. You might, for example, hand-write poems or songs on chart paper, utilize big books, project texts via a document camera, or use digital texts on a smartboard. The goal is to have all of your students looking at the same physical copy of the text as you direct their attention to it during the lesson.

Skills and Strategies

In Table 7.3, you'll find reading goals that are particularly well-served by this lesson structure and how you might plan to teach them.

Table 7.3 How to Teach Different Reading Goals During Shared-Reading Lessons

Reading Goals	How to Teach Them During Shared-Reading Lessons
Concepts about print	You can discuss where the cover is, model left-to-right directionality, invite students to tell you where to start reading or where to go next, or draw attention to punctuation and other features of the text.
Accurate word reading	You can teach or reteach strategies for decoding unfamiliar words, remind children of what they've learned from phonics lessons (see Chapter 4), and introduce or reinforce high-frequency words. Before the lesson begins, for example, you might introduce irregularly spelled high-frequency words they'll encounter in the text by mapping their sounds and spelling using Elkonin boxes (see Figure 4.7). Using tools such as highlighter tape, Wikki Stix (pipe cleaners coated in sticky wax that can be stuck to paper and removed), or interactive whiteboard features, draw students' attention to specific spellings or patterns in words. For example, you might identify words with a silent e or highlight various spellings of the /ō/ sound after reading.
Fluency (phrasing)	You can read short sections at a time (a sentence or a few lines) and ask students to echo read (repeat after you). You might invite children to read chorally (in one voice), pointing under the words. To help them track the print, you might initially point under each word as they are reading it, and then gradually transition to using a scooping motion under a group of words to encourage phrasing, and eventually point in the margin and direct students to read the whole line in one voice, listening to their peers for feedback. Use a thin, inexpensive wooden dowel or a marker with a colored cap for a pointer (avoid pointers with overly decorative or distracting objects on the ends).
Fluency (prosody)	You can model reading with expression, invite students to reread to reflect character emotions, and/or draw their attention to punctuation and prompt them to read in response to it.
Comprehension	You can pause to ask questions; invite students to briefly turn and talk to a partner to summarize, infer, synthesize information on the page to name a main idea; practice retelling the text; and/or model your own thinking.

If the lesson you are planning is for the whole class, you'll need to keep your grade-level standards in mind and weave in various goals aligned to the range of needs in your class, either within one lesson or across a series of lessons (see sample schedules on pages 186–187). If you form a small group based on common needs, you may plan a more focused lesson aligned to those individuals' goals.

Key Terms for Shared Reading:

Choral reading: The teacher and students read aloud together or all students read in one voice while the teacher listens. Hearing others while reading supports students' accuracy, rate, phrasing, and prosody.

Echo reading: The teacher reads aloud a section of material (a sentence or a couple of lines) and students repeat, echoing the same fluent qualities the teacher demonstrated.

Paired reading: Students read with a partner chorally or by taking turns reading portions of text. As one reads, the other listens to give feedback or prompts to correct misread words or to reread for fluency.

Part 2: Lesson Structures

Structure and Timing: Shared-Reading Lessons

The structure and timing for a shared-reading lesson is basically the same whether you're reading with the whole class or with a small group. However, the Read and Teach portion of the lesson will look a bit different depending on whether you decide to focus on a single strategy or work with students to orchestrate multiple strategies.

Shared-reading lessons go like this:

1. Establish a Focus
(1 minute)

Briefly remind students what they've been working on as readers. If it's a whole-class lesson, you'll likely reference one or more unit objectives. For a small group, you will most likely be working on a goal that's based on your assessment of students' individual needs.

2. Warm-Up
(3 minutes)

To give everyone an experience with strong, fluent reading, quickly reread a familiar text with little or no stopping. This rereading is especially important for students who may have found it challenging to join in the first time you read the text. Familiarity helps build fluency and confidence.

3. Read and Teach
(5–10 minutes)

Offer students a single strategy or remind them of a few strategies you've been practicing that you will focus on as you read. Model expressive reading as you read with students or, if the text is very short, you might read it to them first and then return and have them join you in either echo or choral reading. As you read together, interact with both the text and the students to teach whatever you've planned to teach, pausing to offer coaching tips, suggestions, reminders of strategies, and compliments. Be sure to listen closely and observe students as they read, and be ready to switch gears if you see they need extra support. Keep the pace brisk and your eye on engagement; resist the urge to stop too often, and cut the lesson short if you're losing students' attention.

4. Clarify the Takeaways
(1 minute)

Recap the strategy(ies) you practiced in the lesson, encouraging students to continue practicing them any time they read.

Responsive Teaching: Shared-Reading Lessons

Before a shared-reading lesson, you will plan ahead, marking places to stop and check for understanding, identifying vocabulary you want to highlight, making a note to remind students of a strategy you know they need to practice, and/or planning to introduce a new strategy for students to try. While careful planning is key, your *responsiveness* during the lesson is just as critical. You will need to listen to students as they read, answer your questions, and talk about the text and guide them based on what you observe. (For examples, see Table 7.4.)

Table 7.4   Example Language Frames, Responses, and Prompts to Teach Responsively During Shared-Reading Lessons

If You Hear or Observe . . .	Then You Might Say . . .
Students start to mumble through words rather than reading them accurately with automaticity or working to decode.	▶ OK, let's slow down here. I think we're going too fast. I'm hearing some mumbling through words and that tells me we need to spend some time decoding. Let's remember, [remind students of a phonics lesson or accuracy strategy].
The reading sounds staccato, choppy.	▶ Now that we know the words, let's reread to smooth out our reading. [Remind students of a fluency strategy to support their phrasing.]
The reading sounds monotone.	▶ We read that smoothly, but we want to make sure to read with expression, too. [Remind students of a strategy they know for expression and intonation or teach them one and have them reread.]
Students read without attending to punctuation.	▶ Let's make sure we are reading the words *and* the punctuation. Remember to change your voice. [Review strategy for reading with punctuation.]
Some students have stopped reading.	▶ Readers, let's all read together in one voice. ▶ I'll read a few lines, and then I'm going to ask you to repeat the same lines.

If You Hear or Observe . . .	Then You Might Say . . .
Students seem very wiggly, are looking away from the text, or have stopped participating.	▶ OK, readers, I think that might be enough for today. We'll revisit this text tomorrow, reread what we read today, and then continue on. I'm impressed with how you [name one strength you noticed before they became disengaged].
Students read well in unison, matching the rhythm of the text and reading smoothly.	▶ That reading sounds really smooth. You're paying attention to the punctuation [and/or rhythm, if it's a poem].
Students read with good expression.	▶ I can hear the difference between the narrator and the character dialogue! ▶ You all really sound like the character in this part, and I can tell how she's feeling.
Students react or respond to the text in ways that show their comprehension (i.e., giggling, gasping).	▶ I know! I can't believe he did that either! ▶ That silly spider. I wonder what he'll do next!
As students respond to a turn and talk, you listen in and notice they aren't comprehending.	▶ Remember that reading isn't only about sounding good! We have to be thinking while we read. Let's reread this page and think about the words you're reading as you read them.

Lesson in Action: Small-Group Shared-Reading Lesson, First Grade, English Language Arts

This first-grade class was split down the middle—half were working on segmenting, blending, and reading VC (vowel-consonant) and CVC (consonant-vowel-consonant) words and half were working on fluency, reading closer to an end of first-grade level. In this small group, I worked with almost half of the class who were beginning to decode. I decided to use a decodable text to support their careful attention to words and to help coach them out of using pictures to figure out unfamiliar words. At the start of the lesson, I introduced the two high-frequency words they wouldn't be able to decode with their existing phonics knowledge. I also wanted to make sure that I emphasized the importance of thinking while reading and that reading needs to make sense, so I paused to check for understanding and for them to talk about what was happening in the story. This lesson is a nice example of how to help children apply skills they are learning and to orchestrate multiple strategies while reading one text.

Read the lesson plan online or on the opposite page, watch the video (access it using the QR code), then come back to read the post-lesson reflection comments annotating the lesson plan.

Video 7.1 Small-Group Shared-Reading Lesson, First Grade, English Language Arts

Download the lesson plan or a blank template on the companion website https://companion
.corwin.com/
courses/2024_TRAD

Scan this code or go to https://qrs
.ly/ssfg1ro to watch the video.

Notice how my voice dropped out and I was watching the children closely—I wanted to ensure their eyes were on the words (not on me) and that everyone was participating.

Even though this was a warm-up and the reading should have been pretty automatic, I still needed to prompt them several times.

I skipped this second read and the focus on intonation because there was enough work to do with accuracy for this warm-up.

I chose these two words because their spellings had not yet been introduced in their phonics program.

Shared-Reading Lessons: A Planning Template

Literacy Goals:
- Intonation (ending punctuation), decoding and blending, inferring (feelings, traits) about a character; introduce high-frequency words *my* and *she*

Knowledge/Vocabulary Goals:
- *pack* (from text), *forgive/forgave* (talk about text)

Teacher Materials:
- Warm-up text: *Pam Likes to Nap* by Laura Appleton-Smith (2011)
- New text: *Dot and Dan* by Laura Appleton-Smith (2011)
- Pointer
- Smartboard

Student Materials:
- None

Establish a Focus (1 minute):
- Remind: read left to right and blend the sounds together.
- Remind: read the punctuation, changing our voice to match it.
- Introduce the high-frequency words *my* and *she*.

Warm-Up (3 minutes):

What Will Students Do?	What Will You Say?
Choral read *Pam Likes to Nap* (first read)	"Let's read in one voice. I'll sweep my pointer under the line to keep us together."
Choral read (second read)	"I'm wondering if we can add some emotion to our voices as we read it one more time. Let's pay close attention to the punctuation. Question mark—our voice will go up. Exclamation point—our voice will sound excited. Period—our voice will go down."

Read and Teach (5–10 minutes):

Which Pages or Lines?	What Will Students Do?	What Will You Say?
	Practice letter–sound correspondence to orthographically map the high-frequency words *my* and *she*	"Let's learn two new words that will be challenging to decode: *my* and *she*." (Say each word and how many sounds it has, draw a box to represent each sound, and spell the word into the boxes.)
Whole-book first read	Choral read *Dot* and *Dan*	"Let's read the book together. Read with me as I point under the words. Read in one voice. Remember, when we get to a word we don't know, we will blend through the sounds."
	1	Who's the dog? The man ?
	2	How is Dan feeling here?
	3	Read the exclamation marks.
	4	How should we read this? How's the character feeling?
	5	
	6	
Whole-book, second read	Choral read, more automatic with accuracy and expression	"Let's read it again. This time, we'll pause to think about the characters, Dot and Dan." "How should we read this dialogue? With what kind of voice?"
	Discuss	(Turn and talk) "Why do you think he forgave his dog at the end?" "What words would you use to describe Dot?"

Clarify the Takeaways (1 minute):
Remember to read the words and the punctuation. If it's a period, pause. If it's an exclamation mark, sound excited/happy/surprised. Always think about what's happening when you're reading.

In any lesson, you will have some children who find the text fairly easy to read and others for whom it's more challenging. Some might try to zoom ahead, and others might stop reading or echo what those around them say. Try to keep all readers on the same word at the same time, reading in one voice, and redirect them as I did, as needed.

I didn't plan to talk about punctuation, but from listening to their reading, I could tell it would be helpful and important to point it out, so I did.

The children read *bag* instead of *pack* because they were using the pictures, not the letters—this is very common and very important to correct. Notice that I embedded a definition ("*pack*, like a backpack") to make sure they understood the synonym.

When using simple texts to support foundational skills, you can introduce richer vocabulary when you invite students to talk about the text. Notice I used the word *forgave* and elicited words to talk about character traits.

Based on timing, I skipped a reread of the whole book. This will be a good one to revisit with intonation in mind.

I spent a little time talking to them about what was happening so they could understand how the exclamation mark matched the plot and the character's feeling.

Lesson in Action: Whole-Class Shared-Reading Lesson, Second Grade, Social Studies

This shared-reading lesson supports both concept development and vocabulary aligned to social studies as well as the reading goals of summarizing and reading with intonation. This lesson is a nice example of balancing literacy and content goals as well as supporting students as they orchestrate multiple strategies, thus planning with the range of goals in the classroom in mind.

Read the lesson plan online or on the opposite page, watch the video (access it using the QR code), then come back to read the post-lesson reflection comments annotating the lesson plan.

Video 7.2   Whole-Class Shared-Reading Lesson, Second Grade, Social Studies

Shared-Reading Lessons: A Planning Template

Literacy Goals:
- Pause at commas
- Monitor comprehension
- Stop and summarize
- Notice when the topic changes

Knowledge/ Vocabulary Goals:
- a few key features of each of the community types
- urban, rural

Teacher Materials:
- Warm-up text: (Skip a warm-up text—use the new text to reread to improve fluency)
- New text: *Urban and Rural*
- laptop, smartboard

Student Materials:
- None

Establish a Focus (1 minute):

We are learning about different types of communities and the different places where people live. Today, we'll read a text to learn more about the differences in how people live in these two types of communities.

Warm-Up (3 minutes):

What Will Students Do?	What Will You Say?
	(Skip)

Read and Teach (5–10 minutes):

Which Pages or Lines?	What Will Students Do?	What Will You Say?
1	Read chorally	Think aloud at the end: "Lots of people in a small area means *urban*."
2	Read chorally	Think aloud: "You need a big park like this with so many buildings filled with people." Commas mean to pause
3	Read chorally	Longer words—cover and slide.
4	Read chorally Turn and talk	What are all the things we've learned about the city?
5	Read chorally Listen to think aloud	"Notice the topic has changed? We were learning about . . . but now we're learning about . . ."
6–7	Read chorally	
8	Read chorally Turn and talk	What have we learned about rural areas?
9	Read chorally Discuss	Answer the question: Where would you rather live? Why? Use details from the text.
Whole-book, second read	Choral read, more automatic with accuracy and expression	"This time, let's read nice and smooth. Make sure you're paying attention to the punctuation."

Clarify the Takeaways (1 minute):

Make sure we're paying attention to commas to read smoothly. Also, pay attention to what you're reading as you're reading it so you are able to summarize or answer questions about it to show what you've learned.

Callout annotations:

Since their reading was very word-by-word, I decided to model what fluent reading sounds like.

No trouble with the longer words! I ended up not needing to prompt them to do this.

As they talked, I listened in, assessed, and coached. Notice that one student discussed some background knowledge and I redirected him to talk about details from the text.

After a moment of wait time, I noticed very few students had a hand raised, ready to talk. I decided to let them reread to get ready to share. Because *all* children need to participate during turn-and-talk, looking for signs they are ready sets them up to be productive.

I'm always watching the children and noticing if anyone is looking away or if they have stopped reading along. Here, I redirected with "Keep your eyes on the words" to pull a few students' attention back.

I kept my prompting lean ("Can you add on?") to encourage their independence.

On this second read, they read smoothly and accurately and didn't need prompting or redirection.

Notice that I blended positive feedback ("You used details directly from the text") with corrective feedback.

Spin It: Fluency-Oriented Reading Instruction (FORI) Lessons

Fluency-Oriented Reading Instruction (FORI) is a scientifically validated approach to improve students' accuracy, fluency, and comprehension (Kuhn, 2020; Stahl & Huebach, 2005). FORI lessons were developed to support students with reading grade-level complex texts, and this lesson type has been shown to help students gain 1.7+ years of growth in one year of school. The approach is similar to the shared-reading lessons with short texts described in this chapter, but the amount of text and the lesson length are both longer. Each lesson follows a unique but predictable schedule, repeatedly reading the same longer text across a five-day cycle with different focuses and a diminished level of support.

In the classic FORI lesson structure, each lesson is approximately 30–40 minutes in length. On the first day, the focus is on comprehension: The teacher introduces the selection, reads it aloud, and then discusses it with the class. On the second day, the teacher reads shorter portions of the text and, as students echo, introduces comprehension and vocabulary strategies as needed. The third day is for choral reading, and the fourth day is for partner reading where students take turns reading pages or paragraphs, giving each other feedback as the teacher moves around and offers support. On the fifth day, students complete extension activities such as extended discussions or written responses.

Researchers have also validated three variations of the original FORI lessons—Wide Fluency-Oriented Reading Instruction, Fluency-Oriented Oral Reading (FOOR), and Wide Fluency-Oriented Oral Reading (Kuhn, 2020). These lesson structures vary in terms of both the length of lesson (FOOR, for example, is about 15 minutes in length, similar to what you read about in this chapter) and in the number of days students spend with the same text (with FOOR, the same text is used for three days—an introduction day, a choral reading day, and a partner reading day).

You may choose to play with the flow, routines, and length of your shared-reading lessons—revisiting texts or not, varying the length of lessons, layering in new teaching or focuses each time you revisit a text, and more. During lessons, keep an eye on student engagement to find the best rhythm for your students.

Take It to Your Classroom

✓ Consider your text selection. Will you use a story, poem, or informational text from your core program or search for a different supplemental text? Use the advice on page 188 to make sure you're choosing a text with the right supports and challenges, keeping readers' goals and grade-level objectives in mind.

✓ As you teach, watch and listen. Keep an eye on students' levels of engagement, and listen carefully to their ability to read accurately and with appropriate phrasing and expression. Pause the lesson and respond with feedback, a redirection, or a strategy as needed.

✓ Reflect on your text selection. Did the text provide enough challenges for students to stretch themselves with your support?

✓ Reflect about your decision to teach one strategy in the lesson (focus) or several strategies (orchestration). Was your decision right for your students?

✓ Consider how you'll prompt students to transfer what they learned during the shared-reading lesson to their independent reading.

8

Picture It: Seventh Graders Study a Multimodal History Text

"We've been studying the Great Migration and so far, we've only been reading about it from our social studies textbook. Today, I'm going to introduce you to a piece from The History Channel's website that combines text and video to explore the topic with a bit more detail and nuance. We're going to read it together because it's a complex text—but I know you have the skills and knowledge to read and understand it, as long as we take it slow and read with care."

> In addition to literary analysis in reading, you can also utilize close reading to help students make sense of challenging, content-area texts.

Ms. Tan starts the close-reading lesson with her seventh-grade students gathered in the meeting area, near enough that they can all easily see the digital text projected on the smartboard. "What makes this text a bit more challenging is that it doesn't offer a simple chronology. It presents multiple causes (*why*) and effects (*what happens*) and phases of the Great Migration to consider, and our job is to try to understand how the information fits together. Let's start with the short video embedded in the article, which gives a nice foundation for what we'll be reading about in the rest of the text."

> The slow and careful pace of close reading sets it apart from different kinds of reading in the other lesson structures.

> Setting a clear purpose for reading slowly and carefully is key.

After playing the video, Ms. Tan invites the students to turn and explain what they heard, thinking about causes and effects and waves of the Migration. As they talk, she listens in for confusions and understandings, misconceptions, and questions. "OK, it sounds like we have a sense of some of the causes that Professor Williams talks about in the video—that there were unfair labor practices in

> You will remind students of their purpose for reading often in the lesson.

the South at that time. Some of you mentioned an effect—there was a 'flowering' of intellectual and artistic expression known as the Harlem Renaissance. I also heard someone talk about factories, but they weren't sure what they had to do with causes or effects. I'm going to play the video once more; see if there are some additional details you can pick up on about causes, effects, or waves." After the second listen, the students are able to talk about causes and effects with more detail, and Ms. Tan captures some of their thinking in notes on the board.

"Now let's look at the article. In a multimodal text, each portion usually contributes different, complimentary information to make up a whole. As we read, we're going to pause and think, 'How does this add to our understanding of the causes and/or effects and the different waves of the Great Migration?'"

Ms. Tan reads aloud and students join her, reading chorally. She begins with the section titled "What Caused the Great Migration" and thinks aloud, "I think we'll be able to add to some of the causes here, right?" After the first two paragraphs, they add *segregation*, *racial inequality in the Jim Crow South*, and *boll weevil infestation* to their notes about the sharecropping cause they learned from the video. After the third paragraph, Ms. Tan invites students to turn and talk and they add other causes to their notes—violence and lynching. Next, they encounter a callout titled "Did You Know?" with a fact about northern factory wages being three times the typical earnings a Black person could make working the land in the South. Ms. Tan asks, "Is this a cause? An effect? Where should we add this information to our notes?"

They continue on through the text at this slow and careful pace—pausing often to think "What have we learned in this part? How does it fit with the causes and effects we are reading for?" In the next section, Ms. Tan invites the students to read silently, then turn and discuss, reread the section chorally, and finally suggest what to add to their notes (see Figure 8.1).

Figure 8.1   Shared Notes Based on the Multimodal Text

The students contributed to organized notes scribed by Ms. Tan during their close-reading lesson.

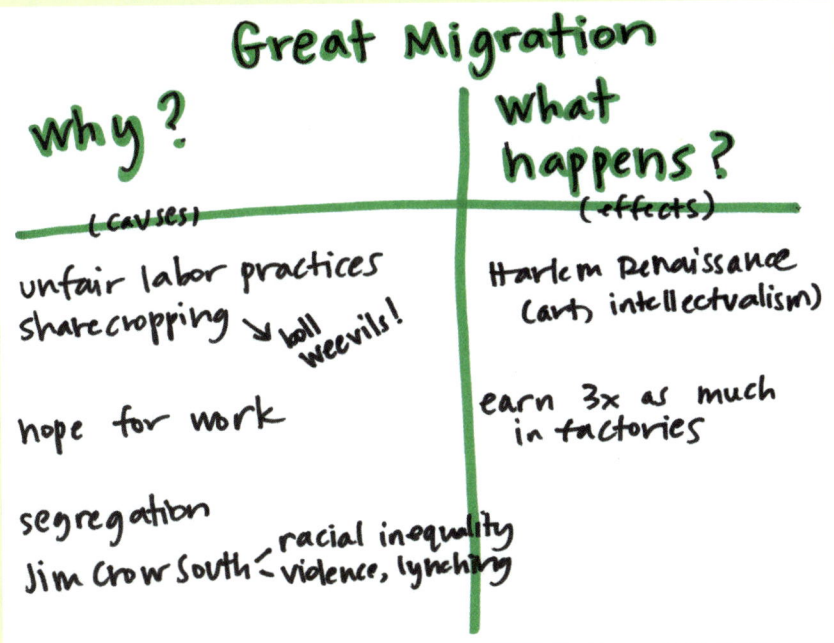

Because you will consider so many details in a close-reading lesson (analysis), it makes sense to synthesize those details into some meaningful take-aways at the end of the lesson.

"Readers, now that we've read the entire text, I'm going to invite you to synthesize—put together—the information in a way that makes the most sense to you. Using our notes to help, can you please turn to your partner and summarize the article and video?"

Embed academic vocabulary in your prompts. Instead of *turn and talk*, you can direct students to *turn and summarize* or *turn and explain*, for example.

Ms. Tan circulates as students talk, coaching them to look back at the notes, reminding them of a detail they left out, praising them for putting relevant information together, asking questions, and inviting them to share what they are still curious about. "Readers, any time you approach a challenging text, if you start with a purpose, take it slow and steady, and check in with that purpose along the way—maybe even talk to a friend—you'll be on your way to understanding it just as you did here today."

Close-Reading Lesson: A Planning Template

Literacy Goals:

- Reading a complex text connected to social studies textbook
- Engaging with a multimodal (video + article) text
- Synthesizing multiple causes and effects, summarizing
- Note-taking

Knowledge/Vocabulary Goals:

- Causes and effects of the Great Migration

Teacher Materials:

- History channel video and article (History.com Editors, 2010)
- Laptop, smartboard
- Note-taking forms

Student Materials:

- None

Establish a Focus (1 minute):

- Connect content to social studies text
- Introduce multimodal text type: video + written article
- Frontload structure—not narrative, multiple causes and effects

Read and Teach (8–13 minutes):

Which Pages or Lines?	What Will Students Do?	What Will You Say?
After playing the video	Turn and talk	Explain what you heard, thinking about causes and effects and waves of the Migration.
After replaying the video the second time	Turn and talk	What additional details did you pick up on during the second watch?
	Observe	[model note-taking on board]
Before reading text	Listen to think aloud	How does the article add to our understanding of causes and effects?
First two paragraphs	Choral reading Think aloud	Let's add to our notes based on what we read.
After third paragraph	Turn and talk	How can we add more to our notes from this paragraph?
After "Did You Know?" box	Turn and talk	Is this a cause or effect? Where will we add this to our notes?
Remainder of the article	Read silently	Read this next part to yourself.
Last portion of text	Read chorally	Now let's reread that same section out loud.
Whole text	Turn and talk	Summarize what we read using notes.

Clarify the Takeaways (1 minute):

Remind students to approach challenging texts with a purpose, to read slowly and deliberately, and to check understanding along the way.

An Overview: Close-Reading Lessons

Close-reading lessons can empower more experienced readers to delve deeper into complex texts, uncovering layers of meaning through careful exploration, examination, textual analysis, and study. Within each lesson, students will have opportunities to process information; learn new vocabulary; ask and answer text-dependent questions; make connections, inferences, and interpretations; learn how to annotate effectively; and/or engage in meaningful discussions with both their peers and you (Mariage et al., 2020; Paddle & Woollett, 2020; Reed et al., 2007). Close reading is not a lesson structure that makes sense for everything you and your students will read together. Instead, it's a structure you'll choose to use with demanding texts while also considering your students' strengths and needs. A close-reading lesson is a great choice, for example, when there is a text you want your students to read but you know they won't be able to read it without a lot of support.

While some argue that close reading should detach the text from its historical context, authorship, and the reader's background knowledge or perspectives and focus only on what's in the text itself (Ransom, 1941; Wimsatt & Beardsley, 1946), others emphasize the importance of the interaction between the text and the reader and purport that meaning is shaped through this transaction (Fish, 1970; Kintsch, 1988; Rosenblatt 1938, 1978). I believe close-reading lessons should encourage students to both draw text-dependent conclusions and teach them how to draw on relevant prior knowledge before, during, and after reading.

In some ways, close-reading lessons can resemble read-aloud lessons (see Chapter 3) as you will pause to think aloud and prompt students to discuss, take notes, and process the text. You can also read aloud portions of a text to students during a close-reading lesson. However, in close-reading lessons, you may find the pace is slower, as you'll pause often to engage in deep analysis. Close-reading lessons can also resemble shared-reading lessons at times (Chapter 7) if you have students read chorally. However, with shared reading, students will spend much more time practicing fluency, accuracy, and exploring print concepts whereas in close reading, the focus is on deeper comprehension and annotation. Close-reading lessons can also look very different from shared-reading lessons—in close-reading lessons, you might decide to give each reader their own copy of the text if you want them to annotate (remember that in shared reading, all eyes must be on the same physical copy). Sometimes, you might ask students to read a portion of the text to themselves during the close-reading lesson—something you wouldn't do in either read-aloud or shared-reading lessons.

You can do close-reading lessons with the whole class or a small group of students, but in either case, the goal is to help readers deeply comprehend the text you're studying as well as to empower them to apply the strategies and skills they learn from the close examination of a specific text to other texts they will read. For example, in the Picture It vignette that opened the chapter, Ms. Tan asked students to track causes and effects as they studied the multimodal text about the Great Migration. But tracking cause and effect is not specific to the study of the Great Migration— it's something students will need to do in a text about any event or period in history. She also taught her students to approach a challenging text with a purpose and to read it deliberately, checking in with that purpose along the way—a great reading habit they can use with any text.

Knowledge and Vocabulary Building
Within Close-Reading Lessons

○ You might choose a short text (or excerpt of a longer text) aligned to topics and concepts you're studying in content areas. With the background knowledge of the topic to support them, students could closely read a text with a more complex structure, more sophisticated vocabulary, and/or one that offers an opportunity for deeper analysis.

○ Look for figurative language in the text you're reading closely and discuss the meaning of each phrase. Teach students strategies to understand figurative language more generally, such as visualizing the two things the author is comparing, noting similarities, and thinking about how the comparison helps you better understand the topic. Challenge them to consider why the author would have chosen to use the figurative language they did in the context of the text's deeper meanings.

○ As with other lesson structures (such as read-aloud lessons and shared-reading lessons), reading texts together allows you to discuss words in context. Remind students of strategies for figuring out vocabulary from information on the page (i.e., definitions embedded within a sentence; words whose meanings are supported by text features, such as illustrations; rereading sentences with words that are repeated to develop a cumulative understanding of the word). Tuck in definitions, think aloud about how you figure out the word using context, and/or guide students to use a strategy to figure out a word and jot its definition or share the definition with a partner.

○ As they engage in close reading, ask students to underline key vocabulary they encounter that is new to them and use strategies they know to figure out the meanings from context. Then, challenge them to use those new words as they discuss the text.

What Research Says
About Close Reading

Interestingly, there is limited empirical research of close reading as a lesson structure, although the practice was a major recommendation in the Common Core State Standards (Hinchman & Moore, 2013). There is, however, a plethora of literature available on closely related topics or key practices often incorporated into close-reading lessons:

➜ Lovett et al. (1996) implemented a reading instruction strategy with students with learning disabilities and found that direct instruction on analyzing a text's main and subordinate ideas allowed students to transfer and successfully apply these skills to unfamiliar texts.

➜ Prompting students to use close-reading strategies such as annotation, referring to the text, generating questions, and building off others' ideas helps to lay a foundation for meaningful Socratic circle discussions (Copeland, 2005). In effective Socratic circle discussions, students— beginning in first grade—can practice critical-thinking skills across a wide range of grade levels (Wolf et al., 2009).

➜ Strategies to slow a reader down, such as annotating or taking notes on a text, are found to increase memory and overall learning (Anderson & Armbruster, 1980).

➜ Boyles and Scherer (2012) found that close reading gives students the opportunity to think critically and analyze more complex texts.

➜ Dedicating time to analyzing the language and message in stories that are centered around humanity prompts students to make connections between literature and their own lives and learn valuable lessons about morality, a process Dr. Maryann Wolf coined "deep reading" (Wolf, 2018).

➜ A survey conducted by Ivey and Broaddus (2001) revealed that middle school students prefer for the teacher to read a complex text aloud first before they reread and analyze it independently.

- Reynolds and Goodwin (2016) found that a reading intervention based in interactional, motivational scaffolding (text discussion, questioning, collaboration with peers) improved students' reading comprehension.

- Yuill and Oakhill (1988) found that for less-skilled seven- and eight-year-old readers, an intervention that focused on inference strategies, such as generating questions and making predictions, helped improve comprehension significantly in comparison to an intervention that focused on decoding strategies.

- Kintsch (1988) explains that comprehension is not automatic for student readers; to build comprehension skills, they must engage in activities that are in line with close-reading strategies—active problem solving, knowledge construction and exploration, and feedback.

- In one study, students who participated in a combined close-reading and strategy instruction intervention improved scores on multiple-choice comprehension quizzes and significantly improved their annotation skills: They asked six times more questions, wrote double the amount of clarification statements, and started commenting on information in the text (Mariage et al., 2020).

- Studies have shown that repeated reading improves the comprehension and reading fluency of students with and without learning disabilities (Therrien, 2004).

- One study that examined close-reading practices found that with groups of both first- and seventh-grade students, reading the text together aided in students' ability to answer text-dependent questions with textual support (Paddle & Woollett, 2020).

- Chen and Chen (2014) found that a digital collaborative annotation tool—one you may use in a close-reading lesson—significantly improved direct and inferential comprehension and increased on-task, higher-level discussion.

Planning: Close-Reading Lessons

Close-reading lessons involve careful guided examination of a text—at times, at the sentence or word level—as well as frequent rereading. You'll want to make sure the text you use is rich enough to lend itself to this lesson type, and you'll want to plan carefully for how you'll support readers' knowledge building and strategy use.

Texts

When you're planning a close-reading lesson, which comes first—the text or the lesson focus? The answer is, it depends. For example, let's say there is a required text that's part of your curriculum, but you know the text is too challenging for most of your students to read independently or that there is so much depth that it warrants a close study. In these cases, you might choose a close-reading lesson structure because it lends itself well to goals such as making sense of complex language or navigating an unfamiliar text structure. Other times, you'll have a skill in mind, such as text analysis and interpretation, that you know your class or a group of students needs and you'll search for a text that will set students up to practice what you want to teach. Here are some other text considerations to have in mind; many of the text considerations you read about in the read-aloud lessons chapter (Chapter 3) apply here as well:

* Texts for close reading need to be **aligned** to what you're teaching; inclusive, relevant, identity-affirming, and culturally responsive and sustaining; engaging; and varied.

* Texts for close reading can be **any genre or text type**—poems, articles, short stories, and so on. Since students will be looking at the text during some or all of the lesson, you can also consider multimodal texts and/or texts with many graphic features that require close examination.

* To keep lessons well-paced and engaging, select **brief texts or short excerpts of longer texts**. For example, you might plan a close-reading lesson around a single page from a book you're reading aloud to students that has some interesting description worth studying. Or, if there is a longer text you want to read closely with your students, plan to read it in small sections across a few days' lessons.

* Texts for close reading should be **complex**—either at or slightly above grade level—and offer students some productive challenge they can meet

with your guidance and support. Texts with some nuance and depth are most likely to lead students to the deeper meaning that should come from a close analysis of a text.

✱ Consider **numbering the lines** of the text you read together to help students refer easily to specific parts in conversation.

Deciding What to Teach: Content

As with most lessons, once you've identified the text, the next planning step is to read it and think about the challenges it will present for your students and the opportunities for teaching. In close-reading lessons, you'll most often be considering the sorts of supports they will need to be able to comprehend and analyze what they read. This is especially important with close-reading lessons because the texts are among the most complex you'll be using, and you'll be prompting and guiding students to grapple with this complexity. You might consider, for example, the demands of vocabulary, sentence structure, key concepts, and background knowledge. Also, think about which parts of the text might lead to interesting, deeper analysis.

Imagine you're a seventh-grade teacher and Langston Hughes's poem "The Negro Speaks of Rivers" is part of your seventh-grade core curriculum. Read it thinking about how you'll guide students' text analysis.

The Negro Speaks of Rivers
by Langston Hughes

I've known rivers:

I've known rivers ancient as the world and older than the flow of human blood in human veins.

My soul has grown deep like the rivers.

I bathed in the Euphrates when dawns were young.

I built my hut near the Congo and it lulled me to sleep.

I looked upon the Nile and raised the pyramids above it.

I heard the singing of the Mississippi when Abe Lincoln went down to New Orleans, and I've seen its muddy bosom turn all golden in the sunset.

I've known rivers:

Ancient, dusky rivers.

My soul has grown deep like the rivers.

While most of the words in the poem are not challenging to read, the short text requires a good bit of background knowledge to make sense of its meaning and—hence—there are lots of opportunities for instruction:

* If they don't have it already, students will need geographical knowledge to make sense of the references to specific rivers (the Congo, Nile, Euphrates, Mississippi) and historical knowledge to consider the connections between them and what some deeper meaning in the poem might be.

* Students might not know much about pyramids and how they were constructed or about Abe Lincoln and why he would have traveled to New Orleans.

* Some of the figurative language (such as "I raised the pyramids") or word choices (such as "The Negro Speaks of Rivers") might pose a challenge.

* Hughes uses simile ("ancient as the world") and parallel construction ("I've known rivers") but doesn't rhyme or a use a specific meter. You'll need to consider what students know about these different poetic devices and what you'll need to share with them.

* If students haven't studied the Harlem Renaissance, they won't be able to use this historical context as perspective in their interpretation.

You can't teach everything, of course, so from your list, you'll need to decide what's most important to focus on for this particular lesson and then consider how you will offer students what they need. Will you introduce some background knowledge? Think aloud for them? Guide their thinking with questions and prompts?

Deciding What to Teach: Strategies

Once you've thought through the challenges of, and opportunities within, this particular text, then you'll think about which strategies you can introduce (or revisit) to help students make sense of both this text and future texts. Remember, strategies offer students a generalizable process that acts as a scaffold they can use with any text that presents similar challenges. For example, with the Hughes poem, you might consider the strategies and specific lines and phrases in Table 8.1.

Table 8.1

Strategy Example	Try It
Think about what the author is describing and the mood or feeling in each part of the text to help you understand individual words and phrases as well as ideas in the text.	Try it in this poem with "I've seen its muddy bosom turn all golden in the sunset."
When the author uses a simile or metaphor, pause and visualize, thinking about the two things that are compared. Picture what the comparison means literally, and then think, "What can I infer it means figuratively, in the context of this text?"	Try it in this poem with "My soul has grown deep like the rivers."
Consider the author's word choices. Think about other words they might have used instead. Then ask, "Why this word and not that one? Or that one?"	Try it in this poem with *dusky* or *ancient* or the phrase *blood in human veins.*

As you read in Chapter 3, when you think aloud in a lesson, you can model strategic thinking and the processes you use to make meaning and recruit students to think along with you. I invite you to revisit the examples of this powerful method (pages 70–72). Similarly, many of the same student engagement techniques you read about in Chapter 3—turn and talk, stop and jot, stop and sketch, acting out—also work well in close-reading lessons. You can reread that section on pages 72–73 for more detail and examples.

As you plan what you will teach in a close-reading lesson and how you will teach it, know that you'll likely need to pause and reread more often and provide more support since the text is so complex and you're asking students for deeper analysis. Because close reading is almost always *slow* reading, it's important to think about your pacing and students' engagement. Consider Billy Collins's cautionary words in "Introduction to Poetry" (2006), where he warns against overburdening a poem with excessive analysis, resembling the act of "tortur[ing] a confession out of it" (p. 58). Close reading should enhance the reading experience, not detract from it, so be careful not to choose a text that's too long or plan to focus on too many objectives; aim for a cadence that keeps you moving through the text and discussing it in a way that feels interesting, not tiring.

Deciding How You Will Read

Once you've planned what you will teach in a close-reading lesson, you'll need to decide how students will read the text. Will they read part or all of it silently to themselves, listen and follow along as you read it aloud, or read it together chorally—or a combination of all three? Also, consider your reading materials. Will each student need their own copy of the text, or can you use a shared (projected) text for the lesson?

Here are some things to keep in mind as you plan how students will read:

✳ Are there opportunities in the text to work on decoding or fluency? If so, you might choose **choral reading**. For example, in Hughes's poem, there is beautiful assonance and consonance and an almost musical rhythm that students might hear better if they read it aloud with the teacher.

* Is the text so complex at the word or sentence level that reading it chorally or asking students to read it silently to themselves might impede their ability to comprehend it? It can be taxing to struggle through many words within the same sentence or to read a long, complex sentence when you aren't sure how to phrase it. In these cases, it probably makes sense to first **read that portion aloud** to students, then reread it together.

* Are you going to ask students to closely examine something visual in the text? In this case, you may choose to have them **read it silently**, probably from their own copy. For example, in one of the video lessons you'll view (see Video 8.2), you'll notice that the students and I spend a lot of time looking at text features in an expository text and then putting the information we find in them together with text to make meaning. In this lesson, I wanted students to have their own copy so they could look at it closely and flip back and forth between pages at their own pace.

* Reflect on past experience: Which way of reading keeps most of your students engaged and focused on the same portion of text at the same time? Whatever it is, utilize that way of reading whenever it makes sense for what you are teaching.

In your lesson plan, along with your think alouds and prompts, be sure to note how students will be reading (or listening) to each section of the text.

Structure and Timing: Close-Reading Lessons

Given the amount of reading and rereading you'll do with students in a close-reading lesson, it's important to keep the lesson brief (10–15 minutes total) and the pacing swift. As with all lessons, you'll begin by establishing a focus and end with clarifying the takeaways. In the Read and Teach section, you'll alternate between modeling ("I do"), guiding practice through prompts and feedback ("we do") and asking students to try reading, thinking about, and/or annotating portions on their own ("you do").

Close-reading lessons go like this:

1. Establish a Focus
(1 minute)

Clearly state the purpose(s) of the close reading you're about to do, explain how the text you've chosen connects to what students are learning about, offer any relevant background information they may need to engage with the text, and/or name any strategy(ies) you'll use as you read.

2. Read and Teach
(8–13 minutes)

Read and reread the text with your students and remind them of the purpose(s) often so the reading and analysis you're doing is focused. As you read, you'll pause often to think aloud, modeling your use of strategies, and/or to prompt students to discuss as a class or in pairs. You can also encourage students to ask questions when something is confusing. You might model taking notes or making annotations to highlight details in the text that match your purpose for close reading, or you can invite students to annotate or take notes on their own copies. Be sure to watch for engagement (or fatigue) and pause the lesson to finish another day if you see students' energy begin to wane.

3. Clarify the Takeaways
(1 minute)

Look back across any notes, annotations, or details that you highlighted, then work together as a class (or have students work in pairs) to synthesize, draw conclusions, and name your takeaways. Repeat the strategy(ies) you practiced during the lesson and encourage students to use them in their independent reading.

Responsive Teaching: Close-Reading Lessons

While you'll plan ahead for much of a close-reading lesson, be sure to be open and ready to respond to things you didn't plan for. For instance, you may notice students having a hard time reading the text fluently, expressing confusion with a key term you thought they would know, or not responding to your questions in ways you'd anticipated. Whatever you see and hear, respond with the support that you see students need, keeping your lesson objective in mind. (See Table 8.2.)

Table 8.2   Example Language Frames, Responses, and Prompts to Teach Responsively During Close-Reading Lessons

If You Hear or Observe . . .	Then You Might Say . . .
Students mumble through a word or part of a text.	▶ OK, let's slow down here. Let's take some time to decode this word. We need to make sure we're reading accurately. ▶ Remember, for long words, take it slow: Break up the word part by part.
Students look confused.	▶ Let's use context to try to understand what this word means in this text. ▶ I can see you're monitoring your comprehension and are realizing it's not making sense. Let's make sure to reread. ▶ Let's take this part slow, pausing after each sentence to make sure we're understanding before moving forward.
Students struggle to answer a question about the text or as students turn and talk, they seem to have misunderstandings about the text.	▶ Let's back up and reread with that question in mind. ▶ I'm going to model using a strategy to help answer that question in this part, and then I'm going to have you try it on the next part.
Students respond to a prompt or question with insight and understanding.	▶ You really thought carefully about what the text says. ▶ Yes! That response makes sense with the details of the text. ▶ I can tell you read and reread with focus and purpose to arrive at that understanding.

Lesson in Action: Small-Group Close-Reading Lesson, Sixth Grade, English Language Arts

This sixth-grade class was beginning a unit focused on reading poetry. They had explored some terms for figurative language (*metaphor*, *simile*, etc.) and examples, but they had not yet read any poetry. I decided to begin with a familiar song to support engagement and to show them that close reading and thinking about song lyrics is something they can do to arrive at deeper meaning—and not only in school!

Read the lesson plan on the opposite page or online, watch the video (access it using the QR code), then come back to read the post-lesson reflection comments annotating the lesson plan.

Video 8.1   Small-Group Close-Reading Lesson, Sixth Grade, English Language Arts

Download the lesson plan or a blank template on the companion website https://companion .corwin.com/ courses/2024_TRAD

Scan the code or go to https://qrs .ly/sgfg1rs to watch the video.

Close-Reading Lesson: A Planning Template

Literacy Goals:
- Understand mood, literal and inferential layers of meaning, and the importance of repetition and character motivation in considering theme

Knowledge/ Vocabulary Goal(s):
- *Ideal*
- Review figurative language terms (simile, metaphor, etc.)

Teacher Materials:
- "What Was I Made For?" song lyrics (Eilish, 2023)

Student Materials:
- Individual copies of the text

Establish a Focus (1 minute):
- You can think of lyrics literally or figuratively.
- Rereading with a new lens helps us to discover new things.

Read and Teach (8–13 minutes):

Which Pages or Lines?	What Will Students Do?	What Will You Say?
First verse	Read independently. Reread after discussing unfamiliar words.	• Are there any words we don't understand? Discuss *ideal*. Reread. • Think about the literal meaning of the first line: "I used to float, now I just fall down." What might those phrases mean figuratively? • What might it mean to realize you're not "an ideal?"
Chorus	Read silently with a focus.	• In a song, the chorus repeats and often holds important main ideas or themes. Read the chorus and think about what the song might be mostly about. • How does "feeling" relate to being "real" in this song?
Second verse	Read silently. Discuss.	• One clue to deeper meaning is to think about what a character really wants and what's standing in their way. What does this character seem to really want?
Third verse	Read silently. Discuss.	• Let's talk about the mood. How is the singer feeling? What feeling do you get from the music? • How does the mood match that feeling?

Clarify the Takeaways (1 minute):
Remind students to approach poems and songs with an expectation that there is a literal and inferential layer, to read (or listen!) slowly and deliberately, and to check their understanding along the way.

Annotation callouts:

I wish I had established this point about literal versus inferential thinking early on; I did come back to it later in the lesson, but it would have been nice to have given students a heads up about it from the beginning.

Half the group had seen *Barbie* (Gerwig, 2023) and could speak to the literal interpretation of the song. In some ways, though, the students who hadn't seen it seemed to access the interpretation more easily and were able to think more globally.

I loved the students' responses! I challenged them to clarify what their interpretation was and I was explicit about moving from literal to more figurative thinking: "That's the literal way of looking at it … but what does it say about *us* as people?"

I had them discuss this next question in pairs because I felt like some students were a bit quieter and I wanted to make sure everyone had a chance to share their thinking. I loved how the students referenced the text as they discussed it.

We didn't get to this part because I didn't want the lesson to run too long. Even though we didn't finish reading through the entire text, I felt like the students understood the concept of reading on literal and inferential levels.

Lesson in Action: Whole-Class Close-Reading Lesson, Fifth Grade, Science

These fifth graders had taken a pretest on concepts and vocabulary related to an upcoming unit on mixtures and solutions and had engaged in one hands-on exploration, but they had not yet done any reading about the topic. The text I chose is complex, so I offered guidance with navigating and synthesizing information in text features, summarizing key information, defining unfamiliar words, and more.

Read the lesson plan on the opposite page or online, watch the video (access it using the QR code), then come back to read the post-lesson reflection comments annotating the lesson plan.

Download the lesson plan or a blank template on the companion website https://companion .corwin.com/ courses/2024_TRAD

Video 8.2   Whole-Class Close-Reading Lesson, Fifth Grade, Science

Scan the code or go to https://qrs .ly/pofg1rt to watch the video.

I looked for opportunities to include Tier 2 and Tier 3 words and their meanings. For example, when one student said "beginning, middle, and end," I said, "Ah, a *sequence*." When another used the word *dissolve*, I checked to make sure they knew what that word meant before proceeding.

Instead of turn and talk, I called on individuals because I wanted them to hear what their peers said and to listen as I coached them through close observation and naming details.

I was going slowly, part-by-part, to help them connect the features and be intentional about how to synthesize them.

I listened in and coached one small group during the turn and talk. When I pulled the students back together, I gave a compliment about using specific information from the text to back up their responses so other students could try this on the next opportunity.

The pair I chose to coach didn't need much redirection or support, so it was a quick talk, and then I resumed the lesson.

Close-Reading Lesson: A Planning Template

Literacy Goal(s):
- Connecting text features to main text
- Using headings to direct reading

Knowledge/Vocabulary Goals:
- Understanding types of mixtures (heterogeneous, homogeneous, colloid, suspension) and the qualities of each
- *Mixtures and solutions*
- *colloid, suspension*

Teacher Materials:
- "What Is a Mixture in Science?" text (Helmenstine, 2019), projected

Student Materials:
- Individual copies of "What Is a Mixture in Science?"

Establish a Focus (1 minute):

In dense texts with features, we need to be sure to read both the features and text and put information from the two together.

Read and Teach (8–13 minutes):

Which Pages or Lines?	What Will Students Do?	What Will You Say?
Photograph and caption	Synthesize photo and caption Discuss	• Images can give us a lot of information. Slow our reading to study them. Three photos showing a sequence: look carefully, read the caption, look back at the images to visualize what's happening.
First heading Intro section	Read the heading. Read the section.	• Heading phrased as a question. Read to be able to answer it. Read, turn to your partner to answer it.
Second heading	Read the heading. Read the section. Listen to the think aloud.	• What is the main information we should plan to learn from this section based on the heading? • This section taught us about two types of mixtures—*heterogeneous* and *homogeneous*. Everyone, say those two words. . . .
Types of mixtures diagram	Study the diagram, part by part. Turn and talk.	• Study the diagram. • Think about the chalk example. Put the photograph with the diagram. Where would it go? • Compare and contrast *heterogeneous* and *homogeneous*, based on what you learned in the section and the diagram.
Caption	Read aloud, then discuss and define *molecule*.	• Listen to me read the caption aloud.
Solution	Read one part at a time, then (with prompting) check for understanding.	• Turn and talk, putting together the diagram with the three definitions.

Clarify the Takeaways (1 minute):

We practiced taking our time with text features such as photos and diagrams and used headings to get ready to read a section and check for understanding.

Prompting them to read and check their understanding on their own released a bit of the support I'd been offering throughout the lesson. When I asked them earlier to synthesize the diagram with the new information, I reminded them of the importance of accumulating new information as they go.

Spin It: Expand the Definition of Text

Consider recasting close-reading lessons as close-listening or close-viewing lessons and invite students to engage in this same way with nonprint texts, such as viewing short video clips or listening to podcasts or songs. For a multilayered analysis, you might also combine two or even three close-reading processes with a single text. For example, first watch a video clip with no sound, then watch and listen to it, then read its transcript, uncovering layers of meaning each time you revisit it.

Take It to Your Classroom

√ Explore the texts included in your curriculum materials to consider which may be more complex than students can handle independently and/or which would offer students opportunities for deeper textual analysis with close-reading lessons.

√ Try planning a close-reading lesson. Consider what, specifically, students will likely find challenging about the text, then plan to offer strategies or prompts to guide them.

√ Reflect after delivering a close-reading lesson. When did students seem most engaged? How was the pacing and length of the lesson? Was the text you selected too complex, too easy, or manageable with your support?

√ Consider the decisions you made. Did you have students read chorally or silently? Did they read from a shared copy or have their own? How did these decisions impact students' engagement with the lesson and overall comprehension? What might you try next time?

Guided Inquiry Lessons

9

Picture It: Fifth Graders Reflect and Set Goals

"Fifth graders, during our next unit, you'll be learning from a variety of sources—print and video—to explore the pros and cons of the important environmental issues you've each chosen to study. After reading broadly, you'll need to take a stand and craft a research-based argument essay. We're going to set goals now for the reading and research part of that work," Ms. Jackson begins.

> Goal-setting is just one type of guided inquiry lesson.

"You have in front of you some of your notebook writing from our focus on informational reading in history two months ago. Remember, you learned to find key details, determine main ideas, learn new vocabulary, and study text features for information about explorers and colonization. As you think back and look at the writing you did then, think about what your strengths were during that study and what you might want to work on now as we engage in similar reading work on a new topic this coming month."

> In guided inquiry, students are always looking at something with a question(s) in mind.

> The purpose behind the inquiry should be very clear—that's what makes it guided.

Ms. Jackson shares a list of some possible goals with kid-friendly definitions (Figure 9.1). "From this list, consider what you feel like you are doing well and with independence and where you might need more support as a reader."

> Sometimes it will make sense to narrow the scope of the inquiry with some options; at other times, you will leave it more open-ended.

Figure 9.1   Student-Facing Chart to Support Goal-Setting

Reading Goal	Short, Student-Friendly Definition or Explanation
Engagement and motivation	Finding books related to the topic that interest you, having a purpose for reading, and feeling "lost in the book" as you read.
Main topics and ideas	Putting information together to be able to say what a part, chapter, or whole text is mostly about.
Key details	Being able to sort through the information to find what's most important and connected to the text's main topics and ideas.
Text features	Learning from features (i.e., photographs, illustrations, maps, graphs, tables, and so on) and being able to connect what you've learned to the main text and other features on the page.
Vocabulary and figurative language	Knowing when a word or phrase is unfamiliar and having strategies to figure out its meaning.
Writing about reading	Using writing to hold onto important information (note-taking, annotating), organizing notes in ways that are useful, and using notes to springboard conversation or more extensive writing.

> Always give students some time to think and process before prompting. It may take a few moments before they are ready to notice and name.

> The prompts you offer are critical scaffolds to guide students toward your lesson objectives. You can anticipate and plan for this.

Ms. Jackson hangs back a moment and watches the children reread some of their notebook writing, glancing back and forth to the list of possible goals. She moves around the meeting area to provide individual coaching and guidance. She prompts students with questions: "What are you noticing comes easy to you as a reader?" and "Do you feel like note-taking and writing down main ideas and details is a strength of yours or something you need support with?" She also gives feedback, "Yes, I agree that you tend to collect a lot of information in your notes. Look to see if you are also synthesizing the information to say what the details are mostly about."

> To make your teaching more efficient, work with several students at once if you see they have the same need.

Three students—David, Jocelyn, and Emi—seem especially stuck and unsure about what to choose as a goal, even with Ms. Jackson's prompting. She pulls them together and uses a skill progression tool to help them reflect (see Figure 9.2). "Let's take a look at this skill progression for understanding main ideas and see if it can help you. After you read a section or chapter, do you feel like you can name the topic, identify an idea about the topic, or figure out a complex idea related to text structure?"

With the progression guiding them, David realizes he was really naming topics and subtopics more than ideas and decides to make this his goal. Jocelyn and Emi realize their main ideas were simple and learning about text structure could help them articulate more complex ideas; this becomes their shared goal.

> Skill progressions can be a helpful tool to guide student self-reflection and goal setting.

Figure 9.2   Skill Progression for Understanding Main Idea(s) in Expository Texts

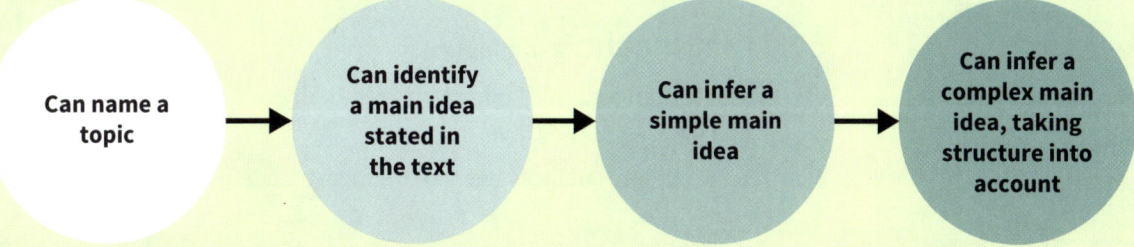

Source: Adapted from *The Reading Strategies Book 2.0*, Serravallo (2023b).

Ms. Jackson returns to address the entire class. "I'm going to give each of you an index card to jot down your name and what you'd like to focus on as your goal. Readers, our unit starts on Monday, and next week, I'll use the goals you set for yourselves today to help us get started with small-group instruction, where I'll start teaching you new strategies."

> Regardless of the type of guided inquiry your students are doing, make sure you always end with some clearly articulated, transferable takeaways.

Guided Inquiry Lessons: A Planning Template

Literacy Goal:

- Reflect on past experience with informational reading to set goals for upcoming informational reading unit

Knowledge/ Vocabulary Goals:

- Names and descriptions of possible goals

Teacher Materials:

- List of goals with kid-friendly definitions
- Skill progressions for each goal (in case students need the support)
- Blank index cards

Student Materials:

- Reading notebooks

Establish a Focus (1 minute):

Introduce the upcoming unit and connect it to the previous one. Introduce the list of goals with kid-friendly definitions.

Guide and Inquire (3–8 minutes):

- Offer children a chance to read through their past work, considering which goal is best for them.
- Use skill progressions as needed to support student reflection.

Possible prompts:

- What do you notice comes easily to you?
- What do you think you might want to work on?
- Is [skill] something you found you were able to do without much support, or is it something you'd like help with?
- Let's look at the skill progression for [goal] and notice how your current work aligns.

Clarify the Takeaways (1 minute):

- Ask students to jot their self-selected goal on an index card.
- Promise follow up with a focus lesson aligned to their goal.

An Overview: Guided Inquiry Lessons

When you choose guided inquiry, you're choosing to teach students to have a "notice and name" habit of mind that will serve them well as learners throughout their lives (Buchanan et al., 2016; Farrell et al., 1999). With your guidance, students look at something with questions in mind, discuss their observations, and draw conclusions. At the end of a guided inquiry lesson, you help students articulate their learning in a way that's replicable.

Some may argue that inquiry-based teaching is the opposite of explicit teaching; however, *guided* inquiry, where you have clear objectives in mind and plan scaffolds, prompts, and questions, can be a useful structure to have in your repertoire. Sometimes, leading students to explore, think, and come to their own conclusions, and being explicit about what they learned and can transfer to other contexts at the end of a lesson, leads to powerful learning and engagement (Chan et al., 2014; Montes et al., 2003; Palincsar et al., 2000; Uphold & Hudson, 2012).

You can guide students to inquire about all kinds of things. They might look at a text with a question in mind: "What word choices (connotations) show the author's stance on their topic? How does the author use figurative language? How is this text organized or structured? What do we notice about the punctuation decisions?" Inquiries like these help students build awareness about new writing techniques they might try in their own writing, and they can also help them analyze and interpret texts from a new lens and can lead to fresh insights and ideas about a text. In a way, guided inquiry about an author's craft can be a form of close reading (see Chapter 8).

Images, of course, are another kind of text, so students might watch a video to notice how the background music impacts the mood or study the illustrations in a picture book to notice how size, shape, and color convey important meaning. Similarly, students might observe an interaction, such as watching a conversation with a question in mind: "How do those in the conversation keep the idea moving and building with each turn?"

Perhaps the most important guided inquiry students can do, however, is to learn to look across their own work—as the students in the lesson description that opens this chapter were doing—and notice and name with a question in mind: "What am I doing well as a reader, and what do I need to work on?" Choosing to make time and space—and provide students with guidance and support—to reflect and set goals will help them develop a habit of mind that will support their growth as readers even when you aren't there to guide them. When you guide students to inquire about their own work, you'll also receive powerful feedback about what they've internalized from lessons— how well they have been able to apply strategies you've taught and how well they understand the skills they need to use to grow as readers (Hattie, 2008; Schunk & Ertmer, 2000).

What Research Says
About Guided Inquiry

Why choose guided inquiry?

➜ To increase students' engagement and ownership over their learning (Buchanan et al., 2016; Chan et al., 2014)

➜ To help students better remember what they've learned (Farrell et al., 1999; Kuhlthau et al., 2015; Margunayasa et al., 2019)

➜ To develop a habit of mind in students that extends beyond any single lesson and helps them self-teach and self-question as they read on their own (Cunningham, 2006; Josephs & Jolivette, 2016; Share, 1995)

Why is it important to help students set goals for themselves as readers?

➜ Your teaching—the strategies you introduce and the feedback you offer—will be more meaningful, effective, and impactful when it's tied to students' goals (Chan et al., 2014; Hattie, 2008).

➜ Clear, actionable, process-oriented goals, together with a plan for how to work toward the goals with strategies, increases self-efficacy, motivation, and comprehension (Cartwright, 2023; Locke & Latham, 1990; Schunk & Rice 1989, 1991).

Knowledge and Vocabulary Building
Within Guided Inquiry Lessons

⚙ Any time you study an author's craft, you will almost certainly talk about word choice as one of the types of decisions authors make. This invites an exploration of the nuanced meanings of words in ways that will deepen students' understandings. For example, whenever you ask, "Why did the author choose this word instead of that one? Why *impatient* instead of *eager*?" you must consider very precise differences in word meanings.

⚙ Students can learn terminology and academic vocabulary related to what they are studying. For example, when setting goals, they may learn and use words such as *infer, synthesize,* or *annotate* to talk about the work they have done or want to do. When studying author's craft, they may use words such as *metaphor, personification,* or *hyperbole* to be precise about naming the figurative language they notice.

⚙ When students name things they've noticed in guided inquiry, you will find many opportunities to offer them richer vocabulary. For example, if a student observing a conversation notices that participants sometimes repeat what the person before them has said, especially when they agree with it, you can say, "Yes, they're *reiterating* a point they think is important."

Planning: Guided Inquiry Lessons

While inquiry may seem open ended, you can actually do quite a bit of planning so you're prepared to guide students skillfully. With your lesson objectives in mind, you can think about the prompts and questions you might offer to guide them (see the Responsive Teaching section later in this chapter), think through how you anticipate they will respond, and consider what material supports and scaffolds they will need. Remember that in a guided inquiry lesson, students are always looking at something with a question in mind, so your planning will always start with the same decision—"What are we going to inquire *about*?"—then you'll figure out what tools and materials you'll need to support that inquiry.

Conversation Fishbowl

If you want students to learn elements of strong conversation, you'll need a conversation for them to observe that has the elements you want them to see. It might be one you've recorded or you could have them watch a conversation as it unfolds in real time. If you observe in real time, be sure you give the students who will have the conversation a heads-up that their classmates will be watching and what they'll be watching for. You might say, for example, "I'm impressed with how you are always able to debate different sides of an issue with respect and compassion for each other's ideas. I'd like your classmates to watch you debate to notice the ways you respond to each other."

As students in the center of the fishbowl converse, or as you play a video of a conversation, the rest of the students will likely take notes on what they see, so they'll need a pen, paper, and a clipboard or notebook. If you are working with younger students, instead of asking them to stop and jot while watching, you might instead pause the conversation for them to discuss what they notice.

Craft Study

In a craft study, you are observing the decisions authors, directors, composers, and so on make when they create so you'll need some kind of text to study. Most of the time it will be a written text, but the "text" you study might also be a video or even a piece of music students can look at and/or listen to closely and then reread or rewatch multiple times, perhaps annotating (if they have their own copies) as they notice and name the decision-making they see. Be sure to choose a text that lends itself well to the goals you've chosen to focus the inquiry—in other words, there needs to be plenty in the text for students to notice. As you plan, you can jot targeted questions aligned to your lesson goals to draw students' attention to specific lines or parts of the text. Sometimes it can be helpful to study contrastive examples in an inquiry, too. For example, if you are studying the way point of view impacts your students' understanding as readers, you might use several excerpts of texts written from different points of view instead of only one, then ask students what they notice about the contrasting examples (see more in Table 9.1).

Table 9.1 Craft Study Lesson Foci and Text Examples

During planning, prepare texts that offer examples, and possibly contrastive examples, aligned to your lesson goal(s).

Example Lesson Focus	Types of Texts to Find
How narrator's point of view (first, second, third person) impacts how a reader relates to the characters	Excerpts of texts with different points of view: ▶ alternating first-person narrators (e.g., *Saving Mr. Terupt* [Buyea, 2015]) ▶ consistent first person (e.g., *New Kid* [Craft, 2019]) ▶ consistent third person (e.g., *A Long Walk to Water* [Park, 2010])
How authors use text features (illustrations, photographs, maps, charts, graphs) to repeat important information visually or add additional information beyond the main text	An assortment of simple and complex informational articles from sources such as *Time for Kids, National Geographic,* and *Cobblestone Magazine*
Different types of figurative language (metaphor, hyperbole, idiom, personification, onomatopoeia, and so on) authors choose and the impact it has on a reader	Excerpts from picture books rich with figurative language (e.g., *I Am Every Good Thing* [Barnes, 2020], *Fry Bread: A Native American Family Story* [Maillard, 2019], *Magnificent Homespun Brown* [Doyon, 2020], *Noisy Night* [Barnett, 2017]), or poetry ("Still I Rise" [Angelou, 2015], "Cynthia in the Snow" [Brooks, 2006])

A common and predictable challenge when students are new to craft study is that they might talk about the content of the text rather than the author's decision-making to create the content. They will say, for example, "I think she really likes that chicken soup!" and you can be ready with an example that will illustrate the difference between content and craft: "When I'm asking you to think about word choice, I'm asking about the author's decisions. For example, the word *delectable* means *delicious*, but what I'm asking is *why* the author may have chosen that word. Why not write *delicious*? Is there a slightly different meaning?"

Students are also likely to use vague language when asked to infer why an author may have made a certain choice. They'll say, "She did it because it makes the writing better" or "Because she likes how it sounds," but you can think ahead about how to explain it: "Long run-on sentences, for example, give us a feeling of trying to catch our breath. It evokes a mood or feeling in us, the reader, that may be similar to what the character is feeling in this moment."

Connected to this, and you can watch this in the small-group Lesson in Action video example (Video 9.3) later in this chapter, students new to craft inquiry are often reluctant to infer an author's motive, likely thinking, "I have no idea why she decided to do that!" If you sense this reluctance, you can be ready to introduce your students to the powerful potential of the word *maybe*: "Maybe she did it because . . ."

Goal Setting

Guided inquiry lessons focused on goal setting can be particularly helpful at the start of a new school year, after a long holiday break, and at the beginning or end of units. If you meet with your students regularly for formative assessments, you might also use guided inquiry any time you see students have made growth or met goals, pulling them individually or in small groups to take stock of their work and plan for the future as needed.

If you're planning guided inquiry to help students reflect and set goals for their work as readers, there are several kinds of materials you might gather for students to use as they inquire.

✳ Based on your own assessments of what goals students need as readers, choose examples of their work that will help them see what you know they need to see. For example, if you know students need to work on fluency, perhaps a recording of them reading aloud would help them notice what they need. If you want them to think about their comprehension, you might have them look at some of their writing about reading or reflect using a recent comprehension assessment.

* Sometimes contrastive examples—a classmate's work or a teacher model—can help students compare their work to work that is more sophisticated and give them a vision for what they might aim for.

* Progressions, rubrics, and/or checklists (see Figures 9.3–9.5) can offer students language to name ways their skills can grow over time and help them see how to place their own work on a pathway to move forward.

Figure 9.3   Single-Point Rubric

Create single-point rubrics by listing the criteria in a center column and asking students to consider if each is a strength or need.

Areas for Improvement	Criteria	Evidence of Excelling
	Attention: I can focus on my book. If I get distracted, I can refocus my attention.	
	Attitude: I look forward to reading and I enjoy it. I choose to read even when it's not assigned.	
	Text and Purpose: I have ways to find texts that fit my purposes, and I focus on my purpose(s) when reading.	

Source: Adapted from the skill progression for engagement and motivation in *The Reading Strategies Book 2.0*, Serravallo (2023b).

Figure 9.4   Self-Assessment Checklist

Use student-facing language and simple text in self-assessment checklists. Be sure to include only statements your students will be able to understand and reflect on, based on what you've already taught.

Yes	No	Self-Assessment Checklist
		I look forward to reading, read with focus, and have a purpose for reading.
		I can figure out most of the words in my book using phonics and decoding strategies.
		I read smoothly and with expression.
		I can retell or summarize when I finish reading.
		I think about characters, themes, and ideas beyond what's literally in the text.
		I write about my reading.
		I enjoy talking with others about my reading, and the conversations go well.

Source: Adapted from the "What Can I Work on As a Reader" self-reflection form available at www.jenniferserravallo.com/downloads

Figure 9.5   Skill Progression for Character

Asking students to sort their responses along a progression or continuum, like this one for deepening ideas about characters, can help them name what they are currently doing as a reader and look ahead to what they might try next.

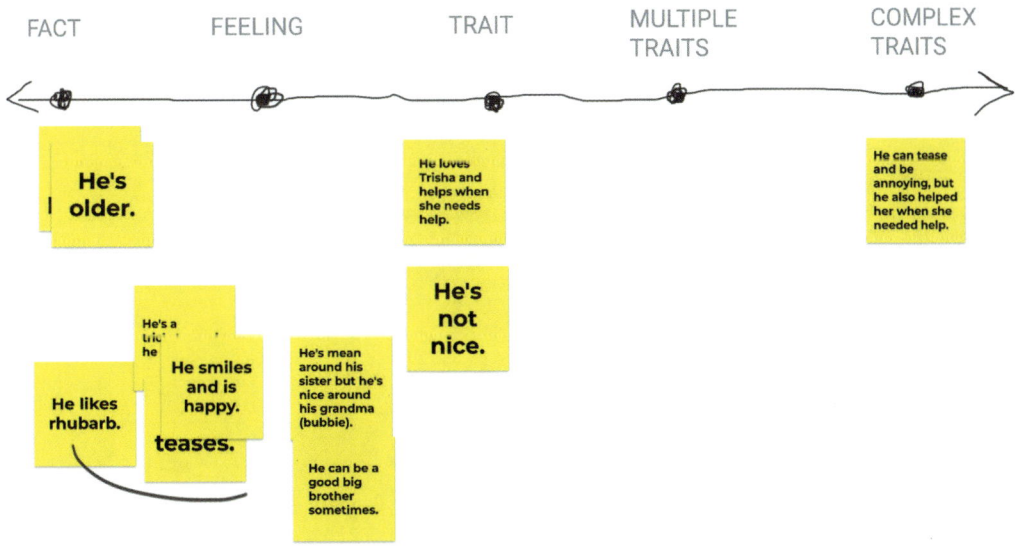

Structure and Timing: Guided Inquiry Lessons

Guided inquiry lessons generally last about 5–10 minutes. The overall lesson structure is sort of an inverted gradual release model. Instead of beginning by showing and telling your teaching point ("I do") and then moving to guided practice ("we do"), you'll begin by asking students to engage with a question right away ("you do"), then guide them as they observe and make discoveries ("we do"). Then, at the end of the lesson, you'll make sure the takeaways are clear. Of course, at any point during the lesson, if you sense they need a quick model or demonstration, you can offer it.

Guided inquiry lessons go like this:

1. Establish a Focus
(1 minute)

Briefly explain what the student(s) will be thinking about or observing (i.e., setting a new goal or checking in on progress with a current goal; noticing an author's craft; observing their peers to notice conversation skills). Introduce them to any materials and/or scaffolds they'll use, such as student-facing skill progressions or rubrics, self-reflection questions, or checklists they can use to evaluate their work.

2. Guide and Inquire
(3–8 minutes)

As students "notice and name," guide them with questions and prompts and offer them any vocabulary they need to articulate what they've noticed. If you find students need more than questions and prompts, you might direct their attention to specific aspects of what they are observing; for example, "What do you notice about what they say when they take a turn? What are their exact words?" You can also offer examples and demonstrations if you find they need even more support.

3. Clarify the Takeaways
(1 minute)

Based on the type of guided inquiry, articulate some key takeaways. If you're goal setting, have students name their new goals and the strategies they'll use to get started working on them. If you're studying an author's craft, you might have students name one thing they want to remember to look for in other texts (or even to try in their own). If you studied a conversation, you might have students name a move they observed and want to try the next time they are in conversation. You might jot down or ask students to jot down a physical reminder they can carry with them from the lesson back to their independent work.

Responsive Teaching: Guided Inquiry Lessons

You'll plan a guided inquiry lesson with outcomes in mind and then prepare materials, questions, and prompts that will help students arrive at the understandings you want them to take away from the lesson. Your guidance during the inquiry is critical, and knowing how to provide feedback that will lead students to make discoveries and draw conclusions requires some skill you'll develop over time. To get you started, in Table 9.2 you can find some prompts and question frames you may find helpful that are aligned to different types of guided inquiry lessons.

Table 9.2   Example Language Frames, Responses, and Prompts to Teach Responsively During Guided Inquiry Lessons

If You Hear or Observe . . .	Then You Might Say . . .
Goal Setting Students need guidance to determine a goal that would be most helpful for them to pursue, based on their current work.	[open-ended prompts] ▶ What are you doing well as a reader? ▶ What seems like a good next step for you as a reader? ▶ What would you most like to work on as a reader? [directed/guided/supportive prompts] ▶ One thing I notice is ____. What are your thoughts about that? ▶ Take a look at the skill progression. What do you think best describes your work? ▶ Look at/listen to ____. Compare what you saw/heard to your work.
Conversation Fishbowl Students need guidance to articulate what they notice as they observe an interaction or to clarify their takeaways.	▶ What do you notice the students are doing to ____? ▶ What effect does it have when a student ____? ▶ What seems to be working well for this group? ▶ How are students supporting each other with ____? ▶ If you were part of this group, what would you do next? ▶ What compliments do you have for the members of this group? ▶ What are students doing to show they are listening? ▶ How are they keeping the conversation going? ▶ What are they doing to build on others' ideas?
Craft Study Students need guidance to begin noticing specific decisions an author has made to craft a text.	▶ What has the author done in this text that feels unique? ▶ How does the author's decision to ____ impact you as a reader? ▶ What would you call/name what the author has done here? ▶ If the author had written this a different way, what effect would that have? What impact does this have on you as a reader? ▶ That's what it's about. What decisions might be behind how it's written? ▶ The author ____ because they wanted to ____. ▶ I know you're not sure, so start with, "Maybe the reason the author did this is ____."

Lesson in Action: Individual Goal Setting Guided Inquiry Lesson, Second Grade, English Language Arts

Violetta's teacher wanted students to start setting goals for themselves as readers to make the strategies they are learning more purposeful. I got things started with this quick four-minute conversation, then each student in the class was to have their own one-on-one conversation with their teacher to be guided through the same reflection process over the next few days.

Read the lesson plan on the opposite page or online, watch the video (access it using the QR code), then come back to read the post-lesson reflection comments annotating the lesson plan.

Download the lesson plan or a blank template on the companion website https://companion .corwin.com/ courses/2024_TRAD

Scan the code or go to https://qrs .ly/3nfg1ru to watch the video.

Video 9.1 Individual Goal-Setting Guided Inquiry Lesson, Second Grade, English Language Arts

Guided Inquiry Lessons: A Planning Template

Literacy Goal:
- Lead Violetta to identify a goal (likely accuracy, based on other assessments)

Knowledge/ Vocabulary Goal(s):
- N/A

Teacher Materials:
- Blank goal bookmark
- Post-its

Student Materials:
- Self-selected books

Establish a Focus (1 minute):
We're going to work together to choose a goal.

Guide and Inquire (3–8 minutes):
- Think about what's going well—easy! Think about what's more challenging.
- Start with an easier text, then move to a more challenging text.

Prompts:
- What feels comfortable for you as a reader?
- What are you doing well as a reader?
- What might you want to work on next?
- Let me read it back the way I heard you read. Do you notice anything?.

Clarify the Takeaways (1 minute):
Leave Violetta with her new goal card and a sticky note with the first strategy.

> I noticed her reading was accurate and fluent, and when I asked her to talk about what she was doing well, she shared all of the things she was thinking about as a reader. There wasn't much work to do in this text at all!

> As the text got harder, her accuracy faltered. Violetta tracked the print as she was reading with her finger and monitored for meaning, but she wasn't catching her word-reading errors. One way to help students recognize the work they need to do is to offer a contrasting example. In this case, I told her what she read, and pointed to the words on the page so she could notice the difference.

> Her goal was bigger than simply paying attention to the words—tracking is one part of what it takes to read accurately. Once she's tracking well and not making omission errors, we'll have her read more complex texts that will challenge her decoding skills, and I can teach her new strategies aligned to that skill to support her.

> Interestingly, after she named her goal, she was able to read the next pages with no help from me at all! Just the awareness and a shift in her attention and tracking was enough.

> Notice I used her own words on this physical reminder.

Lesson in Action: Whole-Class Conversation Fishbowl Guided Inquiry Lesson, Fourth Grade, English Language Arts

By late September, this fourth-grade class had practiced having conversations as a whole class and in partnerships (for more on teaching conversation, see Chapter 11), and they had begun discussing in book clubs when a predictable issue arose: While a couple of the clubs were off to the races—sharing, connecting, and elaborating on ideas and generally having a great talk—some of the other clubs ran out of things to talk about right away. I chose to have one of the more skilled clubs serve as a model for their peers, and I led them to notice and name that group's conversational skills and moves. At the end, I had all of the students set goals for their next club meeting based on what they'd seen.

Read the lesson plan on the opposite page or online, watch the video (access it using the QR code), then come back to read the post-lesson reflection comments annotating the lesson plan.

Download the lesson plan or a blank template on the companion website https://companion .corwin.com/ courses/2024_TRAD

Scan the code or go to https://qrs .ly/1yfg1rx to watch the video.

Video 9.2   Whole-Class Conversation Fishbowl Guided Inquiry Lesson, Fourth Grade, English Language Arts

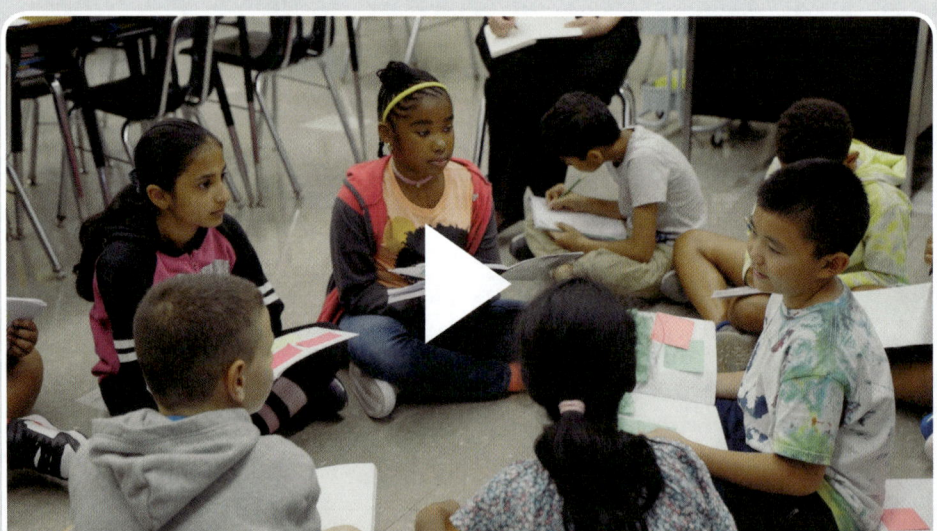

I preselected the students I wanted to serve as the model, and planned to have other students take notes.

I chose this group because I had seen them have rich conversation, but I was ready to jump in if they needed my help. They didn't!

I was taking careful notes in case I needed to prompt the students who were observing.

I am always listening carefully to students' responses thinking, "What are they trying to articulate?" and when I need to, I reframe/rephrase comments to make sure I understood and also to clarify what's been said for the other students.

Most students easily articulated (noticed and named) the group's conversational strengths; I reworded or elaborated only occasionally to help clarify, or attach purpose to a comment.

When one student identified prediction, I saw an opportunity to talk about the content of conversation. "What else did you notice they were talking about?"

I added, "How can you tell?" to my prompts to support close listening.

I may also choose to make a classroom chart with reminders from this quick lesson.

Guided Inquiry Lessons: A Planning Template

Literacy Goals:
- Notice and name elements of effective conversation

Knowledge/ Vocabulary Goal(s):
- N/A

Teacher Materials:
- Note-taking form

Student Materials:
- Nico, Courtney, Akshaya, Nashley— notes from *The Tiger Rising* (DiCamillo, 2001)
- Rest of the class— notebook and pencil

Establish a Focus (1 minute):
We're going to study the conversation of a small group of students to discover what keeps the conversation going and makes it interesting.

Guide and Inquire (3–8 minutes):
- Guide to notice—asking questions, active listening, responding to previous comments, challenging, don't always need to agree
- Ask students watching to take notes and share.

Prompts:
- What do we notice they did to keep the conversation going?
- What do we notice they talked about?
- What is something you might want to try in your conversation?
- Why does that help the conversation?

Clarify the Takeaways (1 minute):
Set goals for your own club based on what you saw.

Lesson in Action: Small-Group Craft Study Guided Inquiry Lesson, Sixth Grade, English Language Arts

Studying the author's craft offered a new lens for this beginning-of-the-year sixth-grade class and, according to their teacher, these four students were ready for the challenge of this deeper analytic work. I chose a text they were already familiar with both to save time in the lesson and to help them see how the kind of reading they'd do in this lesson—reading like a writer—differed from other kinds of reading they'd done so far. I also planned a whole-class conversation (see Lesson in Action, Video 11.1 in Chapter 11) about this story, and I thought if I gave a small group of children extra support with this deeper thinking, they could bring their ideas to enrich the whole class's thinking. Because it was a small group, the four students had a lot of opportunities to think, share their ideas, and get feedback from me and each other.

Read the lesson plan on the opposite page or online, watch the video (access it using the QR code), then come back to read the post-lesson reflection comments annotating the lesson plan.

Video 9.3 Small-Group Craft Study Guided Inquiry Lesson, Sixth Grade, English Language Arts

Download the lesson plan or a blank template on the companion website https://companion.corwin.com/courses/2024_TRAD

Scan the code or go to https://qrs.ly/t3fg1s0 to watch the video.

When I asked what they noticed, the student simply read back the sentence. I then named it for her: "Oh, she listed." Then I followed up with a question to help her think about author's craft: "So why would she do that? Why would she not have just _____." When the students responded, I gently echoed what they said with, "So what you are saying is . . ." In the beginning stages, students need these sorts of support, but over time, they will become more independent.

Guided Inquiry Lessons: A Planning Template

Literacy Goal:
- Examine the author's craft (use of sentence structure, story structure, repetition) to develop ideas about the character and theme

Knowledge/ Vocabulary Goals:
- Run-on sentence
- Metaphor versus simile

Teacher Materials:
- Chart to capture thinking

Student Materials:
- Copy of "Eleven" (Cisneros, 1991)

Establish a Focus (1 minute):
- Connect to prior readings of "Eleven"
- Today, go a little deeper, not only thinking about *what* the author wrote but also considering *how* she wrote it—the decisions she made.
- Consider characters, mood, and theme

Guide and Inquire (3–8 minutes):
- First sentence is a long run-on. Why?
- What's the feeling you get when you read a long sentence?
- So, what do you think about her as a character?
- The rest of paragraph one starts with "And, and, and." Why? What does it make you think about the narrator?

Skip the second paragraph.
- Onion or rings inside a tree trunk or wooden dolls—why use different comparisons here? What does it help you understand about the theme of the story?
- Short sentences—what's the feeling you get from this part?
- "Whose is this"—now we're into the scene. Why only now? Why would she have started off with all of this background first?

Clarify the Takeaways (1 minute):
- Reading to think about the author's decisions is a different way of reading the text.
- Doing this helps us think more deeply about the text and can help with our own writing.
- Ask why and infer decisions.

I am comfortable with wait time, but when I sense hesitation, I find the prompt, "You could say, 'I'm not sure, but maybe . . .'" really frees students up to take risks and move past thinking there is one right answer.

I noticed the students were definitely more comfortable interpreting the character's feelings or traits than talking about the author's decisions.

When I said, "She did that on purpose" and "That's an author move," I was trying to refocus the students on the "reading like a writer" approach we were trying.

It was really helpful that the lines were numbered for easy reference!

Here, again, I was getting them thinking, "Why did she do this?" and "She made this choice as an author, right?"

Spin It: Expand the Definition of Text

If you expand the notion of *text*, students might observe all kinds of things with a question in mind, then notice and name what they see. Studying clouds? Take your students outside and ask them what they notice about how the clouds move through the sky to begin an exploration of weather systems. Learning about the 50 states that make up the nation? Have students study United States maps and ask them what they notice about boundaries and the different sizes of states. Introducing multiplication? Ask students what they notice by looking at a 10 by 10 multiplication table. The Spin It possibilities for guided inquiry are endless!

Take It to Your Classroom

✓   Consider your unit objectives and whether any of the lessons might be more engaging through a guided inquiry approach rather than direct instruction.

✓   Consider when in your unit you might engage readers in self-reflection and goal setting. Look at their assessments or samples of their work before beginning the inquiry so you have a sense of what you'll lead them to notice about their work. Prepare tools such as skill progressions to support their reflection.

✓   Plan to follow up guided inquiry lessons with focus lessons, close reading, read aloud, or other opportunities to explicitly teach strategies (*how*) students can work toward goals or continue to practice applying what they noticed.

Reader's Theater Lessons

10

Picture It: Third Graders Practice Reading a Script About Ancient Egypt

Four third graders sit around a table, scripts of *The Discovery of King Tut* in hand. They decided in their last meeting who would take on the roles of Narrator 1 and 2, Howard Carter (archaeologist), and Arthur Callendar (Carter's assistant), and they highlighted their lines on their own copies of the script. Today, they decide to do the first of several read-throughs to prepare to perform for their kindergarten reading buddies later next week. Mr. Jacobs stands on the outside, ready to observe and offer support as needed.

Hyun, playing Narrator 1, begins. "Born May 9, 1874, Howard Carter Grew up in the town of Kensington, England."

Mr. Jacobs continues to listen as they each take turns. He notices they are able to keep track of their parts without any hiccups, their reading is well-paced, and they are reading the words accurately. "Off to a great start," he thinks. As they begin the scene where characters start talking, with stage directions telling them to read "excitedly" or "with confusion," he notices that while their reading is smooth, they could try to get into character a bit more and reflect character emotions with their voices.

He pauses the group. "Readers, you're all doing a fantastic job of staying in the scene, following along, and joining in when it's your turn. Here's a suggestion as you continue this first read. I want you to think about how your character is feeling and pay close attention

> You'll need to find room in your schedule for reader's theater to unfold over several sessions.

> Rereading is a hallmark of reader's theater, though students do it independently (instead of together, as in other lesson structures such as shared reading).

> Reader's theater helps students improve their prosody—reading with expression, emphasis, and intonation. Look for opportunities to support students with these skills as you listen and coach.

> When you listen and coach, decide on one thing to teach and stay focused on that when you begin coaching.

to any stage directions in parentheses that tell you *how* to read the line—this goes for the narrator, too! Think about what feeling even a narrator might have at this moment in the story—surprise, awe, concern, any feeling really—and try to make your voice match that feeling. Let's actually back up a bit. Read your last line to yourself, thinking about feeling and noticing the stage directions. Everyone ready? OK, let's try it again."

Mr. Jacobs moves to the periphery of the group and watches as they reread the page aloud. He notices that not only are their voices changing to match the feeling, but their faces are, too. He jumps in with a compliment, "Readers! You are really becoming the characters. Your voices and faces are matching how the characters are feeling at this moment in the scene." A few moments later, he notices Carlos, playing Lord Carnavon, reading a section with a flat intonation where the stage directions say "excitedly," and he interrupts to offer some feedback: "Carlos, take a quick look at those stage directions. Think, 'How can I read this part to match not only what the character says but how they say it?'"

Carlos responds, "More excitement!"

Mr. Jacobs says, "Yes! So, as you read it, think about that and try to show that feeling with your voice."

After watching another few turns, Mr. Jacobs leaves a last bit of feedback before moving on to another group of students reading a script about Queen Hatshepsut: "Readers, remember as you keep reading to really stay in character, think about their feelings, notice the stage directions, and make your voice match those feelings!"

> Comprehension and prosody go hand in hand.

> When you're coaching, it's not rude to interrupt! In fact, the art of coaching is knowing when to interrupt, either to confirm that students are getting it or to offer support if they're not.

> Offer a quick, focused summary of what you've taught and leave students to continue working on it.

Reader's Theater Lessons: A Planning Template

Literacy Goals:

- Match voice to character feeling and stage directions

Knowledge/ Vocabulary Goal:

- Reinforce knowledge from social studies unit on Ancient Egypt with scripts aligned to content.

Teacher Materials:

- Note-taking forms

Student Materials:

- Individual copies of script (*Discovery of King Tut*)

Establish a Focus or (Listen and Observe) (1 minute):

- Well-paced, accurate
- Keeping track of lines

Teach and Coach (2–3 minutes):

- Make voice match feeling of character and stage directions

Clarify the Takeaways (1 minute):

- Stay in character, read with feeling!

An Overview: Reader's Theater Lessons

During reader's theater, a pair or a small group of students will practice reading and rereading a script aloud in preparation for a low-stakes performance without memorization, full staging, or props. Reader's theater is both collaborative and interactive and allows students to assume different character roles, practice expressive reading and voice inflections, and use gestures and facial expressions to bring a text to life. Importantly, students are encouraged to read and reread, a practice that has been shown to benefit many areas of reading, including accuracy, oral reading fluency, and comprehension (Chard et al., 2002; Hudson et al., 2020; Stevens et al., 2017). Reader's theater can benefit a wide age range of students and can be used across the day in English language arts and content areas and across genres.

You will likely offer a varying amount of support to readers during these lessons. When students first get their scripts or when your students are new to the routines and rituals of reader's theater, you might offer some direct instruction and guided practice as they read through the script the first time, pausing to help them understand Tier 2 vocabulary words they encounter and to support comprehension. You might even read the script once through with them, chorally, as you would in a shared-reading lesson (see Chapter 7). The fourth-grade Lesson in Action (see Video 10.2) is a good example of what these early setup-type lessons can look like. Additionally, you might decide to teach students strategies, such as those for reading with expression and fluency, before they begin practicing, as you would in a focus lesson (see Chapter 6).

After students are comfortable with the routines and expectations of reader's theater, they will become more independent and need less direct instruction to get started with their reading for the day. At this point, they can read and/or practice their scripts during independent reading while you meet with other students in their class. You might also decide to have a time set aside each day for reader's theater, when everyone in the class is practicing their scripts in their groups and you move around to provide coaching, feedback, and support.

Table 10.1   Strategies to Teach During Reader's Theater

Strategies to Support Students Getting Started With Reader's Theater	Strategies to Help Students Improve Fluency and Comprehension While They Practice Their Reader's Theater Scripts
▶ Orient yourself to the script, understanding that the parentheses contain stage directions. Read stage directions in your head to inform how you'll read your line, and read aloud what comes after the character name and stage directions.	▶ When you have to slow down your reading to figure out a word or when you read and realize your phrasing was awkward, go back and reread. This time, read the words automatically and pay attention to pauses and expression.
▶ Make sure you understand all of the words in your lines. If you don't know a word, work with your group to figure it out. Use strategies such as rereading contextual information, thinking about word part clues, or searching for a word's definition in an outside resource during your first read.	▶ You can be a director to the other members of your group by giving them feedback on their reading. Listen carefully to their phrasing and expression. Compliment them when what you hear sounds smooth and expressive. Give a tip when someone needs it.
▶ Find your character name in the script and highlight your lines (what comes after the name and stage directions). As you practice, make sure you are reading the other characters' lines in your head to follow the script, and read your character's lines aloud when it's your turn.	▶ Make sure you're reading the ending punctuation (not only the words!). Look ahead to the end of the sentence. Notice if there is an exclamation point, question mark, or period. Read the sentence to match the punctuation.

Source: Adapted from *The Reading Strategies Book 2.0*, Serravallo (2023b).

What Research Says
About Reader's Theater

For decades, researchers have found that reader's theater offers a wide range of benefits to developing readers:

➡ Combining authentic repeated reading with an emphasis on meaningful expression improves oral reading fluency—both words correct per minute (WCPM) and prosody (Begeny et al., 2009; Corcoran & Davis, 2005; Mraz et al., 2013; Young & Rasinski, 2018; Young, Valadez et al., 2016).

➡ Repeated reading is one of the most studied interventions, with hundreds of studies yielding moderate to high effect sizes across a range of ages and contexts (Padeliadu & Giazitzidou, 2018). One of the benefits of reader's theater is the opportunity for readers to read the same text again and again (Chard & Tyler, 2000).

➡ Peers of all ages can support each other's fluency from elementary (Marr et al., 2011) to high school (Josephs & Jolivette, 2016). During reader's theater, students can give each other feedback.

➡ Targeted feedback can support the aspects of fluency students most need to improve (Ardoin et al., 2013; Mastrothanasis et al., 2023).

➡ Reading prosody, which readers practice through oral reading and performance, supports comprehension of challenging texts (Benjamin & Schwanenflugel, 2010).

➡ Reader's theater is motivating (Tierney & Readence, 2000) for a wide range of students, including those who are learning English (Liu, 2000; Mastrothanasis et al., 2023), those whom researchers termed "struggling readers" (Drill & Bellini, 2022), and autistic students (Drill & Bellini, 2022).

➡ Reader's theater helps support students' reading confidence, enthusiasm, and motivation for reading (Clark et al., 2009; Corcoran & Davis, 2005; Millin & Rinehart, 1999; Myrset & Drew, 2016; Rinehart, 1999; Tsou, 2011).

Knowledge and Vocabulary Building
Within Reader's Theater Lessons

☼ Choose texts that offer opportunities for vocabulary learning and lead students through a first read, offering student-friendly definitions or strategies to help them figure out word meanings from context, as you would in read-aloud, shared-reading, or close-reading lessons.

☼ Encourage students to talk about the script—not only read it aloud—to clarify any confusion and support comprehension. Teach them to approach the text with word curiosity and discuss meanings of words during the first read (Keehn et al., 2008).

☼ Use scripts that align to content you're studying. You can utilize existing scripts, cocreate them with students, or task students (alone or in pairs or groups) with creating their own dramatic adaptations of historical events, scientific concepts, or mathematical problems.

☼ Revise existing scripts—alone, with colleagues, or with your students' help—to include more sophisticated words. For example, in a script adaptation of the picture book *Paper Bag Princess* (Munsch, 1980), when the dragon says, "Go away! I love to eat princesses, but I have already eaten a whole castle today," *eat* could be revised to *consume* or *devour*.

Planning: Reader's Theater Lessons

Students practice reading individual copies of reader's theater scripts in pairs or small groups. You'll need to make decisions about who will work together, what texts they'll use, and how you'll organize classroom time so they can reread, rehearse, and eventually perform for others.

Groups

Partnerships and groups that work together in reader's theater are flexible and can change often. Students might decide to work together because they are excited about a particular story, they might be in a book club and decide to create a script adaptation of their book, or you might group them because they have a common goal or need you can address with teaching through reader's theater.

Since different parts of a reader's theater text may require different amounts of reading or different levels of reading complexity, students of mixed abilities can work together in a group. Be sensitive to each student's strengths and needs when assigning roles or help them make wise choices if they are deciding parts for themselves. You can create scaffolds for multilingual learners who may need some extra support by buddying them up with a peer to read a part chorally (imagine the narrator from *Discovery of King Tut* performed by two booming voices—like a Greek chorus—instead of one) or by giving them some advanced practice reading the script with you or with a family member at home before reading it with their peers in school.

Texts

You'll need texts that work well for reader's theater, of course—the most obvious choices are published plays/scripts or poems written for two (or more) voices, such as *Joyful Noise* (Fleischman, 1988). With a quick Google Search, you'll find that many scripts are available for free: Check out Chase Young and Tim Rasinski's websites, for example, or sites with digital texts such as Reading A to Z.

You and/or your students might also adapt children's picture books, informational texts, classic stories, or even math story problems into scripts for reader's theater, or students can write their own original scripts (see Figures 10.1 and 10.2). You can also think outside the box. Students might practice reading as a scientist with a voice of authority from an informational text or delivering the news in a news anchor's voice. They can relive famous speeches or even sing (or speak the lyrics of) their favorite songs.

Whatever you use, short texts are best for both those performing and those listening to a no-frills reader's theater performance. And since students

Figure 10.1 A Reader's Theater Script Created During Shared Writing

A class of second graders wrote a script during a shared-writing lesson (Serravallo, 2021)—the teacher did the typing, the students suggested the lines—after their study of honeybees. The class then split into groups of four to practice reading it.

Honeybees and their Honey

Roles: Bee #1, Bee #2, Bee #3, Narrator

Bee #1: The bear is going to sleep for winter.

Bee #2: The turtles are going to sleep for winter.

Bee #3: But we're not going to sleep!

Narrator: Honeybees stay active all winter long.

Bee #1: All spring, summer, and fall, we've been flying for miles in search of flowers and nectar.

Bee #2: We used our proboscis to suck up the nectar.

Bee #3: The nectar went in our stomach where we carried it back to the colony.

Narrator: Once they were back inside the colony, they packed the nectar into hexagon beeswax honey cells. And then they turned the nectar into honey!

Bee #2: That's right! We dried it out by making a warm breeze with our wings!

Bee #3: And when it dried out, we put a lid over it with more beeswax.

Bee #1: (Like a little honey jar!)

Narrator: Bees store their honey so that in the winter, when the flowers have finished blooming, bees can open up these little honey jars and eat the yummy honey they saved.

will read and reread their script many times and they will have the regular support of their peers (as well as occasional support from you), you may also find they can read texts that are more complex (in ideas, concepts, vocabulary, and/or decodability) for reader's theater than what they can read independently without support.

Figure 10.2   A Student-Authored Reader's Theater Script

A pair of fifth graders created this script, an adaptation of the story *Lila and the Crow* by Gabrille Grimard (2016).

Lila and the Crow

Characters: Lila, Narrator

Lila: Hi! I'm Lila and I've just moved.

Narrator: Sometimes Lila likes to go outside, sit on the sidewalk, and poke the dirt with a stick.

Lila: There's this crow that always stands across the road, cawing at me. I don't think it likes me very much.

(Lila looks down at her hands)

Narrator: Lila likes to go outside every day and trap little bugs in a jar, then let them free.

She also likes to play hopscotch and jump rope on the freshly paved driveway.

Narrator: Since she does this every day, it gets boring easily.

Lila: I just wish I had a friend to play with. Just one.

Narrator: On Monday morning, Lila got up extra early and put on a red dress and black leggings. The wind was making her hair fly all over the place.

Lila: I'm REALLY happy. I haven't been this happy since before I moved. I'm happy because I was going to school today. And I am determined to make a friend. And we can play together every day!

Narrator: Lilas teacher, Mr. Nicholas introduced Lila. Lila sees her classmates looking at her and can't wait to get to know them and become their friends.

Lila: I keep squirming in my desk impatient, excited for recess.

Narrator: It's recess time, and all the kids go out to play. Now, Lila can make a friend!

Lila: The kids are NOT as kind as I thought they would be.

Weekly Schedule

As you've read, rereading is a mainstay of reader's theater, so you'll want to make a plan for when students will have opportunities to practice their scripts repeatedly over time and when they'll be able to perform. You might make time daily, or you might earmark a couple of days each week for reader's theater practice and spread the suggested sequence on the sample schedule in Table 10.2 across several weeks. In most cases, children spend at least a few sessions reading and rereading the script before their low-stakes performance (usually for peers in their class, a visiting class, or perhaps some visitors from home). During this time, you will conduct reader's theater lessons with some students, while others work in their groups without your support.

Table 10.2   Sample Five-Day Schedule to Prepare for a Reader's Theater Performance

From receiving a script to a low-stakes performance, students read and reread the same script several times. You do not need to provide time daily; this five-day schedule could be spread over two weeks or more.

Day 1	Day 2	Day 3	Day 4	Day 5
Readers receive (or choose) their script. You assign or let them choose their roles. They read it once through independently, highlighting their lines. You might also convene the group to have a quick discussion about the script, check for understanding, read it together chorally, or help them with vocabulary words. Students can take their script home to practice.	Readers meet to practice reading their script. They can offer each other feedback on their expression, and you can offer support (strategies and feedback; see Tables 10.1 and 10.3). Students can take their script home to practice.	Readers meet again to practice (see Day 2). Students can take their script home to practice.	Readers meet again to practice (see Day 2). Students can take their script home to practice.	Readers perform—no costumes, props, or memorization! They will be reading from the script with minimal (if any) blocking or staging (directions for movement).

Structure and Timing: Reader's Theater Lessons

As you've read, an important part of reader's theater is the opportunity you'll provide for students to read and reread their scripts in groups, practicing their fluency and celebrating their reading with a no-frills performance. The lesson part of reader's theater can come when you introduce a text to a group for the first time (when you'll start by establishing a focus) or when you listen in and choose what to teach (in that case, you'll start by listening and observing). In all cases, these lessons are quick, 5-minute opportunities for direct teaching and guided feedback, taking advantage of the efficiency of a ready-made small group!

Reader's theater lessons go like this:

1. Establish a Focus or Listen and Observe
(1 minute)

If reader's theater is new, the students are reading a new text that will require some support, or there is something you plan to teach before they begin reading, you'll want to establish a focus. If students are familiar with reader's theater routines and/or their script, you can start the lesson by observing students as they are reading/rehearsing. Position yourself on the periphery and encourage students to engage with each other as they practice rather than face you. Listen for strengths and needs.

2. Teach and Coach
(2–3 minutes)

If you established a focus first, you'll observe students as they practice applying what you taught. Interrupt to coach by offering reminders, redirections, corrections, prompts, and compliments to the group (or you can whisper into an individual student's ear as others continue reading their lines). If you listened and observed first, you will name something the students are doing well, offer a strategy to lift the level of their practice, and then coach them as they practice.

3. Clarify the Takeaways
(1 minute)

After a bit of coaching, remind students what they learned with you today. You can also ask them to reflect on how their practice went and discuss what goals they have for moving forward. Students will likely continue practicing as you move to another group (unless you are out of time for the day).

Responsive Teaching: Reader's Theater Lessons

You will spend the majority of time in each lesson engaged in responsive teaching—listening to students read and, as they practice, coaching them based on what you see they need. It's helpful to have a skill progression in mind as you listen, identifying where students' practice falls on the progression and coaching them into the next category. For example, you might have in mind a skill progression for fluency that begins with word-by-word reading, then progresses to short phrases, then to longer phrases, then to expression based on ending punctuation, then to expression based on mid-sentence punctuation, and then expression based on inferring how the character is feeling (Serravallo, 2023b).

Table 10.3   Example Language Frames, Responses, and Prompts to Teach Responsively During Reader's Theater Lessons

If You Hear or Observe . . .	Then You Might Say . . .
A student's reading sounds flat, without intonation or expression.	▶ Reread that line; try to really sound like the character. ▶ Now that you know what the line says, try to show that meaning with your voice. ▶ Think about how they are feeling. Now read it like that.
Students are missing their cues or are getting distracted while others read their lines.	▶ You have your lines highlighted, but you should be reading along (in your head) as your friends read their lines so you know when to jump in.
Students read with expression, sounding like the character.	▶ Yes! Your character is really coming alive because of how you're reading it. ▶ I can tell your character is [emotion] here because you read it with that feeling!
Students are stumbling through words.	▶ I notice you slowed down to figure out words. It's important to back up and reread to smooth out your reading. ▶ Now that you know the words, go back and read with fluency.
Students could use more facial and body expression.	▶ Think about what's happening and what your character is saying. Try to make your face and body act like the character would.
Students seem confused about what is happening in the script.	▶ It's important to understand what's happening before we can perform it. Let's pause after a few lines and discuss what's happening to make sure we're all comprehending before moving on.

Lesson in Action: Small-Group Reader's Theater Lesson, First Grade, English Language Arts

There were a wide range of reading abilities in this class—some students were still working on letter sounds and others were reading above–grade-level texts and working on fluency and comprehension. (You can watch a small-group phonics lesson with other students in this same class as part of the videos in Chapter 4 to better understand the range!) Reader's theater made perfect sense as an engaging and meaningful form of fluency practice for these three readers who were ready to read longer texts.

The three students had been practicing their script for several days, so they didn't need me to establish a focus at the beginning. Instead, I had them begin reading and as I listened and observed, I decided what to teach and coached them to provide support. Note that in this lesson, I used the planning template more as a note-taking form, since I didn't know ahead of time what I would teach. I made notes on the form about the things I noticed, then I went back and filled in both the literacy goal and the takeaway after the lesson so I had a record of both the teaching and what I'd noted that prompted it.

Read the lesson plan online or on the opposite page, watch the video (access it using the QR code), then come back to read the post-lesson reflection comments annotating the lesson plan.

Video 10.1   Small-Group Reader's Theater Lesson, First Grade, English Language Arts

Download the lesson plan or a blank template on the companion website https://companion .corwin.com/ courses/2024_TRAD

Scan the code or go to https://qrs .ly/4ffg1s4 to watch the video.

Reader's Theater Lessons: A Planning Template

Literacy Goals:
- Phrasing and prosody

Knowledge/ Vocabulary Goals:
- N/A

Teacher Materials:
- Note-taking forms

Student Materials:
- Individual copies of script based on (*My Friend Is Sad*) (Willems, 2007)

Establish a Focus or (Listen and Observe) (1 minute):
- Students are losing track of their lines
- Reading is still quite monotone after several days of practice

Teach and Coach (2–3 minutes):
- Follow along and don't lose track
- Think about how character is feeling
- Make your voice match the exclamation mark

Clarify the Takeaways (1 minute):
- Keep track and make sure your voice matches punctuation (period, exclamation, dot–dot–dot)

I suspected they were looking ahead to their own next lines rather than reading silently when a peer was reading, so I made a point to teach them the conventions of reading a script—following along in your head as others read so you don't lose track of where you are.

The text was ripe with opportunities to practice prosody (expression, emphasis). Clueing them in to the exclamation marks, together with thinking about what's happening and how the character is feeling, improved their reading quickly.

Notice I prompted them several times to think about how the exclamation marks communicated different emotions. I also had them practice isolated lines before asking them to read the script in sequence.

This wasn't planned ahead. I crafted a summary of our work together and key takeaways on the spot.

Lesson in Action: Small-Group Reader's Theater Lesson, Fourth Grade, English Language Arts

In this co-taught fourth-grade class, several students needed support with their fluency (phrasing and reading with prosody) and needed support reading grade-level texts, so reader's theater seemed to be a perfect choice. I chose a script with opportunities to teach Tier 2 vocabulary and assigned them roles that would set them up to practice what they needed to work on most: The student who was working on phrasing got the character whose lines included long sentences with commas, and the student who needed to work on prosody got the most emotionally expressive character.

This was the group's first time ever doing reader's theater so, in contrast to the lesson you watched in Video 10.1, I did more up-front planning and provided a good deal more support during this first meeting.

Read the lesson plan online or on the opposite page, watch the video (access it using the QR code), then come back to read the post-lesson reflection comments annotating the lesson plan.

Download the lesson plan or a blank template on the companion website https://companion .corwin.com/ courses/2024_TRAD

Scan the code or go to https://qrs .ly/2ufg1s5 to watch the video.

Video 10.2   Small-Group Reader's Theater Lesson, Fourth Grade, English Language Arts

Reader's Theater Lessons: A Planning Template

Literacy Goals:

- Reading with expression, in character (Skye, Gineen)
- Pausing at commas (Angelique, Aaron)

Knowledge/ Vocabulary Goals:

- Figuring out unknown words from context
- *Duchess, gown, palace, coaxed, splendid, whirled, drove*

Teacher Materials:

- Note-taking forms

Student Materials:

- Individual copies of a script adaptation of *Brave Irene* (Steig, 1988)

Establish a Focus or Listen and Observe (1 minute):

- Introduce the idea of reader's theater—a way to practice their goals of reading with fluency (paying attention to pauses, sounding like the character).
- Work together to read and reread the text, and by Friday, be ready to read it in front of an audience!

Teach and Coach (2–3 minutes):

- Read through once.
- Ask questions to check understanding of what's happening and the meanings of words: *gown, duchess, dumpling, palace, coaxed, splendid, whirled, drove* (the wind drove)
- Think about how the characters are feeling to read the lines with feeling.

Clarify the Takeaways (1 minute):

Help each other with unfamiliar words; practice several times this week during independent reading time to be ready to share at week's end.

Annotations:

Since it was this group's first time with a script, I highlighted their parts ahead of time. I wouldn't do this for them next time.

I had students say *duchess* aloud to connect its pronunciation to its spelling and offered quick definitions.

After discussing *dumpling*, I decided to do a little choral reading with the group. This supported the students with a model of fluent, accurate reading, especially important since the student who first read that line made errors.

After defining *coaxed* for them, I asked her to reread, and I read in a quiet voice to give her a little extra feedback and support to improve her accuracy on the reread.

I left *whirled* and *drove* for them to work on during their next group meeting and asked them to help each other—but I'll be sure to check in to make sure they understand these words.

Pausing to work on prosody helps them to keep meaning-making front and center.

Take It to Your Classroom

√ Find or write your scripts: Decide if you want to use preexisting scripts (probably a good idea for the first few times), create your own, or ask students to create them. Once you have the script(s), split the class into groups and help them choose parts (you might want to assign roles at the beginning).

√ Think about which students might need additional support and work with them in preparation and/or send scripts home to give them extra practice time.

√ Establish classroom expectations for volume during practice time and determine where in the classroom students will be practicing with their groups. Let them know you'll be moving around the room to coach them with strategies as they practice.

√ After students have had a chance to practice (five or so read-throughs), set up a no-frills, low-stakes performance. When students know they will be sharing their work, they are often motivated to practice with more purpose and focus.

√ Consider your students' performances. What additional supports might they need from you the next time they engage in reader's theater? Perhaps a shared reading of the text before splitting up the roles? Discussing text or word meanings before practicing fluency? Additional coaching or support during the days of practice?

Reader's theater is both collaborative and interactive and allows students to assume different character roles, practice expressive reading and voice inflections, and use gestures and facial expressions to bring a text to life.

Conversation Lessons

11

Picture It: Fifth Graders Take Part in a Book Club

Fifth graders in Mr. Wright's class are engaged in a science unit studying different organs and systems of the human body. In addition to the textbook reading everyone has done, they have each chosen a system they want to learn about in more depth and have read an informational trade book to begin their research. Today, they'll meet in book clubs to share information, teach each other about what they've learned, and, as Mr. Wright observes, one club even decides to engage in a debate.

> Across the day, in any content area and whenever students are talking, you can listen in, assess what you see and hear, and offer teaching that is directly responsive to their needs.

"Let's talk about what part of the human body is the most important. I'll start. I think it's what I read about—the brain and nervous system," Jasmine starts.

"Well yeah, the brain is important, but without muscles, you couldn't stand or walk or play or run or do sports or anything like that," Mitchell adds.

"But the brain communicates with muscles, too. So even working muscles would be no good without the brain," Jasmine retorts.

Madison makes a case for the skeletal system—she argues that without bones, you'd be a flat pancake. Sophie says the digestive system is critical because that's how the body gets nutrients to make all the other systems work. Of course, all the children are correct— every system of the human body is essential, Mr. Wright thinks as he listens in on their conversation with a smile, impressed by the clever way they chose to share the information from their books. But he also notices they aren't referencing *specific* information from the books as they make their points, and he notes this on his planning template.

> You have to watch and listen with content and strategies in mind, then respond with teaching that will raise the level of what students are doing.

He interjects, "Readers, I am enjoying listening to your ideas about each of the body's systems we've been learning about. I want to give you a tip to help you with your discussion today. When you're debating, it's important to be *precise*. That means, it's important to have specific facts, examples, and information to back up your arguments. Now I know you've read your books carefully and likely have parts and pages flagged—go ahead and open up to one section and find some specific, precise information that would really *bolster*, or support, your argument. Whoever speaks next can share their idea and then add, 'For example, . . .' or 'in my book, it says . . .' to offer some specifics for your group to consider."

> **Decide on one thing to teach, and then stay focused on that one strategy.**

> **Sentence frames can offer helpful scaffolds as students try new strategies.**

Jasmine's face lights up after hearing his suggestion and she quickly turns to a page in her book about the human brain. She shares, "The brain controls the muscles. For example, it says in my book that motor neurons release a chemical that's picked up by a muscle fiber. That tells the muscle to contract, which makes the muscles move. So, as you can see, the muscles are really nothing without the brain."

Mr. Wright offers some feedback, "That's specific all right. So, the rest of you—evaluate what Jasmine has offered. Do you have a *rebuttal*—something to say back? Remember to offer specific details from the text to support your idea."

> **Precise, specific feedback is most powerful. Sometimes students will "get it" right away, as Jasmine does here, and you can provide positive, reinforcing feedback. Other times, you'll need to offer more support: correcting, redirecting, and prompting students.**

"Well, in my book, it shows a picture of a guy at the Olympics lifting weights, so without muscles you can't lift weights," Mitchell says.

Jasmine responds, "Yes, but what I'm saying is that the weightlifter is also using his brain to lift those weights. That's an example of voluntary muscle control and that starts with the brain!"

> **Take every opportunity to weave sophisticated vocabulary like *bolster* or *rebuttal* into your conversations with students.**

The students continue discussing the human body's systems, and Mr. Wright stays nearby for another couple of minutes, occasionally interjecting to praise their specificity or to remind them to refer to the text details to support their arguments. They are still deep in discussion when Mr. Wright moves away from their group. He leaves them with a reminder of what they practiced: "Your conversation is getting so much richer because it's more specific. Remember to back up those great ideas with details from the text any time you're really trying to prove your point!" He then moves on to coach another group at a nearby table.

> **As you coach, stay focused on the one thing you decided to teach. Don't be distracted by other needs you may see students have, though you may jot down thoughts in your notes as ideas for follow-up in subsequent lessons.**

Conversation Lessons: A Planning Template

Literacy Goals:

- Compare and contrast
- Support ideas with evidence

Knowledge/ Vocabulary Goals:

- Systems of the human body
- Use vocab from texts in their conversations

Teacher Materials:

- Note-taking forms

Student Materials:

- Book club book (assorted books on human body systems)

Establish a Focus or (Listen and Observe) (1–2 minutes):

- Debating
- Talking well across topics
- Precise info needed

Teach and Coach (2–3 minutes):

- Use specific facts, examples, and information to back up your arguments

Clarify the Takeaways (1 minute):

- Convo got richer b/c of detailed support for arguments!

An Overview: Conversation Lessons

During English language arts and content studies, students can and should engage in conversations about texts they have read independently, texts you have read aloud to them, and/or texts you have read together during shared- or close-reading lessons. The quantity and quality of discourse in the classroom has shown to be correlated to student achievement levels, suggesting that conversation can be a powerful tool for learning (Sedova et al., 2019).

But it's not enough to simply make time for conversation. Students will need you to teach them how to have better conversations. While students will likely talk to each other during most lessons explored in this book (read aloud, shared reading, close reading, and so on) with a turn and talk for brief discussions, the lessons in this chapter are about partner, group, and whole-class extended discussions with intentional instruction. Depending on students' experience with and skills related to conversation, you may find that your conversation lessons begin with some up-front teaching you've planned to get students started. You might offer them a model of a recorded conversation, explicitly teach a strategy for a conversation skill, or explain some of what you know they'll need to keep in mind as they talk.

With practice, students will be able to carry on conversations with increased independence, and more of your teaching will be in response to what you observe students do as they talk. In a conversation lesson, you will actively listen, observe, and offer feedback and support to students through coaching. Responsivity (Hardman, 2019) or "spontaneous scaffolding" (Applebee et al., 2003) during discussion has been shown to increase reciprocity, engagement, and learning outcomes.

What Research Says
About Teaching Conversation Skills

When you work to develop speaking and listening skills across all subject areas, you help students to do the following:

→ Articulate their ideas clearly and with confidence as they learn from their peers (Hardman, 2019; Moses & Kelly, 2018)

→ Develop greater self-efficacy about their reading (Venegas, 2018)

→ Be more social and engaged in their reading (Hardman, 2019; Jones, 2020; Kelley & Clausen-Grace, 2010; Protacio, 2019; Sainsbury & Schagen, 2004; Webb et al., 2014) and strengthen peer relationships (Moses & Kelly, 2018; Strommen & Mates, 2004)

→ Support comprehension (Cazden, 2005; Wilkinson et al., 2015)

→ Listen actively and carefully to reply to others in meaningful, relevant ways (Sacks et al., 1978; Weger et al., 2010)

→ Improve the duration and quality of conversation by explicitly teaching the use of sentence stems (Paxton-Buursma & Walker, 2008; Windschitl et al., 2012)

→ Ask high-quality questions during a conversation (Mariage et al., 2020; Scardamalia & Bereiter, 1992)

→ Develop language and vocabulary through elaborating, extending, challenging, and connecting ideas. This is helpful for all students, but especially for those learning a new language (Zwiers & Crawford, 2009).

→ Learn to pick up on social cues to take turns and balance conversation (Clarke & Holwadel, 2007; Ford & Thompson, 1996; Wennerstrom & Siegel, 2003)

→ Navigate disagreement and explore different perspectives and relevant evidence through "constructive controversy," leading to new ideas and understandings (Kamil et al., 2008)

→ Improve cognitive reasoning through debate (Johnson & Johnson, 2015)

→ Develop linguistic and cognitive skills (de Sousa, 2017)

Knowledge and Vocabulary Building
Within Conversation Lessons

☼ Encourage a "questions and clarifications" routine where students can ask each other for help to understand key terms or concepts from the text before they begin talking about their ideas from the text.

☼ Students' vocabulary grows not only when they understand the words they read but also when they use those words to express ideas. Encourage students to incorporate specific words from the text into their conversation and to use the same words the author used to talk about the topic, especially with content area reading in science or social studies.

☼ Conversation can be a great tool for building background knowledge. If you believe some or all students have experiences connected to a topic, consider having them talk about their experiences and look for both commonalities and differences. Then coach them to bring that prior knowledge back to their reading and see how it adds to, confirms, or is rejected by the text.

☼ Direct students to pay attention to the author's craft and discuss the language the author uses (specific words and/or figurative language) to help them arrive at their ideas about a text. This can help them go beyond the literal to think about connotative meanings or how words can have multiple meanings that can change based on context.

Planning: Conversation Lessons

Because you will plan for students to talk as part of almost every lesson you teach, you will often listen and coach into brief conversation—especially when students are in partnerships—in the midst of other lessons. In those cases, the conversations will be about the learning objectives you've planned and the texts you've selected for the lesson. You likely won't plan what you'll say to students during quick turn-and-talk conversations; instead, your teaching will be in response to what you see and hear. Still, the teacher and student moves you learn about in this chapter can guide you as you listen to students and coach them during these moments.

In contrast, you will often plan for students to engage in extended conversations, where the deepened insight and understanding that comes from conversation—and the more advanced conversational skills—are the point. These conversations will frequently follow other lessons. For example, after a close-reading lesson (see Chapter 8) where students explore a portion of a shared textbook, you might ask them to meet in small groups to discuss questions and ideas or, after a read-aloud lesson (see Chapter 3) where you asked students to stop and jot their thinking, you might follow up with a 15-minute whole-class conversation (sitting in a big circle) about the text and the thinking students noted as they read. You also might plan time for students to talk about texts they have read independently, such as a book club that read four chapters at home and is ready to discuss the chapters together. Extended conversation takes time, of course, so you'll need to plan intentionally for it to happen—the text(s) students will be talking about, how they'll be grouped, and the sorts of skills and strategies you might offer to support their conversation.

Texts

Students will most often be talking about the same text(s)—a set of poems, a chapter in a science textbook, a novel or a group of chapters in a novel—though it's possible to have productive conversations across texts that have some common thread, such as books in the same series or books that are conceptually related. Texts that lend themselves to strong conversation are ones that allow students to go beyond the literal details of the text and to explore ideas and their own thinking. This means that in the primary grades, the texts about which students have longer discussions will most likely be the more rich and complex texts you read to them. (You won't get very far with a conversation about a decodable book used in a kindergarten phonics lesson such as, "I am Sam. This is a hat. I can get it.") In upper elementary and middle school, you may find students can have meaningful extended conversations about shared class texts and may also be ready for book clubs where they read the texts on their own, then come together to talk.

Grouping

One important planning decision you will need to make is how to group students for the types of conversations you'd like them to have—will they discuss as a whole class, in partnerships, or small groups?

Whole-Class Conversations

In a whole-class conversation, also known as a *grand conversation* (Eeds & Peterson, 1991; Eeds & Wells, 1989), the entire class community engages in a discussion, and the approach has been shown to be highly effective at promoting literal and inferential comprehension, critical thinking, reasoning, and argumentation (Murphy et al., 2009). Most often, students will discuss a text you've read aloud, though you might engage students in a discussion of a core text that everyone has read independently, such as a novel or a science or social studies textbook chapter. With so many students participating, the responsibility for generating questions and ideas is shared by more students, creating a safe space for everyone to learn about and engage in productive conversation.

In whole-class conversations, you can teach students the skills and strategies they need to have successful, more independent conversations in partnerships or clubs. And since you are there to listen and coach for the entire conversation as it unfolds, you'll help students orchestrate conversation and comprehension skills using a variety of strategies (rather than focusing on a single strategy, as you do when you coach small groups or pairs).

Partnerships

When students discuss texts in pairs, they learn to listen, take turns, and share their thinking. You might start them out with turn-and-talk partnerships during whole-class focus or read-aloud lessons. In these partnerships, students turn and briefly discuss something (1–2 minutes), often based on a direct prompt—"Turn and share your thinking about how the character is changing with your partner"—but sometimes with a more open-ended one—"What's on your mind? Turn and tell your partner." As students discuss, you can listen in to one or two of the partnerships and either coach them directly or use what you observe to offer a suggestion to the whole class—or both! To help manage turn-and-talk partnerships, consider seating students with their partners in the same spots each time you gather for a whole-class lesson so they develop a relationship over time and learn each other's conversational style. You might also find that assigning each a name such as Partner A and Partner B allows you to better direct them and ensure more even, equal participation ("Partner A, tell Partner B . . ." or "Partner B, you're going to go first this time").

Beyond the quick turn-and-talk partnerships, you might establish partnerships that meet for a more extended discussion time. In elementary classrooms, partners might meet several times a week (~10 minutes each time) to share ideas about what they've read and to talk to deepen each other's thinking. For example, students might read a chapter in a social studies textbook on their own, then come together in a partnership to share questions, practice summarizing, or compare and contrast concepts within the chapter. Partners might each read a book in an early chapter book series and then come together to compare and contrast how the character dealt with the problem in each story. In partnerships like these, students can get more practice with the speaking and listening skills you've taught them during whole-class conversations and also get ready for discussions in larger clubs.

Small Groups or Clubs

For more extended conversation, consider grouping three to six students into a club, sometimes called *book clubs*, *literature circles*, or *discussion groups* (Daniels, 1994; Raphael & McMahon 1994; Short & Pierce, 1990). Clubs can meet to discuss a text you've read to them (sometimes called *read-aloud clubs*), or they can prepare notes with thoughts and questions to discuss texts they've read independently. Because the group engaged in conversation is larger, clubs are a next step from discussion partnerships and students will likely need coaching to support a good balance of participation, invite quieter voices, and keep the conversation on topic.

Skills and Strategies

Your conversation lessons need to support both students' conversation skills (speaking and listening skills) as well as their comprehension skills (so they have better things to talk about) with strategies and feedback as they practice (Zwiers, 2019; Zwiers & Crawford, 2011). In one large study, researchers observed classroom talk and considered how it related to the academic rigor of reading comprehension lessons. One finding was that the quality of student responses during conversation depended on the ideas and questions that began the conversation, showing that taking time to plan and prepare for conversation can yield higher-quality talk (Wolf et al., 2005). That said, there's also a reciprocal relationship between comprehension and conversation—readers need to come prepared with thoughts and ideas in order to have a good conversation and through conversation, they can deepen comprehension as they learn from peers (McKeown & Beck, 2015; see Table 11.1).

Table 11.1   The Reciprocal Relationship Between Comprehension and Conversation Skills

Conversations Are Stronger When Comprehension Is Strong.	Comprehension Can Develop Through Conversation.
▶ Good conversation is often about ideas—original thoughts, inferences, and interpretations. If students discuss only literal understandings, it may make conversational stamina difficult. ▶ Ideally, having already read and understood the text, students come ready to talk and are looking to explore ideas and deepen thinking.	▶ Skilled comprehenders ask questions of the author, the text, and their own responses as they read. Conversation can be a place to explore how others might answer those questions. ▶ In conversation, students benefit from hearing new perspectives and ideas and can practice considering these new ideas to possibly revise their own.

Help students set goals for inferential comprehension of plot, characters, and theme (in narrative texts); understanding main ideas, key details, and text features (in expository texts); and vocabulary and figurative language (in all texts). Then, using other lesson types, offer students comprehension strategies before, after, and even during their conversation groups, where you'll listen and coach as needed. As you listen to students during conversation lessons, you can also teach strategies for deepening their conversation so they have better ideas to talk about.

Students will also need to be prepared for conversations. Teach students how to annotate and take notes, perhaps beginning with modeling these skills during read-aloud lessons, shared-reading lessons, or close-reading lessons, and then reteach strategies during focus lessons before asking them to take notes independently. Encourage students to come prepared with written thoughts, questions, conclusions, or key information they'd like to discuss or with parts of their texts underlined, highlighted, or flagged. When they're engaged in conversation, listen and coach students to show them how to use their notes to support an engaging discussion.

Figure 11.1   Conversation Playing Board

One helpful strategy to get students started with accountable talk is to introduce the conversation playing board (Serravallo, 2023b). Students take notes as they read and bring the notes to the conversation, placing them on the outside squares. The group decides who will talk first, and they place a sticky note in the center. When in the center, that is the topic under discussion. When they are out of things to say about the sticky note in the center, they move a new one into the center. This serves as a concrete scaffold to focus conversation and support turn-taking.

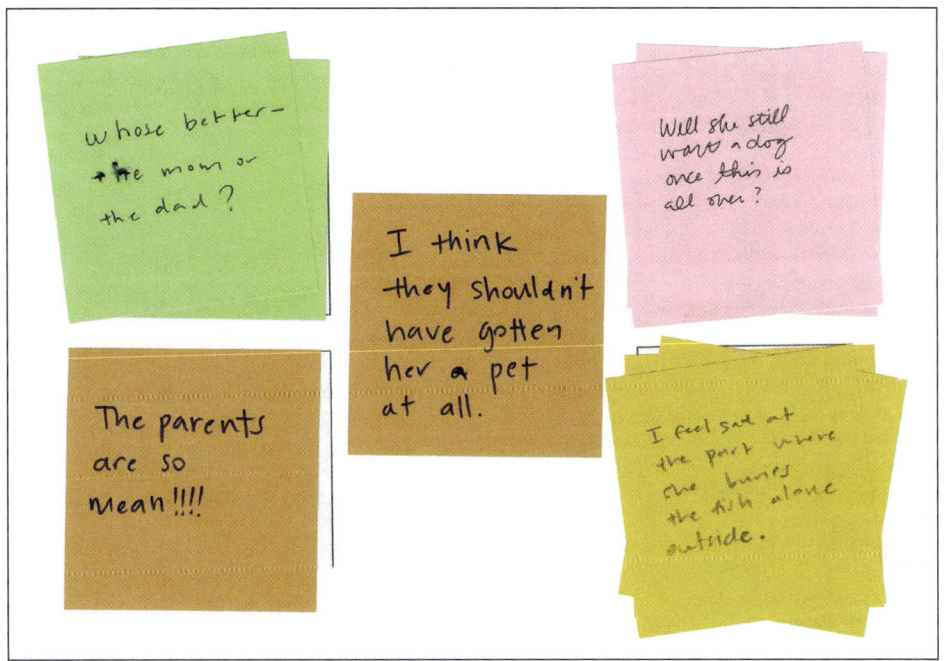

Structure and Timing: Conversation Lessons

In an extensive literature review about small-group conversation, Webb (2009) found that structuring interactions and offering specific activities for students to do during discussions improved group collaboration, task performance, and, often, academic achievement. Therefore, whether they meet in partnerships, groups, or as a whole class, students will likely benefit from a consistent structure and set of routines. If conversations are a new routine or if you know students will need extra support to get started, you might establish a focus and offer them a strategy before they begin a conversation. Alternatively, you might simply direct students to sit in a circle or disperse in partnerships or groups around the room and start talking. Then as you listen, you can interrupt to coach by offering a strategy to improve their conversation, followed by feedback and support as they practice. Before you move away, help students reflect and/or repeat what you worked on together.

Conversation lessons go like this:

1. Establish a Focus or Listen and Observe
(1–2 minutes)*

When the routines of conversation are new or past experience has shown that students need a lot of support, you'll begin by establishing a focus. You might get students started by teaching a strategy and/or articulating a plan for their talk time. In most cases, however, you'll start by listening and observing as students take the first few turns in their discussion. Position yourself on the periphery and encourage them to talk to each other, not to you. Listen for strengths and needs in both comprehension and conversation skills.

2. Teach and Coach
(2–3 minutes)*

Name something the students are doing well and offer a strategy to lift the level of their conversation. This might be a strategy to support their speaking and listening or, if their conversation seems to be stalled because they need something better to talk about, you might teach a comprehension strategy to get them thinking about the text. Continue observing students as they attempt to apply the strategy you taught them, making sure they talk to each other rather than directing comments to you. Interrupt to offer reminders, redirections, corrections, prompts, sentence starters, and compliments to the group (or you can whisper into an individual student's ear as the conversation continues).

3. Clarify the Takeaways
(1 minute)

After a bit of coaching, remind students what they learned with you today. You can also ask them to reflect on how their conversation has gone so far and discuss what goals they have for moving forward. Students may continue their discussion as you move on to listen and coach another group or partnership.

*In whole-class conversations, which last 10 minutes or more, you might repeat the Listen and Observe–Teach and Coach cycle multiple times, offering support with more than one strategy.

Responsive Teaching: Conversation Lessons

While you might plan to teach a strategy to set children up to have a good conversation (likely based on something you noticed they needed during their last conversation or because you want to introduce a new routine), once they start talking, you'll choose your teaching based on what you see, listening for both the conversation and comprehension skills students need to support them. It can be helpful to have a progression of skills in mind as you listen to students talk (to help you think about where to take them next). For example, you might first look to see if students are listening actively, staying on topic, and taking turns; then, if they have ideas worth talking about and if they can elaborate on their ideas and those of others; then if they are asking questions; and then if they are ready for more sophisticated conversations such as debates (Serravallo, 2023b; see Table 11.2).

Table 11.2   Example Language Frames, Responses, and Prompts to Teach Responsively During Conversation Lessons

If You Hear or Observe . . .	Then You Might Say . . .
Students are taking turns sharing different ideas, as if they are not yet listening to each other.	▶ Let's make a decision about what conversation topic to focus on. I'm hearing several options, and we'll want to choose one and try to deepen our thinking.
Students are talking mostly about literal information from the text.	▶ I notice you are sharing what you remember from the text. That can be helpful to clarify the literal information. When you feel clear about what you read, please move on to your *ideas* about what you read. ▶ You're mostly talking about literal information in the text. I'm going to teach you a strategy to help you get ideas about the topic . . .
Students are focused on one topic, deepening their ideas, and offering differing perspectives.	▶ Your conversation is rich! When you each come with your own perspectives but really listen to each other, you'll often find you come to new thinking and maybe even have your mind changed! ▶ Can anyone share something new you're thinking, based on the conversation?
Students are sharing their own ideas but aren't yet inviting others to speak.	▶ You all have been really clear on what your ideas are and what you think. I wonder if you have any questions about what one of your friends has said?
Students are speaking with vague language or misusing key terms from their reading selection.	▶ Let's spend a little time making sure we understand some key vocabulary from this text. Let's identify the words we'll need to use to talk knowledgably about this topic, and we can do a little rereading to get clear.

Lesson in Action: Whole-Class Conversation Lesson, Sixth Grade, English Language Arts

This class had been studying Sandra Cisneros's "Eleven" and were moving into a poetry study, so I found a poem with similar themes and ideas ("On Turning Ten" by Billy Collins) so they could talk across texts. Prior to this conversation, four of the students also participated in a small group with me (see Chapter 9, Video 9.3) to study the author's craft in "Eleven"—work I hoped would lead to some deeper ideas they could bring to this group. I visited their class at the start of the school year, so the routine of a whole-class conversation was new. Therefore, I positioned myself as part of the circle and was prepared to do a good deal of coaching. Prior to the conversation, I asked the students to read the poem, reread the short story, and jot down ideas they wanted to talk about.

Notice I used the planning template as both a place to record plans before the lesson as well as a note-taking form to jot observations and record the teaching that happened in response to those observations.

Read the lesson plan on the opposite page or online, watch the video (access it using the QR code), then come back to read the post-lesson reflection comments annotating the lesson plan.

Video 11.1   Whole-Class Conversation Lesson, Sixth Grade, English Language Arts

online resources

Download the lesson plan or a blank template on the companion website https://companion .corwin.com/ courses/2024_TRAD

Scan the code or go to https:// qrs.ly/gvfg1s8 to watch the video

Conversation Lessons: A Planning Template

Literacy Goals:
- Compare and contrast themes and ideas
- Use details from the text to support answers
- Build on ideas from others

Knowledge/ Vocabulary Goals:
- N/A

Teacher Materials:
- Note-taking form

Student Materials:
- "Eleven" (Cisneros, 1991) and "On Turning Ten" (Collins, 1995)

(Establish a Focus) or Listen and Observe (1–2 minutes):
- Plant the idea that the two texts have some things in common
- Introduce the procedure—anyone with an idea worth talking about can talk, don't look to me to call on you
- A couple students doing most of the talking

Teach and Coach (2–3 minutes):
- Ask questions to invite quieter voices
- Look for opportunities to support conversation and/or comprehension skills.
- Put students into turn-and-talk pairs if there is a lull or there are dominant voices.

Clarify the Takeaways (1 minute):
Important to ask questions. Come prepared for the next conversation not only with ideas but also with questions. Keep an eye on balancing the conversation and inviting quieter voices.

I chose to teach this based on my observation to help them invite in quieter voices and to try to help them outgrow their first ideas, allowing new thoughts to emerge through the discussion.

Notice that the student to my right brought up something he remembered from a prior close-reading lesson about a different poem (Video 8.2)! I loved the transfer.

I chose to do this fairly early—within the first three minutes of the conversation. Partner talk sometimes helps shyer students rehearse what they want to say and feel more confident to share and gives me an opportunity to coach some students who may need support.

When I called them back together, I provided a lot of support with what to do with a question—share, think, respond, or ask another question.

I'll remind them of these points before we start the next whole-class conversation.

Eight minutes into the conversation, a few students were still doing the majority of the talking, so I decided to ask them to turn and talk again as I moved to coach a partnership that hadn't yet shared.

Lesson in Action: Partnership Conversation Lesson, Second Grade, English Language Arts

In a second-grade classroom, the teacher was starting partner conversations to support her students' comprehension and engagement with series books. Providing support and feedback to each pair during their first conversation helps establish expectations and sets them up with strategies to be more independent. While this conversation was taking place, the other students in the class were reading on their own, getting ready to meet with their partners. Once students demonstrate that they can hold a productive conversation without support, there can be a routine "partner time" when everyone in the class is engaged in discussion as the teacher meets with a few partnerships to provide strategies, feedback, and support.

Notice I used the planning template as a note-taking form to save a record of my teaching.

Read the lesson plan on the opposite page or online, watch the video (access it using the QR code), then come back to read the post-lesson reflection comments annotating the lesson plan.

Download the lesson plan or a blank template on the companion website https://companion .corwin.com/ courses/2024_TRAD

Video 11.2   Partnership Conversation Lesson, Second Grade, English Language Arts

Scan the code or go to https://qrs .ly/i2fg1s9 to watch the video.

I began by naming what students were already doing, and connected their next move to an existing strength using the phrase, "I noticed you . . . and now, to have a strong conversation, we need to . . ."

After telling them what I wanted them to try, I gave them a moment to think about it and get ready.

After the first student spoke, I waited to see what would happen next. Would they need me to coach them to keep it going, or would they naturally take turns?

Conversation Lessons: A Planning Template

Literacy Goals:
- Determined in response to student needs

Establish a Focus or (Listen and Observe) (1–2 minutes):

"The main thing that happened → Summary"

Knowledge/ Vocabulary Goals:
- N/A

Teach and Coach (2–3 minutes):

What happened → Idea about what happened

Needed support to practice strategy

Needed redirection to talk to each other.

Teacher Materials:
- Note-taking form

Student Materials:
- Series books

Clarify the Takeaways (1 minute):

Write down ideas to bring to conversation

I jumped in with a coaching prompt: "After someone shares an idea . . ."

For a while, they did a great job of talking to each other and not to me. However, the more I coached with prompts—"Because . . . ?"—the more they started to address their comments to me.

I left them with some work to do as they continued to read their books and prepare for their next conversation.

Lesson in Action: Small-Group Book Club Conversation Lesson, Fifth Grade, Science

After reading a book aloud to the whole class, I divided the students into groups of four to have a quick conversation. Small-group discussions after a read aloud are a great way to get students ready for more traditional book clubs, where they'll need to read and prepare discussion topics with more independence. Also, they give all students an opportunity to speak up and share their thinking, and through discussion, students often come to cement their understandings and develop deeper ideas. During an interactive read aloud, I'd intentionally laid the groundwork for rich conversation by asking questions along the way to get them thinking more deeply (to see the video of that read aloud or to read more about read-aloud lessons, see Chapter 3).

Notice I used the planning template as a note-taking form to save a record of my teaching.

Read the lesson plan on the opposite page or online, watch the video (access it using the QR code), then come back to read the post-lesson reflection comments annotating the lesson plan.

Download the lesson plan or a blank template on the companion website https://companion .corwin.com/ courses/2024_TRAD

Scan the code or go to https://qrs .ly/tnfg1sa to watch the video.

Video 11.3   Small-Group Book Club Conversation Lesson, Fifth Grade, Science

The conversation was already in progress when I sat down. I stayed quiet, taking notes and observing, thinking about what I wanted to teach.

A habit of backing up ideas with text evidence will come in handy when they write about what they are learning or thinking in science or any other subject. What students learn to do in conversation can serve as helpful preparation for writing.

Conversation Lessons: A Planning Template

Literacy Goals:
- Determined after observation, but I'll be looking for evidence of comprehension, extending ideas from the read aloud, and qualities of good conversation

Knowledge/ Vocabulary Goals:
- Traits of a scientist (*persevere, curious, methodical,* etc.)
- Scientific method (ask questions, hypothesize, experiment, collect evidence, etc.)

Teacher Materials:
- Note-taking forms

Student Materials:
- N/A

Establish a Focus or (Listen and Observe (1–2 minutes):
- Conversation feels general, not specific → back up ideas with evidence

Teach and Coach (2–3 minutes):
- Redirect away from speaking to T → talk S-to-S
- Easily incorporated text evidence with ideas

Clarify the Takeaways (1 minute):
- Knowing where ideas come from makes your argument clearer to those you're in conversation with.

Notice that aside from redirecting their attention to each other, they didn't need much coaching from me. It's not always like this—sometimes students will need a lot of prompting and support with the new strategy.

After interjecting and explaining a strategy, sometimes students will start directing their attention to the teacher, as did the student on my left, who spoke first. Always direct them back to student-to-student interactions and independent conversation.

In retrospect, I wish I'd asked the students to stop and jot during the read aloud that preceded this conversation so they would have something written down to refer to during the conversation. Next time!

I decided to offer a little bit of a why in this takeaway to help them remember to do it again next time.

Take It to Your Classroom

√ If your students are new to discussions, begin with whole-class conversations so you can observe and support them, modeling and offering strategies for successful speaking and listening as needed. Use partnerships at other times of the day and intermittently during a whole-class conversation so students can practice talking in pairs.

√ Teach students how to prepare for conversation with written notes. Consider doing shared writing or modeled writing from read aloud, shared reading, or close reading as a first step (see Serravallo, 2021).

√ In any grouping, take notes as you listen. Note-taking will help you home in on what's most important in the conversation and will give you a record to return to as you reflect and make decisions about what to teach. You can use the planning templates for this if you choose.

√ Plan how you'll teach across a unit or across a week. Layer in strategies for speaking and listening all month long, and plan for opportunities for students to talk in the whole class, in small groups, and in pairs.

√ After you Listen and Observe, reflect on what additional supports students might need to have better conversations. If they need support with comprehension, consider teaching them additional strategies (outside of conversations) as extra support or starting off the next lesson with some direct teaching.

Appendix

Lesson Planning Templates

Throughout the book, you've seen planning templates filled in to accompany each Picture It lesson description and each Lesson in Action video lesson. These templates are available for you to use, either by photocopying from this appendix or downloading or printing from online if you prefer a writeable PDF format. If you choose to use them, you may find they help you to organize your thinking and make a quick record of your decisions as you plan. They also follow the structure and pacing of the lesson and can be a handy reference as you teach; you may have noticed I referred to my plans during the recorded lessons you watched. In addition to recording your plans on templates, you may also choose to use sticky notes directly on the text you'll be using as you teach for some lesson types—I do this during read-aloud and close-reading lessons almost every time. I find that notes on the text help me remember to stop where I'd planned to highlight vocabulary, model my thinking, or prompt for student engagement.

Over time, as the different lesson types become very familiar, you should find that you need to include less and less written detail, though you will continue to think through each of these planning decisions every time you teach a lesson.

In cases where you need to submit lesson plans to an administrator, you'll need to consider their expectations and guidelines in terms of the amount of detail and formatting required, of course. In these cases, it may help to ask yourself, "What does someone who will not be teaching or observing the lesson need to know about my plans?" The answer to this question may be different from what you need to write down in order to teach it well.

Download these lesson plan templates in editable PDF format at https://companion.corwin.com/courses/2024_TRAD

Note that every planning template can also be used as a note-taking form. You may already have a note-taking system you prefer, but you may like the simplicity of adding notes to your plan as you teach, since you'll have it with you during the lesson. You might have a designated space on the form to make notes of observations, ideas, student responses, and so on, but you might also add marginal notes related to specific parts of the plan, strike through things students didn't need, circle or highlight parts you want to come back to—really, anything that can inform your future teaching. And, of course, with some teaching (such as reader's theater lessons and conversation lessons), you often won't make detailed plans ahead of time because much of what you teach will be in response to seeing students in action for a bit. In these cases, you might fill out the key parts of the template both as you teach (making notes on what you observe) and after the lesson is over (noting what you taught).

Read-Aloud Lessons: A Planning Template

Literacy Goal(s):

Knowledge/ Vocabulary Goal(s):

Teacher Materials:

Student Materials:

Establish a Focus (1 minute):

Read Aloud and Engage (7–15 minutes):

Page #	What Will Students Do?	What Will You Say?

Clarify the Takeaways (1 minute):

Phonics and Spelling Lessons: A Planning Template

Goal(s):

Teacher Materials:

Student Materials:

Warm-Up and Review (2 minutes):

Introduce a New Concept (2 minutes):

Spell Words/Word Work (3 minutes):

Read Words (3 minutes):

Write Connected Text (5 minutes):

Read Connected Text (10 minutes):

Clarify the Takeaways (1 minute):

Vocabulary Lessons: A Planning Template

Goal(s):

Teacher Materials:

Student Materials:

Introduce and Explain (2 minutes):

Focus Word:

Initial Context:

Examples/Non-examples:

Synonyms/Antonyms:

Part of Speech:

Visual:

Other:

Apply (3 minutes):

Choose:

Yes/No/Why Questions:

Word in Context:

Sentence Completion:

Synonyms/Antonyms:

Other:

Extend (5 minutes):

Circle One:

word sums

word matrix

word web

concept map

Clarify the Takeaways (1 minute):

Focus Lessons: A Planning Template

Literacy Goal(s):

Knowledge/ Vocabulary Goal(s):

Teacher Materials:

Student Materials:

Establish a Focus (30 seconds):

Teach (1–4 minutes):
Strategy:

Coach (2–5 minutes):

Clarify the Takeaways (1 minute):

Shared-Reading Lessons: A Planning Template

Literacy Goal(s):

Knowledge/ Vocabulary Goal(s):

Teacher Materials:

Student Materials:

Establish a Focus (1 minute):

Warm-Up (3 minutes):

What Will Students Do?	What Will You Say?

Read and Teach (5–10 minutes):

Which Pages or Lines?	What Will Students Do?	What Will You Say?

Clarify the Takeaways (1 minute):

Close-Reading Lessons: A Planning Template

Literacy Goal(s):

Knowledge/ Vocabulary Goal(s):

Teacher Materials:

Student Materials:

Establish a Focus (1 minute):

Read and Teach (8–13 minutes):

Which Pages or Lines?	What Will Students Do?	What Will You Say?

Clarify the Takeaways (1 minute):

Guided Inquiry Lessons: A Planning Template

Literacy Goal(s):

Knowledge/ Vocabulary Goal(s):

Teacher Materials:

Student Materials:

Establish a Focus (1 minute):

Guide and Inquire (3–8 minutes):

Clarify the Takeaways (1 minute):

Reader's Theater: A Planning Template

Literacy Goal(s):

Knowledge/Vocabulary Goal(s):

Teacher Materials:

Student Materials:

Establish a Focus or Listen and Observe (1 minute):

Teach and Coach (2–3 minutes):

Clarify the Takeaways (1 minute):

Conversation Lessons: A Planning Template

Literacy Goal(s):

Establish a Focus or Listen and Observe (1–2 minutes)*:

**Knowledge/
Vocabulary Goal(s):**

Teach and Coach (2–3 minutes)*:

Teacher Materials:

Clarify the Takeaways (1 minute):

Student Materials:

In whole-class conversations, which last 10 minutes or more, you might repeat the Listen and Observe–Teach and Coach cycle multiple times, offering support with more than one strategy.

References

Adams, M. J. (1990). *Beginning to read: Thinking and learning about print.* Massachusetts Institute of Technology.

Alexander, A. W., Anderson, H. G., & Heilman, P. C. (1991). Phonological awareness training and remediation of analytic decoding deficits in a group of severe dyslexics. *Annals of Dyslexia, 41*, 193–206.

Amendum, S. J., Li, Y., & Creamer, K. H. (2009). Reading lesson instruction characteristics. *Reading Psychology, 30*(1), 119–143.

Amendum, S. J., Li, Y., Hall, L. A., Fitzgerald, J., Creamer, K. H., Head-Reeves, D. M., & Hollingsworth, H. L. (2009). Which reading lesson instruction characteristics matter for early reading achievement? *Reading Psychology, 30*(2), 119–147.

Anderson, L. M., Carolyn, M. E., & Jere, E. B. (1979). An experimental study of effective teaching in first-grade reading groups. *The Elementary School Journal, 79*(4), 193–223.

Anderson, R. C., & Nagy, W. E. (1992). The vocabulary conundrum. *American Educator: The Professional Journal of the American Federation of Teachers, 16*(4).

Anderson, T. H., & Armbruster, B. B. (1980). Studying. *Center for the Study of Reading Technical Report*, 155.

Angelou, M. (2015). Still I rise. *The complete collected poems of Maya Angelou.* Random House.

Applebee, A. N., Langer, J. A., Nystrand, M., & Gamoran, A. (2003). Discussion-based approaches to developing understanding: Classroom instruction and student performance in middle and high school English. *American Educational Research Journal, 40*(3), 685–730.

Appleton-Smith, L. (2011). *Dot and Dan.* Flyleaf. Available at https://portal.flyleafpublishing.com/wp-content/uploads/books/9-Dot-and-Dan/mobile/index.html#p=1

Appleton-Smith, L. (2011). *Pam likes to nap.* Flyleaf. Available at https://portal.flyleafpublishing.com/wp-content/uploads/books/6-Pam-Likes-to-Nap/mobile/index.html#p=18

Archer, A. L., & Hughes, C. A. (2011). Explicit instruction: Effective and efficient teaching (what works for special-needs learners). *Journal of Special Education, 36*(4), 186–205.

Ardoin, S. P., Morena, L. S., Binder, K. S., & Foster, T. E. (2013). Examining the impact of feedback and repeated readings on oral reading fluency: Let's not forget prosody. *School Psychology Quarterly, 28*(4), 391–404.

Armbruster, B., Lehr, F., & Osborn, J. (2001). *Put reading first: The research building blocks for teaching children to read.* Education Publishing Centre.

August, D., Artzi, L., Barr, C., & Francis, D. (2018). The moderating influence of instructional intensity and word type on the acquisition of academic vocabulary in young English language learners. *Reading and Writing, 31*, 965–989.

Baker, D. L., Santoro, L., Biancarosa, G., Baker, S. K., Fien, H., & Otterstedt, J. (2020). Effects of a read aloud intervention on first grade student vocabulary, listening comprehension, and language proficiency. *Reading and Writing, 33,* 2697–2724.

Bandura, A., & Cervone, D. (1983). Self-evaluative and self-efficacy mechanisms governing the motivational effects of goal systems. *Journal of Personality and Social Psychology, 45*(5), 1017–1028.

Barnes, D. (2017). *Crown: An ode to the fresh cut.* Agate Bolden.

Barnes, D. (2020). *I am every good thing.* Nancy Paulsen Books.

Barnett, M. (2017). *Noisy night.* Roaring Brook Press.

Barrentine, S. J. (1996). Engaging with reading through interactive read-alouds. *The Reading Teacher, 50*(1), 36–43.

Barron, B. J., Schwartz, D. L., Vye, N. J., Moore, A., Petrosino, A., Zech, L., & Bransford, J. D. (1998). Doing with understanding: Lessons from research on problem-and project-based learning. *Journal of the Learning Sciences, 7*(3–4), 271–311.

Barton, D., Hamilton, M., & Ivanic, R. (2000). *Situated literacies: Theorising reading and writing in context.* Routledge.

Baumann, J. F., Edwards, E. C., Font, G., Tereshinski, C. A., Kame'enui, E. J., & Olejnki, S. (2002). Teaching morphemic and contextual analysis to fifth-grade students. *Reading Research Quarterly, 37*(2), 150–176.

Baumann, J. F., Kame'enui, E. J., & Ash, G. E. (2003). Research on vocabulary instruction: Voltaire redux. In J. Flood, D. Lapp, J. R. Squire, & J. M. Jensen (Eds.), *Handbook of research on teaching the English language arts* (2nd ed., pp. 752–785). Lawrence Erlbaum.

Beard, R. (1991). Learning to read like a writer. *Educational Review, 43*(1), 17–24.

Beck, I. L., & Beck, M. E. (2013). *Making sense of phonics: The hows and whys.* Guilford Publications.

Beck, I. L., & McKeown, M. G. (1991). Conditions of vocabulary acquisition. In R. Barr, M. L. Kamil, P. B. Mosenthal, & P. D. Pearson (Eds.), *Handbook of reading research* (Vol. 2, pp. 789–814). Lawrence Erlbaum.

Beck, I. L., & McKeown, M. G. (2007). Increasing young low-income children's oral vocabulary repertoires through rich and focused instruction. *The Elementary School Journal, 107,* 251–271.

Beck, I. L, McKeown, M. G., & Kucan, L. (1987). *Bringing words to life: Robust vocabulary instruction* (1st ed.). Guilford Publications.

Beck, I. L., McKeown, M. G., & Kucan, L. (2013). *Bringing words to life: Robust vocabulary instruction* (2nd ed.). Guilford Press.

Beck, I. L., McKeown, M. G., & Omanson, R. C. (1987). The effects and uses of diverse vocabulary instructional techniques. In M. G. McKeown & M. E. Curtis (Eds.), *The nature of vocabulary acquisition* (pp. 147–163). Lawrence Erlbaum Associates.

Beck, I. L., McKeown, M. G., & Sandora, C. A. (2020). *Robust comprehension instruction with questioning the author: 15 years smarter.* Guildford Press.

Beck, I. L., Perfetti, C. A., & McKeown, M. G. (1982). Effects of long-term vocabulary instruction on lexical access and reading comprehension. *Journal of Educational Psychology, 74*(4), 506–521.

Begeny, J. C., Krouse, H. E., Ross, S. G., & Mitchell, R. C. (2009). Increasing elementary-aged students' reading fluency with small-group interventions: A comparison of repeated reading, listening passage preview, and listening only strategies. *Journal of Behavioral Education, 18*(3), 211–228.

Begeny, J. C., Levy, R. A., & Field, S. A. (2018). Using small-group instruction to improve students' reading fluency: An evaluation of the existing research. *Journal of Applied School Psychology, 34*(1), 36–64.

Benjamin, R. G., & Schwanenflugel, P. J. (2010). Test complexity and oral reading prosody in young readers. *Reading Research Quarterly, 45*(4), 388–404.

Berninger, V. W., Abbott, R. D., Abbott, S. P., Graham, S., & Richards, T. (2002). Writing and reading: Connections between language by hand and language by eye. *Journal of Learning Disabilities, 35*(1), 39–56.

Biber, D., & Conrad, S. (2019). *Register, genre, and style* (2nd ed.). Cambridge University Press.

Biemiller, A. (2001). Teaching vocabulary: Early, direct, and sequential. *American Educator, 25.*

Bishop, R. S. (1990). Mirrors, windows, and sliding glass doors. *Perspectives: Choosing and Using Books for the Classroom, 6*(3), ix–xi.

Blevins, W. (2016). *A fresh look at phonics, Grades K–2: Common causes of failure and 7 ingredients for success.* Corwin.

Bowers, P. N., Kirby, J. R., & Deacon, S. H. (2010). The effects of morphological instruction on literacy skills: A systematic review of the literature. *Review of Educational Research, 80*, 144–179.

Boyer, N., & Ehri, L. C. (2011). Contribution of phonemic segmentation instruction with letters and articulation pictures to word reading and spelling in beginners. *Scientific Studies of Reading, 15*(5), 440–470.

Boyles, N., & Scherer, M. (2012). Closing in on close reading. *On developing readers: Readings from educational leadership (EL essentials)* (pp. 89–99). ASCD.

Bråten, I., & Samuelstuen, M. S. (2004). Does the influence of reading purpose on reports of strategic text processing depend on students' topic knowledge? *Journal of Educational Psychology, 96*(2), 324–336.

Braunger, J., & Lewis, J. P. (1997). *Building a knowledge base in reading.* International Reading Association and the National Council for Teachers of English.

Brooks, G. E. (2006). Cynthia in the snow. *Selected poems.* Harper Perennial.

Bryant, D. P., Linan-Thompson, S., Ugel, N., Hamff, A., & Hougen, M. (2001). The effects of professional development for middle school general and special education teachers on implementation of reading strategies in inclusive content area classes. *Learning Disability Quarterly, 24*(4), 251–264.

Buchanan, S., Harlan, M., Bruce, C., & Edwards, S. (2016). Inquiry-based learning models, information literacy, and student engagement: A literature review. *School Libraries Worldwide, 22*(2), 23–39.

Burns, M. K., & Gibbons, K. (2008). *Implementing response-to-intervention in elementary and secondary schools: Procedures to assure scientific-based practices* (1st ed.). Routledge.

Buyea, R. (2015). *Saving Mr. Terupt.* Delacorte Press.

Carlisle, J., Kelcey, B., Berebitsky, D., & Phelps, G. (2011). Embracing the complexity of instruction: A study of the effects of teachers' instruction on students' reading comprehension. *Scientific Studies of Reading, 15*(5), 409–439.

Carlisle, N. B., Arita, J. T., Pardo, D., & Woodman, G. F. (2011). Attentional templates in visual working memory. *Journal of Neuroscience, 31*(25), 9315–9322.

Carnine, D. W. (1976). Effects of two teacher-presentation rates on off-task behavior, answering correctly, and participating. *Journal of Applied Behavior Analysis, 9*(2), 199–206.

Cartwright, K. (2023). *Executive skills and reading comprehension: A guide for educators* (2nd ed.). Guilford Press.

CAST. (n.d.). *About universal design for learning.* www.cast.org/our-work/about-udl.html#.XybYfC85Q4c.

Castiglioni-Spalten, M., & Ehri, L. (2003). Phonemic awareness instruction: Contribution of articulatory segmentation to novice beginners' reading and spelling. *Scientific Studies of Reading, 7*, 25–52.

Cazden, C. B. (2005). The value of conversations for language development and reading comprehension. *Literacy Teaching and Learning, 9*(1), 1–6.

Cervetti, G. N., & Hiebert, E. H. (2015). Knowledge, literacy, and the common core. *Language Arts, 92*(4), 256–269.

Cervetti, G. N., & Wright, T. S. (2020). The role of knowledge in understanding and learning from text. *Handbook of reading research* (Vol. 5, pp. 237–260). Routledge.

Cervetti, G. N., Wright, T. S., & Hwang, H. (2016). Conceptual coherence, comprehension, and vocabulary acquisition: A knowledge effect? *Reading and Writing, 29*(4), 761–779.

Chall, J. S. (1967). *Reading: The great debate.* McGraw-Hill.

Chan, P. E., Graham-Day, K. J., Ressa, V. A., Peters, M. T., & Konrad, M. (2014). Beyond involvement. *Intervention in School and Clinic, 50*(2), 105–113.

Chard, B-J., & Tyler, D. J. (2000). Focus on inclusion: Using readers theatre to foster fluency in struggling readers: A twist on the repeated reading strategy. *Reading & Writing Quarterly, 16*(2), 163–168.

Chard, D. J., Vaughn, S., & Tyler, B. J. (2002). A synthesis of research on effective interventions for building reading fluency with elementary students with learning disabilities. *Journal of Learning Disabilities, 35*(5), 386–406.

Cheatham, J. P., Allor, J. H., & Roberts, J. K. (2014). How does independent practice of multiple-criterion text influence the reading performance and development of second graders? *Learning Disability Quarterly, 37*(1), 3–14.

Chen, C. M., & Chen, F. Y. (2014). Enhancing digital reading performance with a collaborative reading annotation system. *Computers & Education, 77,* 67–81.

Christ, T., & Chiu, M. M. (2018). Hearing words, learning words: How different presentations of novel vocabulary words affect children's incidental learning. *Early Education and Development, 29*(6), 831–851.

Cisneros, S. (1991). Eleven. *Woman hollering creek.* Available at https://academyolmc.org/wp-content/uploads/sites/2/2020/09/eleven.sandra.cisneros.pdf

Clark, R., Morrison, T., & Wilcox, B. (2009). Readers' theater: A process of developing fourth-graders' reading fluency. *Reading Psychology, 30*(4), 359–385.

Clarke, L. W., & Holwadel, J. (2007). Help! What is wrong with these literature circles and how can we fix them? *The Reading Teacher, 61*(1), 20–29.

Coelho, E. (2012). *Language and learning in multilingual classrooms: A practical approach* (No. 16). Multilingual Matters.

Collins, B. (1995). On turning ten. *The art of drowning.* University of Pittsburgh Press. Available at https://upittpress.org/wp-content/uploads/2019/07/9780822938934exr.pdf

Collins, B. (2006). Introduction to poetry. *The apple that astonished Paris.* Available at https://www.poetryfoundation.org/poems/46712/introduction-to-poetry

Connor, C. M., Spencer, M., Day, S. L., Giuliani, S., Ingebrand, S. W., McLean, L., & Morrison, F. J. (2014). Capturing the complexity: Content, type, and amount of instruction and quality of the classroom learning environment synergistically predict third graders' vocabulary and reading comprehension outcomes. *Journal of Educational Psychology, 106*(3), 762.

Conradi Smith, K., Amendum, S. J., & Williams, T. W. (2022), Maximizing small-group reading instruction. *The Reading Teacher, 76*(3), 348–356.

Copeland, M. (2005). *Socratic circles: Fostering critical and creative thinking in middle and high school.* Stenhouse Publishers.

Corcoran, C. A., & Davis, A. (2005). A study of the effects of readers' theater on second and third grade special education students' fluency growth. *Reading Improvement, 42*(2), 105–111.

CORE Learning. (2008). *CORE's assessing reading: Multiple measures* (rev. 2nd ed.). Academic Therapy Publications. https://www.corelearn.com/store/cores-assessing-reading-multiple-measures-revised-2nd-ed/

Coxhead, A. (2000). A new academic word list. *TESOL Quarterly, 34*(2), 213–238.

Craft, J. (2019). *New kid.* Quill Tree Books.

Cromley, J. G., & Azevedo, R. (2007). Testing and refining the direct and inferential mediation model of reading comprehension. *Journal of Educational Psychology, 99*(2), 311.

Crosson, A. C., & McKeown, M. G. (2016). Middle school learners' use of Latin roots to infer the meaning of unfamiliar words. *Cognition and Instruction, 34*(2), 148–171.

Cunningham, A. E. (2006). Accounting for children's orthographic learning while reading text: Do children self-teach? *Journal of Experimental Child Psychology, 95*(1), 56–77.

Cunningham, A. E., & Stanovich, K. E. (1998). What reading does for the mind. *American Educator, 22*, 8–17.

Cunningham, K., Burkins, J., & Yates, K. (2023). *Shifting the balance: Bringing the science of reading to the upper elementary classroom, 3–5.* Stenhouse.

Daniels, H. (1994). *Literature circles.* Stenhouse Publishers.

de Sousa, E. (2017). Promoting the contributions of multilingual preschoolers. *Linguistics and Education, 39*, 1–13.

Denton, C., Fletcher, J., Anthony, J., & Francis, D. (2006). An evaluation of intensive intervention for students with persistent reading difficulties. *Journal of Learning Disabilities, 39*, 447–466.

Diamond, A., & Lee, K. (2011). Interventions shown to aid executive function development in children 4 to 12 years old. *Science, 333*(6045), 959–964.

DiCamillo, K. (2001). *The tiger rising.* Candlewick.

Dolch, E. W. (1936). A basic sight vocabulary. *The Elementary School Journal, 36*(6), 456–460.

Doyon, S. C. (2020). *Magnificent homespun brown: A celebration.* Tilbury House Publishers.

Drill, R. B., & Bellini, S. (2022). Combining readers theater, story mapping and video self-modeling interventions to improve narrative reading comprehension in children with autism spectrum disorder. *Journal of Autism and Developmental Disorders, 52*(1), 1–15.

Duff, D., Tomblin, B. J., & Catts, H. (2015). The influence of reading on vocabulary growth: A case for a Matthew effect. *Journal of Speech, Language, and Hearing Research, 58*(3), 853–864.

Duke, N. K., & Cartwright, K. B. (2021). The science of reading progresses: Communicating advances beyond the simple view of reading. *Reading Research Quarterly, 56*(1), S25–S44.

Duke, N. K., Ward, A. E., & Pearson, P. D. (2021). The science of reading comprehension instruction. *The Reading Teacher, 74*(6), 663–672.

Ebarvia, T., Germán, L., Parker, K. N., & Torres, J. (2020). #Disrupttexts: An introduction. *English Journal, 110*(1), 100–102.

Eeds, M., & Peterson, R. (1991). Teacher as curator: Learning to talk about literature. *The Reading Teacher, 45*(1), 18–126.

Eeds, M., & Wells, D. (1989). Grand conversations: An exploration of meaning construction in literature study groups. *Research in the Teaching of English, 23*(1), 4–29.

Ehri, L. C. (1997). Learning to read and learning to spell are one and the same, almost. *Learning to Spell: Research, Theory, and Practice Across Languages, 13*, 237–268.

Ehri, L. C. (2004). Teaching phonemic awareness and phonics: An explanation of the national reading panel meta-analyses. In P. McCardle & V. Chhabra (Eds.), *The voice of evidence in reading research* (pp. 153–186). Paul H. Brookes Publishing Co.

Ehri, L. C. (2014). Orthographic mapping in the acquisition of sight word reading, spelling memory, and vocabulary learning. *Scientific Studies of Reading, 18*(1), 5–21.

Ehri, L. C. (2017). Orthographic mapping and literacy development revisited. In K. Cain, D. Compton & R. Parrila (Eds.), *Theories of reading development* (pp. 127–145). John Benjamins.

Ehri, L. C. (2020). *The science of learning to read words: A case for systematic phonics instruction.* Reading Research Quarterly.

Ehri, L. C., Nunes, S. R., Stahl, S. A., & Willows, D. M. (2001). Systematic phonics instruction helps students learn to read: Evidence from the National Reading Panel's meta-analysis. *Review of Educational Research, 71*, 393–447.

Eilish O'Connell, B., & O'Connell, F. (2023). What was I made for? [Song]. Atlantic.

Elbaum, B., Vaughn, S., Hughes, M., & Moody, S. W. (1999). Grouping practices and reading outcomes for students with disabilities. *Exceptional Children, 65*(3), 399–415.

Elbaum, B., Vaughn, S., Tejero Hughes, M., & Watson, M. S. (2000). How effective are one-to-one tutoring programs in reading for elementary students at risk for reading failure? A meta-analysis of the intervention research. *Journal of Educational Psychology, 92*(4), 605–619.

Elleman, A. M., & Oslund, E. L. (2019). Reading comprehension research: Implications for practice and policy. *Policy Insights from the Behavioral and Brain Sciences, 6*(1), 3–11.

Ellis, E. S., & Graves, A. W. (1990). Teaching rural students with learning disabilities: A paraphrasing strategy to increase comprehension of main ideas. *Rural Special Education Quarterly, 10*(2), 2–10.

Ericsson, K. A., & Kintsch, W. (1995). Long-term working memory. *Psychological Review, 102*(2), 211–245.

España, C., & Herrera, L. Y. (2020). *En comunidad: Lessons for centering the voices and experiences of bilingual Latinx students.* Heinemann.

Farrell, J. J., Moog, R. S., & Spencer, J. N. (1999). A guided-inquiry general chemistry course. *Journal of Chemical Education, 76*(4), 570.

Fish, S. (1970). Literature in the reader: Affective stylistics. *New Literary History, 2*(1), 123–162.

Fisher, D., Flood, J., Lapp, D., & Frey, N. (2004). Interactive read-alouds: Is there a common set of implementation practices? *The Reading Teacher, 58*(1), 8–17.

Fleischman, P. (1988). *Joyful noise.* HarperCollins.

Flood, J., Lapp, D., & Fisher, D. (2005). Neurological impress method PLUS. *Reading Psychology, 26*(2), 147–160.

Foorman, B. R., & Torgesen, J. (2001). Critical elements of classroom and small-group instruction promote reading success in all children. *Learning Disabilities Research & Practice, 16*(4), 203–212.

Ford, C. E., & Thompson, S. A. (1996). Interactional units in conversation: Syntactic, intonational, and pragmatic resources for the management of turns. *Studies in Interactional Sociolinguistics, 13*, 134–184.

Frayer, D., Frederick, W. C., & Klausmeier, H. J. (1969). *A schema for testing the level of cognitive mastery.* Wisconsin Center for Education Research.

Fry, E. (1979). *1000 instant words: The most common words for teaching reading, writing, and spelling.* Teacher Created Resources.

Gambrell, L. B., Palmer, B. M., & Codling, R. M. (1993). *Motivation to read.* Office of Educational Research and Improvement.

Garnett, S. (2020). *Cognitive load theory: A handbook for teachers.* Crown House Publishing Ltd.

Gersten, R., Newman-Gonchar, R. A., Haymond, K. S., & Dimino, J. A. (2017). *What is the evidence base to support reading interventions for improving student outcomes in Grades 1–3* (REL2017–271). Institute of Education Sciences, National Center for Education Evaluation and Regional Assistance, Regional Educational Laboratory Southeast.

Gerwig, G. (Director). (2023). *Barbie* [Film]. Warner Bros.

Goldschmidt, P., & Jung, H. (2011). *Evaluation of seeds of science/roots of reading: Effective tools* for developing literacy through science in the early grades—light energy unit. (CRESST Report 781). University of California, National Center for Research on Evaluation, Standards, and Student Testing (CRESST).

Goodwin, A. P., & Ahn, S. (2013). A meta-analysis of morphological interventions in English: Effects on literacy outcomes for school-age children. *Scientific Studies of Reading, 17*(4), 257–285.

Gough, P. B., & Tunmer, W. E. (1986). Decoding, reading, and reading disability. *Remedial and Special Education, 7*(1), 6–10.

Graaff, S., Bosman, A., Hasselman, F., & Verhoeven, L. (2009). Benefits of systematic phonics instruction. *Scientific Studies of Reading, 13*, 318–333.

Graesser, A. C., Singer, M., & Trabasso, T. (1994). Constructing inferences during narrative text comprehension. *Psychological Review, 101*(3), 371.

Graham, S., & Santangelo, T. (2014). Does spelling instruction make students better spellers, readers, and writers? A meta-analytic review. *Reading and Writing, 27*, 1703–1743.

Gratz, A. (2012). *Ground zero: A novel of 9/11*. Scholastic Press.

Greenleaf, C. L., Litman, C., Hanson, T. L., Rosen, R., Boscardin, C. K., Herman, J., Schneider, S. A., Madden, S., & Jones, B. (2011). Integrating literacy and science in biology: Teaching and learning impacts of reading apprenticeship professional development. *American Educational Research Journal, 48*(3), 647–717.

Griffith, R. R. (2010). Students learn to read like writers: A framework for teachers of writing. *Reading Horizons: A Journal of Literacy and Language Arts, 50*(1).

Grimard, G. (2016). *Lila and the crow*. Annick Press.

Guthrie, J. T., Wigfield, A., & You, W. (2012). Instructional contexts for engagement and achievement in reading. In S. L. Christenson, A. L. Rescgly, & C. Wylie (Eds.), *Handbook of research on student engagement* (pp. 601–634). Springer.

Hagaman, J. L., Luschen, K., & Reid, R. (2010). The "RAP" on reading comprehension. *Teaching Exceptional Children, 43*(1), 22–29.

Hall, M. S., & Burns, M. K. (2018). Meta-analysis of targeted small-group reading interventions. *Journal of School Psychology, 66*, 54–66.

Hammond, Z. (2015). *Culturally responsive teaching and the brain: Promoting authentic engagement and rigor among culturally and linguistically diverse students*. Corwin.

Hardman, J. (2019). Developing and supporting implementation of a dialogic pedagogy in primary schools in England. *Teaching and Teacher Education, 86*.

Hatcher, P. J., Hulme, C., Miles, J. N., Carroll, J. M., Hatcher, J., Gibbs, S., Smith, G., Bowyer-Crane, C., & Snowling, M. J. (2006). Efficacy of small group reading intervention for beginning readers with reading-delay: A randomized controlled trial. *Journal of Child Psychology and Psychiatry, 47*(8), 820–827.

Hattie, J. (2008). *Visible learning*. Routledge.

Hattie, J. (2009). The black box of tertiary assessment: An impending revolution. In L. Meyer, S. Davidson, H. Anderson, R. Fletcher, P. Johnston, & M. Rees (Eds.), *Tertiary Assessment and Higher Education Student Outcomes: Policy, Practice & Research* (pp. 259–276). Ako Aotearoa.

Hattie, J., & Clarke, S. (2018). *Visible learning: Feedback*. Routledge.

Hattie, J., & Clarke, S. (2019). *Visible learning: Feedback* (2nd ed.) Routledge

Hattie, J., & Timperley, H. (2007). The power of feedback. *Review of Educational Research, 77*(1), 81–112.

Hayes, D. P., & Ahrens, M. G. (1988). Vocabulary simplification for children: A special case of 'motherese'? *Journal of Child Language, 15*(2), 395–410.

Heath, M. A., Smith, K., & Young, E. L. (2017). Using children's literature to strengthen social and emotional learning. *School Psychology International, 38*(5), 541–561.

Helmenstine, A. M. (2019, September 19). What is a mixture in science? *Newsela.* Available at https://shorturl.at/imv78

Hickman, P., Pollard-Durodola, S., & Vaughn, S. (2004). Storybook reading: Improving vocabulary and comprehension for English-language learners. *The Reading Teacher, 57*(8), 720–730.

Hiebert, E. H. (2011). Using multiple sources of information in establishing text complexity. *Reading Research Report,* no. 11.03. Text Project and University of California, Santa Cruz. Available at https://files.eric.ed.gov/fulltext/ED521661.pdf

Hinchman, K. A., & Moore, D. W. (2013). Close reading: A cautionary interpretation. *Journal of Adolescent & Adult Literacy, 56*(6), 441–450.

History.com Editors. (2010). The Great Migration. *History Channel.* https://www.history.com/topics/black-history/great-migration

Holdaway, D. (1979). *The foundations of literacy.* Heinemann.

Hollingsworth, J. R., & Ybarra, S. E. (2017). *Explicit direct instruction (EDI): The power of the well-crafted, well-taught lesson* (2nd ed.). Corwin.

Howard, J. R., Milner-McCall, T., & Howard, T. C. (2020). *Not this but that: No more teaching without positive relationships.* Heinemann.

Hudson, A., Koh, P. W., Moore, K. A., & Binks-Cantrell, E. (2020). Fluency interventions for elementary students with reading difficulties: A synthesis of research from 2000–2019. *Education Sciences, 10*(3), 52.

Hurst, S., & Griffity, P. (2015). Examining the effect of teacher read-aloud on adolescent attitudes and learning. *Middle Grades Research Journal, 10*(1), 31–47.

Hwang, H., Cabell, S. Q., & Joyner, R. E. (2022). Effects of integrated literacy and content-area instruction on vocabulary and comprehension in the elementary years: A meta-analysis. *Scientific Studies of Reading, 26*(3), 223–249.

Hwang, H., Cabell, S. Q., & Joyner, R. E. (2023). Does cultivating content knowledge during literacy instruction support vocabulary and comprehension in the elementary school years? A systematic review. *Reading Psychology, 44*(2), 145–174.

Hwang, H., McMaster, K. L., & Kendeou, P. (2023). A longitudinal investigation of directional relations between domain knowledge and reading in the elementary years. *Reading Research Quarterly, 58*(1), 59–77.

Invernizzi, M. A., Johnston, F. R., Templeton, S., & Bear, D. R. (2017). *Words their way* (3rd ed.). Pearson.

Ivey, G., & Broaddus, K. (2001). "Just plain reading": A survey of what makes students want to read in middle school classrooms. *Reading Research Quarterly, 36*(4), 350–377.

Johnson, D., & Johnson, R. (2015). Cooperative learning: Improving university instruction by basing practice on validated theory. *Journal on Excellence in College Teaching, 25,* 85–118.

Jones, S. P. (2020). *Ending curriculum violence.* Learning for Justice. Available at https://www.learningforjustice.org/magazine/spring-2020/ending-curriculum-violence

Josephs, N. L., & Jolivette, K. (2016). Effects of peer mediated instruction on the oral reading fluency skills of high school aged struggling readers. *Insights Into Learning Disabilities, 13*(1), 39–59.

Joshi, R. M., & Aaron, P. G. (2000). The component model of reading: Simple view of reading made a little more complex. *Reading Psychology, 21*(2), 85–97.

Justice, L. M., & Ezell, H. K. (2002). Use of storybook reading to increase print awareness in at-risk children. *American Journal of Speech: Language Pathology, 11*(1), 17.

Kame'enui, E., Carnine, D., & Freschi, R. (1982). Effects of text construction and instructional procedures for teaching word meanings on comprehension and recall. *Reading Research Quarterly, 17*, 367.

Kamil, M. L., Borman, G. D., Dole, J., Kral, C. C., Salinger, T., & Torgesen, J. (2008). *Improving adolescent literacy: Effective classroom and intervention practices*. National Center for Education Evaluation and Regional Assistance.

Katims, D. S., & Harris, S. (1997). Improving the reading comprehension of middle school students in inclusive classrooms. *Journal of Adolescent & Adult Literacy, 41*(2), 116–123.

Keehn, S., Harmon, J., & Shoho, A. (2008). A study of readers theater in eighth grade: Issues of fluency, comprehension, and vocabulary. *Reading & Writing Quarterly, 24*(4), 335–362.

Kelley, M. J., & Clausen-Grace, N. (2010). Guiding students through expository text with text feature walks. *The Reading Teacher, 64*(3), 191–195.

Kenneth L. J., & Kieffer, M. J. (2017). Evaluating the role of polysemous word knowledge in reading comprehension among bilingual adolescents. *Reading and Writing: An Interdisciplinary Journal, 30*(8), 1687–1704.

Kim, Y-S. (2020). Toward integrative reading science: The direct and indirect effects model of reading. *Journal of Learning Disabilities, 53*(6), 469–491.

Kim, Y-S. (2023). Executive functions and morphological awareness explain the shared variance between word reading and listening comprehension. *Scientific Studies of Reading, 27*(5), 451–474.

King, S. (1982). *The running man*. Signet.

Kintsch, W. (1986). Learning from text. *Cognition and Instruction, 3*(2), 87–108.

Kintsch, W. (1988). The role of knowledge in discourse comprehension: A construction-integration model. *Psychological Review, 95*(2), 163–182.

Kintsch, W. (2005). An overview of top-down and bottom-up effects in comprehension: The CI

perspective. *Discourse Processes, 39*(2–3), 125–128.

Kirkland, M. R., & Saunders, M. A. P. (1991). Maximizing student performance in summary writing: Managing cognitive load. *TESOL Quarterly, 25*(1), 105–121.

Kirschner, P. A., Sweller, J., & Clark, R. E. (2006). Why minimal guidance during instruction does not work: An analysis of the failure of constructivist, discovery, problem-based, experiential, and inquiry-based teaching. *Educational Psychologist, 41*(2), 75–86.

Kline, S. (2016). *Horrible Harry and the birthday girl*. Viking Books for Young Readers.

Kosanovich, M., Ladinsky, K., Nelson, L., & Torgesen, J. (2007). *Differentiated reading instruction: Small group alternative lesson structures for all students*. Florida Center for Reading Research. https://files.eric.ed.gov/fulltext/ED498777.pdf

Kraemer, L., McCabe, P., & Sinatra, R. (2012). The effects of read-alouds of expository text on first graders' listening comprehension and book choice. *Literacy Research and Instruction, 51*(2), 165–178.

Krashen, S. D. (2004). *The power of reading: Insights from the research*. Bloomsbury Publishing.

Kuhlthau, C. C., Maniotes, L. K., & Caspari, A. K. (2015). *Guided inquiry: Learning in the 21st century*. Bloomsbury Publishing.

Kuhn, M. R. (2020). Whole class or small group fluency instruction: A tutorial of four effective approaches. *Education Sciences, 10*(5), 145.

Ladson-Billings, G. (1995). But that's just good teaching! The case for culturally relevant pedagogy. *Theory Into Practice, 34*(3), 159–165.

Ladson-Billings, G. (2006). Yes, but how do we do it? Practicing culturally relevant pedagogy. In J. Landsman & C. Lewis (Eds.), *White teachers/diverse classrooms* (pp. 29–41). Stylus Publishers.

Landreth, S. J., & Young, C. (2021). Developing fluency and comprehension with the secondary fluency routine. *The Journal of Educational Research, 114*(3), 252–262.

Lane, H. B., & Comtesse, V. (2022). *UFLI Foundations: An explicit and systematic phonics program.* Ventris Learning.

Lane, H. B., Pullen, P. C., Hudson, R. F., & Konold, T. R. (2009). Identifying essential instructional components of literacy tutoring for struggling beginning readers. *Literacy Research and Instruction, 48*(4), 277–297.

Larsen-Freeman, D. (2012). On the roles of repetition in language teaching and learning. *Applied Linguistics Review, 3*(2), 195–210.

Lauterbach, S. L., & Bender, W. N. (1995). Cognitive strategy instruction for reading comprehension: A success for high school freshmen. *The High School Journal, 79*(1), 58–64.

Lawrence-Brown, D. (2004). Differentiated instruction: Inclusive strategies for standards-based learning that benefit the whole class. *American Secondary Education, 32*(3), 34–62.

Lindsay, J. B. (2023). *Reading above the fray.* Scholastic.

Liu, J. (2000). The power of readers theater: From reading to writing. *English Language Teaching Journal, 54*(4), 354–361.

Locke, E. A., & Latham, G. P. (1990). *A theory of goal setting & task performance.* Prentice.

Lovell, O. (2020). *Sweller's cognitive load theory in action.* John Catt Educational.

Lovett, M. W., Borden, S. L., Warren-Chaplin, P. M., Lacerenza, L., DeLuca, T., & Giovinazzo, R. (1996). Text comprehension training for disabled readers: An evaluation of reciprocal teaching and text analysis training programs. *Brain and Language, 54*(3), 447–480.

Lubliner, S., & Smetana, L. (2005). The effects of comprehensive vocabulary instruction on Title I students' metacognitive word-learning skills and reading comprehension. *Journal of Literacy Research, 37*(2), 163–200.

Lupo, S. M., Berry, A., Thacker, E., Sawyer, A., & Merritt, J. (2019). Rethinking text sets to support knowledge building and interdisciplinary learning. *The Reading Teacher, 73*(4), 1–12.

Maillard, K. N. (2019). *Fry bread: A Native American family story.* Roaring Brook Press.

Mancilla-Martinez, J., & McClain, J. B. (2020). What do we know today about the complexity of vocabulary gaps and what do we not know? *In Handbook of Reading Research* (Vol. 5, pp. 216–236). Routledge.

Margunayasa, I. G., Dantes, N., Marhaeni, A., & Suastra, I. W. (2019). The effect of guided inquiry learning and cognitive style on science learning achievement. *International Journal of Instruction, 12*(1), 737–750.

Mariage, T. V., Englert, C. S., & Mariage, M. F. (2020). Comprehension instruction for Tier 2 early learners: A scaffolded apprenticeship for close reading of informational text. *Learning Disability Quarterly, 43*(1), 29–42.

Marr, M. B., Algozzine, B., Nicholson, K., & Keller Dugan, K. (2011). Building oral reading fluency with peer coaching. *Remedial and Special Education, 32*(3), 256–264.

Martin, A. (2005). *A dog's life.* Scholastic.

Mastrothanasis, K., Kladaki, M., & Andreou, A. (2023). A systematic review and meta-analysis of the readers' theatre impact on the development of reading skills. *International Journal of Educational Research Open, 4.*

McKenna, M. C., & Robinson, R. D. (1990). Content literacy: A definition and implications. *Journal of Reading, 34*(3), 184–186.

McKeown, M. G. (1993). Creating effective definitions for young word learners. *Reading Research Quarterly, 28*(1), 17–31.

McKeown, M. G. (2019). Effective vocabulary instruction fosters knowing words, using words, and understanding how words work. *Language, Speech, and Hearing Services in Schools, 50*, 466–476.

McKeown, M. G., & Beck, I. L. (2014). Effects of vocabulary instruction on measures of language processing: Comparing two approaches. *Early Childhood Research Quarterly, 29*(4), 520–530.

McKeown, M. G., & Beck, I. L. (2015). Effective classroom talk is reading comprehension instruction. In L. B. Resnick, C. A. Asterhan, & S. N. Clarke (Eds.), *Socializing intelligence through academic talk and dialogue* (pp. 51–62). American Educational Research Association.

McKeown, M. G., Beck, I. L., Sinatra, G. M., & Loxterman, J. A. (1992). The contribution of prior knowledge and coherent text to comprehension. *Reading Research Quarterly, 27*(1), 78–93.

Meadows, D. (2009). *Trixie the Halloween fairy.* Scholastic.

Meltzer, L., & Krishnan, K. (2007). Executive function difficulties and learning disabilities. *Executive Function in Education: From Theory to Practice, 77,* 105.

Mesmer, H. A. E. (2005). Text decodability and the first-grade reader. *Reading & Writing Quarterly, 21*(1), 61–86.

Miller, G. A. (1999). On knowing a word. *Annual Review of Psychology, 50,* 1–19.

Millin, S. K., & Rinehart, S. D. (1999). Some of the benefits of readers theater participation for second-grade Title I students. *Reading Research and Instruction, 39*(1), 71–88.

Minor, C. (2018). *We got this: Equity, access, and the quest to be who our students need us to be.* Heinemann.

Mol, S. E., Bus, A. G., De Jong, M. T., & Smeets, D. J. (2008). Added value of dialogic parent–child book readings: A meta-analysis. *Early Education and Development, 19*(1), 7–26.

Moll, L. C., Amanti, C., Neff, D., & Gonzalez, N. (1992). Funds of knowledge for teaching reading: Using a qualitative approach to connect homes and classrooms. *Theory Into Practice, 31*(2), 132–141.

Montes, I., Lai, C., & Sanabria, D. (2003). Like dissolves like: A guided inquiry experiment for organic chemistry. *Journal of Chemical Education, 80*(4), 447.

Moses, L., & Kelly, L. B. (2018). "We're a little loud. That's because we like to read!": Developing positive views of reading in a diverse, urban first grade. *Journal of Early Childhood Literacy, 18*(3), 307–337.

Mraz, M., Nichols, W., Caldwell, S., Beisley, R., Sargent, S., & Rupley, W. (2013). Improving oral reading fluency through readers theatre. *Reading Horizons: A Journal of Literacy and Language Arts, 52*(2), 5.

Munsch, R. (1980). *The paper bag princess.* Annick Press.

Murphy, P. K., Wilkinson, I. A. G., Soter, A. O., Hennessey, M. N., & Alexander, J. F. (2009). Examining the effects of classroom discussion on students' comprehension of text: A meta-analysis. *Journal of Educational Psychology, 101*(3), 740–764.

Myrset, A., & Drew, I. (2016). A case study of readers theatre in a primary Norwegian EFL class. *Nordic Journal of Modern Language Methodology, 4*(1), 49–66.

Nagy, W. E., Anderson, R. C., & Herman, P. A. (1987). Learning word meanings from context during normal reading. *American Educational Research Journal, 24*(2), 237–270.

Nash, H., & Snowling, M. (2006). Teaching new words to children with poor existing vocabulary knowledge: A controlled evaluation of the definition and context methods. *International Journal of Language and Communication Disorders, 41,* 335–354.

Nation, I. S., & Nation, I. S. P. (2001). *Learning vocabulary in another language.* Cambridge University Press.

National Reading Panel (US), National Institute of Child Health & Human Development (US). (2000). *Teaching children to read: An evidence-based assessment of the scientific research* literature on reading and its implications for reading instruction: Reports of the subgroups. National Institute of Child Health and Human Development, National Institutes of Health.

Neitzel, A. J., Lake, C., Pellegrini, M., & Slavin, R. E. (2022). A synthesis of quantitative research on programs for struggling readers in elementary schools. *Reading Research Quarterly, 57*(1), 149–179.

Nieto, S. (2017). Becoming sociocultural mediators: What all educators can learn from bilingual and ESL teachers. *Issues in Teacher Education, 26*(2), 129–141.

O'Neil, K. (2010). Once upon today: Teaching for social justice with postmodern picture books. *Children's Literature in Education, 41*(1), 40–51.

Paas, F., & Sweller, J. (2012). An evolutionary upgrade of cognitive load theory: Using the human motor system and collaboration to support the learning of complex cognitive tasks. *Educational Psychology Review, 24*, 27–45.

Paddle, H., & Woollett, O. (2020). Close reading across the curriculum. *Literacy Learning: The Middle Years, 28*(3), 53–63.

Padeliadu, S., & Giazitzidou, S. (2018). A synthesis of research on reading fluency development: Study of eight meta-analyses. *European Journal of Special Education Research, 7*(2), 34–45.

Paige, D. D. (2011). 16 minutes of "eyes-on-text" can make a difference: Whole-class choral reading as an adolescent fluency strategy. *Reading Horizons: A Journal of Literacy and Language Arts, 51*(1), 33–46.

Paige, D. D., Young, C., Rasinski, T. V., Rupley, W. H., Nichols, W. D., & Valerio, M. (2021). Teaching reading is more than a science: It's also an art. *Reading Research Quarterly, 56*(1), 1–12.

Palincsar, A. S., Collins, K. M., Marano, N. L., & Magnusson, S. J. (2000). Investigating the engagement and learning of students with learning disabilities in guided inquiry science

teaching. *Language, Speech, and Hearing Services in Schools, 31*(3), 240–251.

Park, L. S. (2010). *A long walk to water: Based on a true story*. Clarion Books.

Parkes, B. (2000). *Read it again! Revisiting shared reading*. Stenhouse Publishers.

Paul, B., & Paul, M. (2019). *I am farmer: Growing an environmental movement in Cameroon*. Millbrook Press.

Paxton-Buursma, D., & Walker, M. (2008). Piggybacking: A strategy to increase participation in classroom discussions by students with learning disabilities. *Teaching Exceptional Children, 40*(3), 28–34.

Pearson, P. D., & Gallagher, M. C. (1983). The instruction of reading comprehension. *Contemporary Educational Psychology, 8*(3), 317–344.

Peng, P., Wang, W., Filderman, M. J., Zhang, W., & Lin, L. (2023). The active ingredient in reading comprehension strategy intervention for struggling readers: A Bayesian network meta-analysis. *Review of Educational Research, 1*(1), 25–38.

Pressley, M. (2002a). Comprehension strategies instruction: A turn-of-the-century status report. In C. C. Block & M. Pressley (Eds.), *Comprehension instruction: Research-based best practices* (pp. 11–27). Guilford.

Pressley, M. (2002b). Metacognition and self-regulated comprehension. In A. E. Farstrup & S. J. Samuels (Eds.), *What research has to say about reading instruction* (3rd ed., pp. 291–309). International Reading Association.

Pressley, M., & Allington, R. (2014). *Reading instruction that works: The case for balanced teaching*. Guilford Publications.

Protacio, M. S. (2019). How positioning affects English learners' social interactions around reading. *Theory Into Practice, 58*(3), 217–225.

Pugh, A., Kearns, D. M., & Hiebert, E. H. (2023). Text types and their relation to efficacy in beginning reading interventions. *Reading Research Quarterly, 58*(4), 710–732.

Quadri, J., Masson, J., & Poncelet, M. (2023). The effect of a reading aloud program on reading rate and reading prosody in a group of sixth-grade low-achievement, language-minority, and/or low-SES readers. *Reading and Writing* (pp. 1–27). Springer

Ransom, J. C. (1941). *The new criticism.* New Directions Publishing Corporation.

Rasinski, T. (2004). *Assessing reading fluency.* Pacific Resources for Learning.

Raphael, T. E., & McMahon, S. I. (1994). Book club: An alternative framework for reading instruction. *The Reading Teacher, 48*(2), 102–116.

Rappolt-Schlichtmann, G. (2020, March 18). Distance learning: 6 UDL best practices for online learning. *Understood.org.* http://www.understood.org/en/school-learning/for-educators/universal-design-for-learning/video-distance-learning-udl-best-practices

Reed, J. M., Marchand-Martella, N. E., Martella, R. C., & Kolts, R. L. (2007). Assessing the effects of the reading success Level A program with fourth-grade students at a Title I elementary school. *Education and Treatment of Children, 30*(1), 45–68.

Rehfeld, D. M., Kirkpatrick, M., O'Guinn, N., & Renbarger, R. (2022, October 6). A meta-analysis of phonemic awareness instruction provided to children suspected of having a reading disability. *Language, Speech, and Hearing Services in Schools, 53*(4), 1177–1201.

Reutzel, D. R., Fawson, P. C., & Smith, J. A. (2008). Reconsidering silent sustained reading: An exploratory study of scaffolded silent reading. *The Journal of Educational Research, 102*(1), 37–50.

Reynolds, D., & Goodwin, A. (2016). Supporting students reading complex texts: Evidence for motivational scaffolding. *American Education Research Association Open, 2*(4).

Rinehart, S. D. (1999). "Don't think for a minute that I'm getting up there": Opportunities for readers' theater in a tutorial for children with reading problems. *Reading Psychology, 20*(1), 71–89.

Rivera, S., & Oliveira, A. (2021). "Why would Benjamin Franklin want to know if lightning was electricity?" Elementary teachers and students making sense of the nature of science during interactive read-alouds. *Cultural Studies of Science Education, 16*(1), 47–69.

Rizzuto, K. C., & Steiner, L. M. (2022). Creating multicultural community spaces for all children: Transformative read-alouds in the early childhood classroom. *School Community Journal, 32*(1), 187–200.

Robertson, D. A. (2021). Explicit instruction. In S. A. Parsons & M. Vaughn (Eds.), *Principles of effective literacy instruction, Grades K–5* (pp. 139–149). Guilford Press.

Roessingh, H. (2020). Read-alouds in the upper elementary classroom: Developing academic vocabulary. *TESOL Journal, 11*(1), e00445.

Rosenblatt, L. M. (1938). *Literature as exploration.* Modern Language Association of America.

Rosenblatt, L. M. (1978). *The reader, the text, the poem: The transactional theory of the literary work.* Southern Illinois University Press.

Rosenshine, B. (1971). *Teaching behaviours and student achievement.* National Foundation for Educational Research.

Rosenshine, B. (1986). Synthesis of research on explicit teaching. *Educational Leadership, 43*(7), 60–69.

Rosenshine, B. (2012). Principles of instruction: Research-based strategies that all teachers should know. *American Educator, 36*(1), 12.

Rowen, D., Biggs, D., Watkins, N., & Rasinski, T. (2015). Choral reading theater: Bridging accuracy, automaticity, and prosody in reading fluency across an academic unit of study. *Journal of Teacher Action Research, 1*, 53–69.

Rupley, W. H., Logan, J. W., & Nichols, W. D. (1999). Vocabulary instruction in a balanced reading program. *The Reading Teacher, 52*(4), 114–124.

Sacks, H., Schegloff, E. A., & Jefferson, G. (1978). *A simplest systematics for the organization of turn taking for conversation.* Academic Press.

Sadler, D. R. (1989). Formative assessment and the design of instructional systems. *Instructional Science, 18*, 119–144.

Sainsbury, M., & Schagen, I. (2004). Attitudes to reading at ages nine and eleven. *Journal of Research in Reading, 27*(4), 373–386.

Sampson, M. R., Valmont, W. J., & Van Allen, R. (1982). The effects of instructional cloze on the comprehension, vocabulary, and divergent production of third-grade students. *Reading Research Quarterly, 17*(3), 389–399.

Santoro, L. E., Chard, D. J., Howard, L., & Baker, S. K. (2008). Making the "very" most of classroom read-alouds to promote comprehension and vocabulary. *Reading Teacher, 61*(5), 396–408.

Scarborough, H. S. (2001). Connecting early language and literacy to later reading (dis)abilities: Evidence, theory, and practice. In S. Neuman & D. Dickinson (Eds.), *Handbook for research in early literacy* (pp. 97–110). Taylor and Francis.

Scardamalia, M., & Bereiter, C. (1992). Text-based and knowledge-based questioning by children. *Cognition and Instruction, 9*(3), 177–199.

Schnotz, W., & Kürschner, C. (2007). A reconsideration of cognitive load theory. *Educational Psychology Review, 19*(4), 469–508.

Schumaker, J. B., Denton, P. H., & Deshler, D. D. (1984). *The paraphrasing strategy: Instructor's manual.* University of Kansas Institute for Research in Learning Disabilities.

Schunk, D. H., & Ertmer, P. A. (2000). Self-regulation and academic learning: Self-efficacy enhancing interventions. In M. Boekaerts, P. R. Pintrich, & M. Zeidner (Eds.), *Handbook of self-regulation* (pp. 631–649). Academic Press.

Schunk, D. H., & Rice, J. M. (1989). Learning goals and children's reading comprehension. *Journal of Reading Behavior, 21*(3), 279–293.

Schunk, D. H., & Rice, J. M. (1991). Learning goals and progress feedback during reading comprehension instruction. *Journal of Reading Behavior, 23*(3), 351–364.

Scott, J. A., Miller, T. F., & Flinspach, S. L. (2012). Developing word consciousness: Lessons from highly diverse fourth-grade classrooms. In E. J. Kame'enui & J. F. Baumann (Eds.), *Vocabulary instruction: Research to practice* (2nd ed., pp. 169–188). Guildford.

Scott, J. A., & Nagy, W. E. (1997). Understanding the definitions of unfamiliar verbs. *Reading Research Quarterly, 32*(2), 184–200.

Sedova, K., Sedlacek, M., Svaricek, R., Majcik, M., Navratilova, J., Drexlerova, A., Kychler, J., & Salamounova, Z. (2019). Do those who talk more learn more? The relationship between student classroom talk and student achievement. *Learning and Instruction, 63.*

Serravallo, J. (2010). *Teaching reading in small groups.* Heinemann.

Serravallo, J. (2018). *Understanding texts and readers.* Heinemann.

Serravallo, J. (2019). *A teacher's guide to reading conferences.* Heinemann.

Serravallo, J. (2021). *Teaching writing in small groups.* Heinemann.

Serravallo, J. (Host). (2023a, November 20). Dr. P. David Pearson (Episode 27) [Audio podcast episode]. In *To the classroom podcast.* https://podcasts.apple.com/us/podcast/to-the-classroom-conversations-with/id1671184358?i=1000635382636

Serravallo, J. (2023b). *The reading strategies book 2.0.* Heinemann.

Shakory, S., Chen, X., & Deacon, S. H. (2021). Learning orthographic and semantic representations simultaneously during shared reading. *Journal of Speech, Language & Hearing Research, 64*(3), 909–921.

Share, D. L. (1995). Phonological recoding and self-teaching: Sine qua non of reading acquisition. *Cognition, 55*(2), 151–226.

Share, D. L. (2008). On the Anglocentricities of current reading research and practice: The perils of overreliance on an "outlier" orthography. *Psychological Bulletin, 134*(4), 584–615.

Short, K. G., & Pierce, K. M. (Eds.). (1990). *Talking about books: Creating literate communities.* Heinemann.

Silverman, R., Crandell, J. D., & Carlis, L. (2013). Read alouds and beyond: The effects of read aloud extension activities on vocabulary in Head Start classrooms. *Early Education & Development, 24*(2), 98–122.

Snow, C. E., & Juel, C. (2005). Teaching children to read: What do we know about how to do it? In M. J. Snowling & C. Hulme (Eds.), *The science of reading: A handbook* (pp. 501–520). Blackwell Publishing.

Souto-Manning, M. (2010). Teaching English learners: Building on cultural and linguistic strengths. *English Education, 42*(3), 249–263.

Souto-Manning, M., Llerena, C. L., Martell, J., Maguire, A. S., & Arce-Boardman, A. (2018). *No more culturally irrelevant teaching.* Heinemann.

Souto-Manning, M., & Martell, J. (2016). *Reading, writing, and talk: Inclusive teaching strategies for diverse learners, K–2.* Teachers College Press.

Stahl, S. A., & Fairbanks, M. (1986). The effects of vocabulary instruction: A model-based meta-analysis. *Review of Educational Research, 56,* 72–110.

Stahl, S. A., & Heubach, K. M. (2005). Fluency-oriented reading instruction. *Journal of Literacy Research, 37*(1), 25–60.

Stahl, S. A., & Nagy, W. E. (2005). *Teaching word meanings.* Routledge.

Stahl, S. A., & Shiel, T. G. (1992). Teaching meaning vocabulary: Productive approaches for poor readers. *Reading and Writing Quarterly: Overcoming Learning Difficulties, 8*(2), 223–241.

Stanovich, K. E. (1986). Matthew effects in reading: Some consequences of individual differences in the acquisition of literacy. *Reading Research Quarterly, 22,* 360–407.

Stanovich, K. E. (1993). Romance and reality. *Reading Teacher, 47,* 280–280.

Steacy, L. M., Wade-Woolley, L., Rueckl, J. G., Pugh, K., Elliott, J. D., & Compton, D. L. (2019). The role of set for variability in irregular word reading: Word and child predictors in typically developing readers and students at-risk for reading disabilities. *Scientific Studies of Reading, 23*(6), 523–532.

Steele, S. C., & Mills, M. T. (2011). Vocabulary intervention for school-age children with language impairment: A review of evidence and good practice. *Child Language Teaching and Therapy, 27*(3), 354–370.

Steig, W. (1988). *Brave Irene* (Sunburst ed.). Farrar, Straus & Giroux.

Steinbeck, J. (1939). *The grapes of wrath.* Penguin Classics.

Stevens, E. A., Walker, M. A., & Vaughn, S. (2017). The effects of reading fluency interventions on the reading fluency and reading comprehension performance of elementary students with learning disabilities: A synthesis of the research from 2001 to 2014. *Journal of Learning Disabilities, 50*(5), 576–590.

Strommen, L. T., & Mates, B. F. (2004). Learning to love reading: Interviews with older children and teens. *Journal of Adolescent & Adult Literacy, 48*(3), 188–200.

Sulzby, E. (1985). Children's emergent reading of favorite storybooks: A developmental study. *Reading Research Quarterly, 20*(4), 458–481.

Sulzby, E. (1991). Assessment of emergent literacy: Storybook reading. *The Reading Teacher, 44*(7), 498–500.

Sulzby, E., & Teale, W. H. (2003). The development of the young child and the emergence of literacy. In J. Flood, D. Lapp, J. Squire, & J. Jensen (Eds.), *Handbook of research on teaching the English language arts* (2nd ed., pp. 300–313). Erlbaum.

Swanson, E., Hairrell, A., Kent, S., Ciullo, S., Wanzek, J. A., & Vaughn, S. (2014). A synthesis and meta-analysis of reading interventions using social studies content for students with learning disabilities. *Journal of Learning Disabilities, 47*(2), 178–195.

Swanson, H. L. (1999). Instructional components that predict treatment outcomes for students with learning disabilities: Support for a combined strategy and direct instruction model. *Learning Disabilities Research and Practice, 14*(3), 129–140.

Sweller, J. (1988). Cognitive load during problem solving: Effects on learning. *Cognitive Science, 12*(2), 257–285.

Therrien, W. J. (2004). Fluency and comprehension gains as a result of repeated reading: A meta-analysis. *Remedial and Special Education, 25*(4), 252–261.

Tierney, R. J., & Pearson, P. D. (2021). *A history of literacy education: Waves of research and practice.* Teachers College Press.

Tierney, R. J., & Readence, J. E. (2000). *Reading strategies and practices: A compendium* (5th ed.). Allyn and Bacon.

Tilly, W. D. (2008). The evolution of school psychology to science-based practice: Problem solving and the three-tiered model. *Best Practices in School Psychology, 1,* 17–36.

Torcasio, S., & Sweller, J. (2010). The use of illustrations when learning to read: A cognitive load theory approach. *Applied Cognitive Psychology, 24*(5), 659–672.

Torgesen, J. K., Alexander, A. W., Wagner, R. K., Rashotte, K., Voeller, K. S., & Conway, T. (2001). Intensive remedial instruction for children with severe reading disabilities: Immediate and long-term outcomes from two instructional approaches. *Journal of Learning Disabilities, 34*(1), 33–58, 78.

Tsou, W. (2011). The application of readers theater to FLES (foreign language in the elementary schools) reading and writing. *Foreign Language Annals, 44*(4), 727–748.

Tunmer, W. E., & Arrow, A. W. (2013). Reading: Phonics instruction. In J. Hattie & E. Anderman (Eds.), *International guide to student achievement* (pp. 316–319). Routledge.

Turner, F. D. (2010). Evaluating the effectiveness of fluency-oriented reading instruction with increasing Black and Latino reading fluency, as compared to Asian and White second-grade students' reading fluency. *The Journal of Negro Education, 79*(2), 112–124.

Uphold, N., & Hudson, M. (2012). Student-focused planning. In D. West (Ed.), *Evidence-based instructional strategies for transition: Brookes transition to adulthood series* (pp. 55–78). Brookes.

USHistory.org. (2017, May 1). How government works: Comparing governments. *Newsela.* https://newsela.com/view/ck9noofvf041q0iqjybuct1gx/

Vaughn, S., Cirino, P. T., Wanzek, J., Wexler, J., Fletcher, J. M., Denton, C. D., Barth, A., Romain, M., & Francis, D. J. (2010). Response to intervention for middle school students with reading difficulties: Effects of a primary and secondary intervention. *School Psychology Review, 39*(1), 3–21.

Vaughn, S., Swanson, E. A., Roberts, G., Wanzek, J., Stillman-Spisak, S. J., Solis, M., & Simmons, D. (2013). Improving reading comprehension and social studies knowledge in middle school. *Reading Research Quarterly, 48*(1), 77–93.

Venegas, E. M. (2018). Strengthening the reader self-efficacies of reluctant and struggling readers through literature circles. *Reading and Writing Quarterly, 34*(5), 419–435.

Vernon-Feagans, L., Gallagher, K., Ginsberg, M. C., Amendum, S. J., Kainz, K., Rose, J., & Burchinal, M. R. (2010). A diagnostic teaching intervention for classroom teachers: Helping struggling readers in early elementary school. *Learning Disabilities Research & Practice, 25*(4), 183–193.

Wagner, R. K., & Ridgewell, C. (2009). A large-scale study of specific reading comprehension disability. *Perspectives on Language and Literacy, 35*(5), 27–31.

Walpole, S., & McKenna, M. C. (2017). *How to plan differentiated reading instruction: Resources for Grades K–3.* Guilford Publications.

Wanzek, J., Petscher, Y., Otaiba, S. A., Rivas, B. K., Jones, F. G., Kent, S. C., Schatschneider, C., & Mehta, P. (2017). Effects of a yearlong supplemental reading intervention for students with reading difficulties in fourth grade. *Journal of Educational Psychology, 109*(8), 1103–1119.

Wanzek, J., Vaughn, S., Scammacca, N., Gatlin, B., Walker, M. A., & Capin, P. (2016). Meta-analyses of the effects of Tier 2 type reading interventions in Grades K–3. *Educational Psychology Review, 28*, 551–576.

Wanzek, J., Wood, C., & Schatschneider, C. (2023). Teacher vocabulary use and student language and literacy achievement. *Journal of Speech, Language, and Hearing Research* (*JSLHR*), *66*(9), 3574–3587.

Wasik, B. (2008). When fewer is more: Small groups in early childhood classrooms. *Early Childhood Education Journal, 35*, 515–521.

Wasik, B., Bond, M. A., & Hindman, A. (2006). The effects of a language and literacy intervention on Head Start children and teachers. *Journal of Educational Psychology, 98*(1), 63.

Wasowicz, J. (2021). A speech-to-print approach to teaching reading. *Learning Difficulties Australia Bulletin, 53*(2), 10–18.

Watts-Taffe, S., Fisher, P., & Blachowicz, C. (2017). Vocabulary instruction: Research and practice.

In D. Fisher & D. Lapp (Eds.), *Handbook of research on teaching the English language arts* (4th ed.). Routledge.

Webb, N. M. (2009). The teacher's role in promoting collaborative dialogue in the classroom. *British Journal of Educational Psychology, 79*(1), 1–28.

Webb, N. M., Franke, M. L., Ing, M., Wong, J., Fernandez, C. H., Shin, N., & Turrou, A. C. (2014). Engaging with others' mathematical ideas: Interrelationships among student participation, teachers' instructional practices, and learning. *International Journal of Educational Research, 63*, 79–93.

Wegener, S., Wang, H., De Lissa, P., Robidoux, S., Nation, K., & Castles, A. (2018). Children reading spoken words: Interactions between vocabulary and orthographic expectancy. *Developmental Science, 21*(3), 1.

Weger Jr., H., Castle, G. R., & Emmett, M. C. (2010). Active listening in peer interviews: The influence of message paraphrasing on perceptions of listening skill. *The International Journal of Listening, 24*(1), 34–49.

Weisler, B., & Mathes, P. (2011). Using encoding instruction to improve the reading and spelling performances of elementary students at risk for literacy difficulties: A best-evidence synthesis. *Review of Educational Research, 81*(2), 17–200.

Wennerstrom, A., & Siegel, A. F. (2003). Keeping the floor in multiparty conversations: Intonation, syntax, and pause. *Discourse Processes, 36*(2), 77–107.

Whitehurst, G. J., Arnold, D. S., Epstein, J. N., Angell, A. L., Smith, M., & Fischl, J. E. (1994). A picture book reading intervention in day care and home for children from low-income families. *Developmental Psychology, 30*(5), 679–689.

Whitehurst, G. J., Zevenbergen, A. A., Crone, D. A., Schultz, M. D., Velting, O. N., & Fischel, J. E. (1999). Outcomes of an emergent literacy intervention from Head Start through second grade. *Journal of Educational Psychology, 91*(2), 261–272.

Whitten, C., Labby, S., & Sullivan, S. L. (2019). The impact of pleasure reading on academic success. *Journal of Multidisciplinary Graduate Research, 2*(1), 48–64.

Wilkinson, I. A., Murphy, P. K., & Binici, S. (2015). Dialogue-intensive pedagogies for promoting reading comprehension: What we know, what we need to know. In L. B. Resnick, C. A. Asterhan, & S. N. Clarke (Eds.), *Socializing intelligence through academic talk and dialogue* (pp. 37–50). American Educational Research Association.

Willems, M. (2007). *My friend is sad.* Hyperion Books for Children.

Williams, J. P. (1991). Comprehension by learning-disabled and nondisabled adolescents of personal/social problems presented in text. *The American Journal of Psychology, 104*(4), 563–586.

Willingham, D. T. (2006). How knowledge helps. *American Educator.* https://www.aft.org/ae/spring2006/willingham

Wimsatt, W. K., & Beardsley, M. C. (1946). The intentional fallacy. *The Sewanee Review, 54*(3), 468–488.

Windschitl, M., Thompson, J., Braaten, M., & Stroupe, D. (2012). Proposing a core set of instructional practices and tools for teachers of science. *Science Education, 96*(5), 878–903.

Wise, B., Ring, J., & Olson, R. (1999). Training phonological awareness with and without explicit attention to articulation. *Journal of Experimental Child Psychology, 72,* 271–304.

Wisniewski, B., Zierer, K., & Hattie, J. (2019). The power of feedback revisited: A meta-analysis of educational feedback research. *Frontiers in Psychology, 10,* 3087.

Wolf, M. (2018). The science and poetry in learning (and teaching) to read. *Phi Delta Kappan, 100*(4), 13–17.

Wolf, M., Barzillai, M., & Dunne, J. (2009). The importance of deep reading. *Challenging the Whole Child: Reflections on Best Practices in Learning, Teaching, and Leadership, 130,* 21.

Wolf, M., Crosson, A. C., & Resnick, L. B. (2005). Classroom talk for rigorous reading comprehension instruction. *Reading Psychology, 26*(1), 27–53.

Worthy, J., Chamberlain, K., Peterson, K., Sharp, C., & Shih, P. Y. (2012). The importance of read-aloud and dialogue in an era of narrowed curriculum: An examination of literature discussions in a second-grade classroom. *Literacy Research and Instruction, 51*(4), 308–322.

Wright, T. S. (2020). *A teacher's guide to vocabulary development across the day.* Heinemann.

Wright, T. S., & Cervetti, G. N. (2017). A systematic review of the research on vocabulary instruction that impacts text comprehension. *Reading Research Quarterly, 52*(2), 203–226.

Wright, T. S., Cervetti, G. N., Wise, C., & McClung, N. A. (2022). The impact of knowledge-building through conceptually coherent read alouds on vocabulary and comprehension. *Reading Psychology, 4*(1), 70–84.

Wright, T. S., & Gotwals, A. W. (2017). Supporting kindergartners' science talk in the context of an integrated science and disciplinary literacy curriculum. *The Elementary School Journal, 117*(3), 513–537.

Young, C., & Rasinski, T. (2018). Readers theatre: Effects on word recognition automaticity and reading prosody. *Journal of Research in Reading, 41*(3), 475–485.

Young, C., Rasinski, T., & Mohr, K. A. J. (2016). Read Two Impress: An intervention for disfluent readers. *The Reading Teacher, 69*(6), 633–636.

Young, C., Valadez, C., & Gandara, C. (2016). Using performance methods to enhance students' reading fluency. *Journal of Educational Research, 109*(6), 624–630.

Yuill, N., & Oakhill, J. (1988). Effects of inference awareness training on poor reading comprehension. *Applied Cognitive Psychology, 2*(1), 33–45.

Zwiers, J. (2019). *Next steps with academic conversations: New ideas for improving learning through classroom talk.* Stenhouse Publishers.

Zwiers, J., & Crawford, M. (2009). How to start academic conversations. *Educational Leadership, 66*(7), 70–73.

Zwiers, J., & Crawford, M. (2011). *Academic conversations: Classroom talk that fosters critical thinking and content understandings.* Stenhouse Publishers.

Index

Active View of Reading model, 3, 20, 42, 51
  components, 21, 21–24 (table)
  Duke and Cartwright's, 20 (figure)
  reader–text questions, 26–27
  sociocultural context, 28–29
  tasks, 27–28
  teach strategies and build knowledge,
    30–31
  texts, 25–27
Activities and games (phonics and spelling), 109
  Elkonin boxes, 109, 109 (figure)
  read connected text, 113–114
  read words, 111–112, 111 (figure), 112 (figure)
  review and warm-up, 109
  spell words/word work, 110–111, 110 (figure)
  word chains, 111
  write connected text, 112
Affix, 133
Alphabetic principle, 91
"April Rain Song" (Hughes), 179–180
Archer, A. L., 33
Authentic texts, 91, 114

Bardoe, C., 61
Barnes, D., 127
Beck, I. L., 116, 135
Beck, M. E., 116
Behold the Beautiful Dung Beetle
    (Bardoe), 61
Blending, 91
Blevins, W., 116
Bound base, 133
Boyles, N., 208
Broaddus, K., 208

Callendar, A., 249
Carter, H., 249
Charlotte's Web, 65
Chen, C. M., 209
Chen, F. Y., 209
Choral reading, 190, 214
Cisneros, S., 282

Close-reading lessons, 42, 163
  deciding to teach (content), 211–213
  deciding to teach (strategies), 213–214, 213 (table)
  expand definition of text, 222
  knowledge and vocabulary building, 207
  multimodal text, Great Migration, 203 (figure), 206
  overview, 205–206
  planning template, 204, 219, 221, 296
  read, deciding to, 214–215
  research, 208–209
  responsive teaching, 217, 217 (table)
  seventh graders, 201–203
  shared-reading and read aloud, 184
  small-group (sixth grade, ELA), 218
  structure and timing, 216
  texts, 210–211
  whole-class (fifth grade, science), 220
Coherent text sets, 56, 57 (figure)
Collins, B., 214
Common Core State Standards, 208
Componential Model of Reading, 20
Construction-Integration Model, 20
Conversation lessons
  fifth graders, 269–270
  knowledge and vocabulary building, 274
  overview, 272
  partnerships, 277
  partnerships (second grade, ELA), 284
  planning template, 271, 283, 285, 287, 299
  playing board, 279 (figure)
  research, 273
  responsive teaching, 281, 281 (table)
  skills and strategies, 278–279, 278 (table)
  small-group book club (fifth grade, science), 286
  small groups/clubs, 277
  structure and timing, 280
  texts, 275–276
  whole-class (sixth grade, ELA), 282
  whole-class conversation, 276
CORE Learning, 100, 116
Crown: An Ode to the Fresh Cut (Barnes), 127
Cultural competence, 29

Decodable texts, 91, 113
Decode, 91
Decoding inventories, 101
Deep orthography, 91
Deep reading, 208
Dialogic reading, 65
Direct and Indirect Effects Model of
    Reading (DIER), 20
The Discovery of King Tut (Carter), 249

Echo reading, 190
"Eleven" (Cisneros), 282
Encode, 91
English language arts (ELA), 1, 21, 28–29, 38, 56, 69
    individual goal setting guided inquiry
        lesson, 240
    partnership conversation lesson, 284
    small-group close-reading lesson, 218
    small-group craft study guided inquiry lesson, 244
    small-group reader's theater lesson, 262, 264
    whole-class conversation fishbowl guided inquiry
        lesson, 242
    whole-class conversation lesson, 282
    whole-class read-aloud lesson, 80
Etymology, 133
Explicit instruction, 33, 132
    elements of, 34, 36–37 (figure)
    focused practice *vs.* orchestration, 42
    individual lessons, 55
    lesson structures for, 38–39, 40–41 (table)
    morphology, 34
    planning and responsiveness, 43–45, 44 (figure),
        45 (figure)
    practice, selecting texts for, 56, 57 (figure)
    scaffolding. *See* Scaffolding methods
    small-group lessons, 54–55
    whole-class lessons, 54
Extension, focus words, 140
    concept map, 141 (figure)
    connections, 140 (figure)
    semantic map, 141 (figure)
    shades of meaning, 140 (figure)
    vocabulary board, 142 (figure)
    which one doesn't belong, 140 (figure)
    word matrix, 142 (figure)
    word web, 142 (figure)

Florian, D., 179
Fluency-Oriented Oral Reading (FOOR), 198

Fluency-Oriented Reading Instruction (FORI), 198
Focus lessons, 42, 47
    anchor chart, 154 (figure)
    articulating strategy, 161, 161 (table)
    comparing pacing, 164 (figure)
    demonstration, texts for, 162
    by different names, 159 (table)
    individual lesson (sixth grade, social studies), 168
    individual student reminder cards, 155, 155 (figure)
    knowledge and vocabulary building, 160
    overview, 157
    planning template, 156, 169, 171, 173, 294
    research, 158
    responsive teaching, 166, 167 (table)
    small-group (first grade, fluency), 172
    structure and timing, 164–165
    student engagement, texts for, 162–163
    student-led, 174–175, 174 (figure), 175 (figure)
    visual anchors, 163
    whole-class (fourth grade, science), 170
Focus words
    extension. *See* Extension, focus words
    indignant, teaching, 137 (table)
    vocabulary lessons, choosing, 134–135
Formative assessment and progress monitoring
    (phonics and spelling), 97
    alphabet and letter–sound assessment, 100,
        100 (table)
    assessment summaries, 102, 102 (figure),
        103 (figure)
    phonics survey, 101, 101 (table)
    spelling inventory, 98, 98 (table)
    writing sample, 99, 99 (table)
Frayer model
    for *indignant,* 139, 139 (figure)
    for *rearrange,* 128 (figure)
Free base, 133
A Fresh Look at Phonics (Blevins), 116

Goodwin, A., 209
Grand conversation, 276
The Grapes of Wrath (Steinbeck), 26
Grapheme, 91
Grapheme–phoneme correspondence, 97
Grimard, G., 258
Guided inquiry lessons, 42, 47
    conversation fishbowl, 233
    craft study, 233–235, 234 (table)
    expand definition of text, 246

fifth graders and set goals, 225–227, 226 (figure)
goal setting, 235–237, 236 (figure), 237 (figure)
individual goal setting (second grade, ELA), 240
knowledge and vocabulary building, 232
overview, 229–230
planning template, 228, 241, 243, 245, 297
research, 231
responsive teaching, 239, 239 (table)
small-group craft study (sixth grade, ELA), 244
structure and timing, 238
whole-class conversation fishbowl (fourth grade, ELA), 242

Harlem Renaissance, 202
High-frequency words (HFWs), 92, 114–115
Holdaway, D., 182
Hollingsworth, J. R., 33
Horrible Harry and the Birthday Girl (Kline), 26
Hughes, C. A., 33
Hughes, L., 179, 212–213

I Am Farmer: Growing an Environmental Movement in Cameroon (Paul & Paul), 72–73
Individual lessons, 55
focus (sixth grade, social studies), 168
guided inquiry, goal setting (second grade, ELA), 240
Instructional read aloud, 65
Interactive read aloud, 65
"Introduction to Poetry" (Collins), 214
Ivey, G., 208

Joyful Noise (Fleischman), 256

King, S., 26
Kintsch, W., 209
Knowledge and building, 30–31

Ladson-Billings, G., 29
Lessons
planning templates, 10, 10 (figure), 289–290
types, 3. *See also specific type of lessons*
Lesson structures, 50
to adapt program/curriculum, 50–51
to support individual needs, 51
Lila and the Crow (Grimard), 258 (figure)
Lindsay, J. B., 116
Literacy practices, 29
Lovett, M. W., 208

Making Sense of Phonics (Beck & Beck), 116
Moment-to-moment decisions, 6
Morpheme, 133
Morphological awareness, 133
Morphology, 133
Multiple criterion texts (phonics and spelling), 113

National Reading Panel, 95
"The Negro Speaks of Rivers" (Hughes), 212–213

Oakhill, J., 209
Online resources, 8
video lessons, 8, 8 (table)
Orthographic mapping, 92

Paige, D. D., 2
Paired reading, 190
Paper Bag Princess (Munsch), 255
Parkes, B., 182
Partnerships, 277
conversation (second grade, ELA), 284
Pearson, P. D., 31
Phoneme, 92
Phonemic awareness, 92
Phonics and spelling lessons, 42
activities and games, 109–114
formative assessments and progress monitoring, 97–103
general progression, 94, 94 (table)
high-frequency words (HFWs), 114–115
introducing /sh/ to group of first graders, 87–89
knowledge and vocabulary building, 96
overview, 93–94
planning template, 90, 121, 123, 292
research, 95
responsive teaching, 118, 118–119 (table)
small-group (first grade, /ŏ/), 120
structure and timing, 116–117
student engagement, 107
teaching articulatory gestures, 108
tools and materials, 104–106
vocabulary, 91–92
whole-class (second grade, VCe review), 122

Quantitative leveling, 26

Read-aloud lessons, 38, 42, 163, 206
interactive, 65–66
knowledge and vocabulary building, 68

overview, 65

planning template, 64, 79, 81, 83, 291

research, 66

responsive teaching, 76, 76–77 (table)

shared and close reading, 184

small-group (fourth grade, social studies), 78

strategies and prompt examples, 72, 72 (table)

structure and timing, 75

student engagement, 72–73

text marked up with prompts, 74 (figure)

texts, 69–70

think aloud, 70–72, 71 (table)

third grade (science), 61–63

video aloud, 84

whole-class (fifth grade, science), 82

whole-class (first grade, ELA), 80

Readers models, 20. *See also* Active View of Reading model

Reader's theater lessons

groups, 256

knowledge and vocabulary building, 255

overview, 252

planning template, 251, 263, 265, 298

research, 254

responsive teaching, 261, 261 (table)

small-group (first grade, ELA), 262

small-group (fourth grade, ELA), 264

strategies to teach, 253 (table)

structure and timing, 260

texts, 256–258, 257 (figure), 258 (figure)

third graders practice, 249–250

weekly schedule, 259, 259 (table)

Reading, 1

choral, 190, 214

deep, 208

dialogic, 65

echo, 190

paired, 190

successful, 19

Reading Above the Fray (Lindsay), 116

The Reading Strategies Book 2.0 (Serravallo), reading goals, 51, 52–53 (table)

Responsive teaching, 3, 45, 45 (figure)

close-reading lessons, 217, 217 (table)

conversation lessons, 281, 281 (table)

focus lessons, 166, 167 (table)

guided inquiry lessons, 239, 239 (table)

phonics and spelling lessons, 118, 118–119 (table)

read-aloud lessons, 76, 76–77 (table)

reader's theater lessons, 261, 261 (table)

shared-reading lessons, 192, 192–193 (table)

vocabulary lessons, 145, 145 (table)

Reynolds, D., 209

Robertson, D. A., 30

Rosenshine, B., 33

The Running Man (King), 26

Scaffolding methods, 39, 42, 45–46

demonstration, 46

example and explanation, 47

guided inquiry, 47

prompting and feedback, 47–49, 49 (table)

shared practice, 46–47

Scarborough, H. S., 20

Scherer, M., 208

Segmenting, 92

Shared book reading, 65

Shared-reading lessons, 42, 163, 206

close reading and read aloud, 184

Fluency-Oriented Reading Instruction (FORI), 198

key terms for, 190

knowledge and vocabulary building, 185

overview, 182

planning template, 181, 195, 197, 295

research, 183

responsive teaching, 192, 192–193 (table)

schedule, 186 (table), 187, 187 (table)

second graders practice, 179–180

skills and strategies, 189, 189 (table)

small-group (first grade; decoding, fluency & inferring), 194

structure and timing, 191

texts, 188

whole-class (second grade, social studies), 196

Sight words, 92

Simple View of Reading, 20

Skill progressions, 44, 44 (figure), 47, 227 (figure), 237 (figure)

Small-group lessons, 8, 13, 54–55, 67

book club, 277

close-reading (sixth grade, ELA), 218

conversation (fifth grade, science), book club, 286

focus (first grade, fluency), 172

guided inquiry craft study (sixth grade, ELA), 244

phonics and spelling (first grade, /ŏ/), 120

phonics and spelling assessments, 102, 102 (figure), 103 (figure) read-aloud lesson (fourth grade, social studies), 78

reader's theater (first grade, ELA), 262

reader's theater (fourth grade, ELA), 264

shared-reading (first grade; decoding, fluency, and inferring), 194

vocabulary (second grade, social studies), 148

Sociocultural context, 28–29

Speech-to-print approach, 92

Spellings, 92

Steinbeck, J., 26

Struggling readers, 254

Systematic instruction, 92

Teacher-curated text, 57 (figure)

Teaching

art of, 2

responsive. *See* Responsive teaching

Teaching Reading Across the Day (*TRAD*)

guidance, 14 (table)

as professional learning/supplemental resource, 11, 11–12 (table)

reader models, 20–21

teach strategies and build knowledge, 30–31

Teaching Reading in Small Groups (Serravallo), 13

Tools and materials (phonics and spelling), 104

digital word work mat, 105 (figure)

magnetic letters, 104 (figure)

whiteboards, markers, and erasers, 105

words on cards/slips of paper, 106, 106 (figure)

word work mat, 104 (figure)

Translanguaging, 29

Trixie the Halloween Fairy (Meadows), 26

UFLI Foundations (Lane & Contesse), 116

Universal Design for Learning, 54

Virtuous cycle, 31

Vocabulary lessons

choosing focus words, 134–135

deep processing, 138–139, 138 (table)

explaining, 137

extending, 140–143

with morphology, 127–129

online tools for, 143

overview, 131

planning template, 130, 147, 149, 293

research, 132

responsive teaching, 145, 145 (table)

small-group (second grade, social studies), 148

structure and timing, 144

three tiers of, 135 (figure)

vocabulary, 133

whole-class (fifth grade, tier 3 words in science), 146

word lists to support selection, online tools and, 136

Walker, J., 108, 116

Wascowicz, J., 116

Webb, N. M., 280

Whole-class lessons, 8, 54, 67, 75, 97

assessments, phonics and spelling, 102, 102 (figure), 103 (figure)

close-reading (fifth grade, science), 220

conversation, 42, 276

conversation (sixth grade, ELA), 282

guided inquiry conversation fishbowl (fourth grade, ELA), 242

phonics and spelling (second grade, VCe review), 122

read-aloud lesson (fifth grade, science), 80

read-aloud lesson (first grade, ELA), 80

shared-reading (second grade, social studies), 196

vocabulary (fifth grade, tier 3 words in science), 146

Wide Fluency-Oriented Oral Reading, 198

Wide Fluency-Oriented Reading Instruction, 198

Wolf, M., 208

Word matrix for arrange, 129, 129 (figure)

Ybarra, S. E., 33

Yuill, N., 209

Because...
ALL TEACHERS ARE LEADERS

WILEY BLEVINS

Implement effective phonics instruction with these powerful routines that help teachers differentiate whole-class lessons, so students at every skill level can engage.

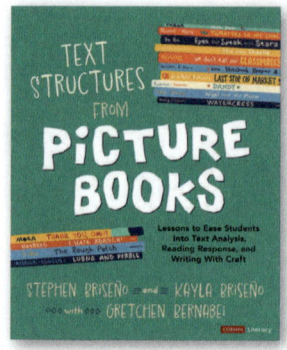

STEPHEN BRISEÑO, KAYLA BRISEÑO, WITH GRETCHEN BERNABEI

Boost students' reading comprehension and writing skills with 50 low-prep, quick-access lessons within the context of beautifully illustrated, engaging picture books.

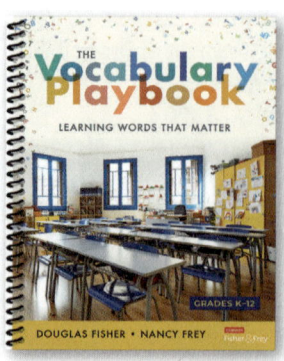

DOUGLAS FISHER, NANCY FREY

Put away the word-list mindset, and embrace active modeling, peer work, and independent practice to build vocabulary success.

TRICIA EBARVIA

Make important intentional anti-bias shifts in pedagogy to help students become more critical readers, writers, and thinkers.

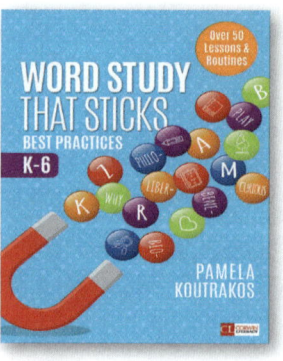

PAMELA KOUTRAKOS

Make word learning jubilant and fun and encourage students to take ownership of word learning with this step-by-step approach.

SONJA CHERRY-PAUL

Foster identity-inspiring learning experiences where students can show up completely as themselves and recognize the full humanity of all people.

At Corwin Literacy we have put together a collection of just-in-time, classroom-tested, practical resources from trusted experts that allow you to quickly find the information you need when you need it.

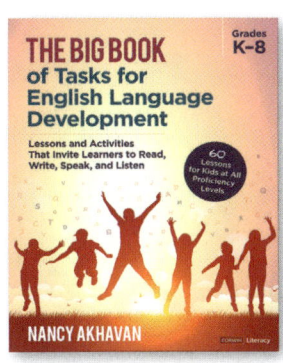

NANCY AKHAVAN
Support students at all levels of English language proficiency as they learn and grow more confident.

JUSTIN M. STYGLES
Learn how to build relationships so shame-bound readers trust enough to risk enough to grow.

High-Impact Professional Learning with Jennifer Serravallo

Jennifer Serrravallo helps literacy educators around the globe develop skillful, enthusiastic readers and writers by translating research and complex theories into easy-to-implement practices that fit today's classrooms.

No matter your curriculum, approach to literacy instruction, or the student population you support, Jen and her team of literacy experts tailor professional development to meet your needs. Customized experiences—in-person and online— in either English or Spanish are specifically designed to address both your district's vision and the individual goals of educators and students in your building.

For more information, contact Jen and her team @ **jenniferserravallo.com**

CORWIN
A Sage Company

CORWIN HAS ONE MISSION: to enhance education through intentional professional learning.

We build long-term relationships with our authors, educators, clients, and associations who partner with us to develop and continuously improve the best evidence-based practices that establish and support lifelong learning.